IMAGES
of America

RARITAN

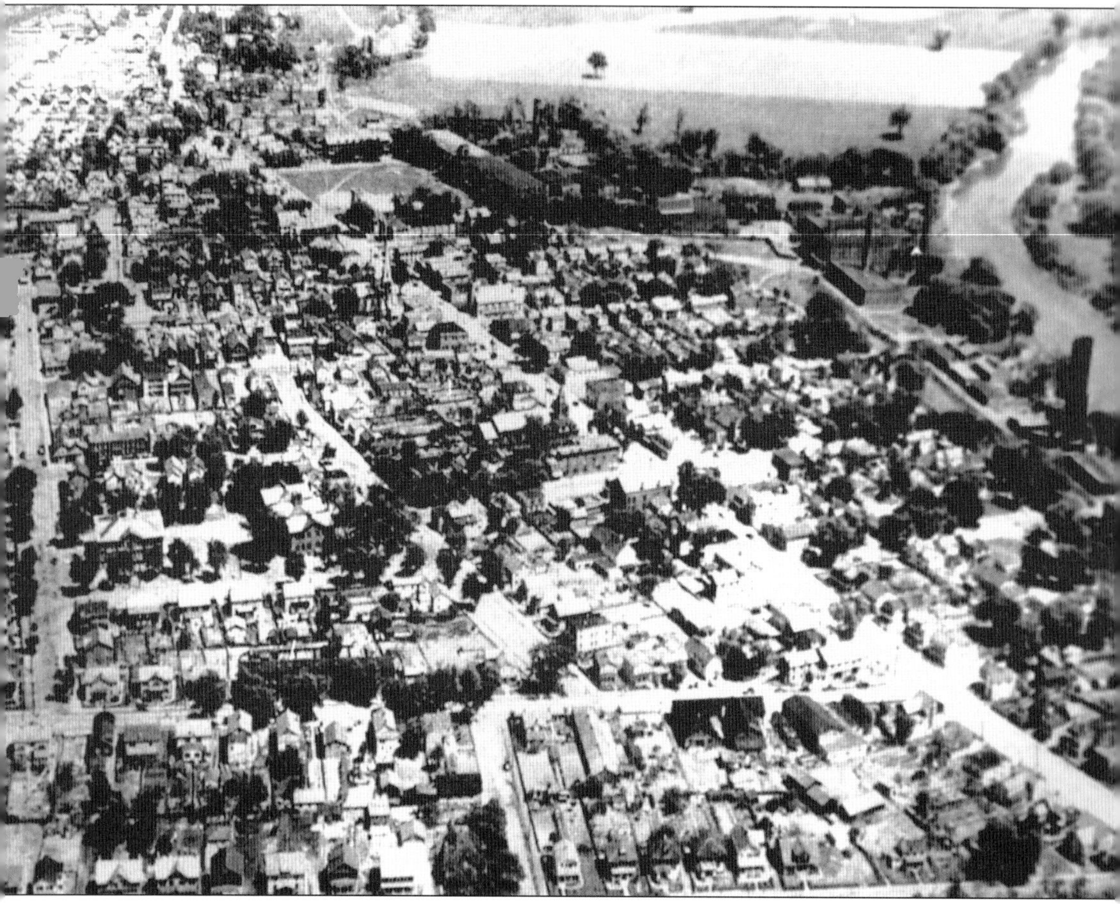

Raritan, "the Friendly Town of Friendly People," is seen here in the 1920s. This aerial view shows the main residential, business, and industrial areas, as well as the canal and river.

IMAGES
of America

RARITAN

M. Frieda Helmstetter and Jo-Ann Liptak

ARCADIA
PUBLISHING

ISBN 978-0-7385-3451-0

Published by Arcadia Publishing
Charleston SC, Chicago IL, Portsmouth NH, San Francisco CA

Printed in the United States of America

Library of Congress Catalog Card Number: 2003110756

For all general information contact Arcadia Publishing at:
Telephone 843-853-2070
Fax 843-853-0044
E-mail sales@arcadiapublishing.com
For customer service and orders:
Toll-Free 1-888-313-2665

Visit us on the Internet at www.arcadiapublishing.com

Contents

ACKNOWLEDGMENTS

Many people shared their treasured photographs, postcards, and information with us. We would like to thank Frank Tropiano, Linda Barth, Barbara Navatto, Lilyan Navatto, William Dudeck, Bernard Navatto Sr., Mary Carlino Soriano, Michael Deak, Mrs. Dante Alberghini, Evelyn Schweitzer, Ann Navatto, and Robert Strauss. We would also like to thank the Raritan Public Library, the *Somerset Messenger Gazette*, and the Raritan Senior Citizens.

Special thanks go to Jerry and Jim for encouraging us and permitting us to spend the time and energy needed to complete this book.

A final acknowledgment goes to the third- and fourth-grade students of John F. Kennedy School, who in 1984, wrote the original photographic history of Raritan as part of a special school project.

Please note that the names in parentheses at the end of the captions indicate the source of the photograph, not the source of the information.

INTRODUCTION

The first people to settle the Raritan Valley were the Naraticongs, a peace-loving branch of the Lenape who were part of the Iroquois Nation. Numbering about 1,200, the Naraticongs lived mostly along the north side of the river. They roamed the forest to hunt, fished in the river, and planted corn in the fertile valley.

In 1683, when the Dutch and English arrived, the Naraticongs met them with friendly advances and a ready sale of land. The Dutch shortened and altered the name of the Naraticongs and named the area Raritan, or "forked river." Other versions of history state that Raritan translates to "where the stream overflows."

The Dutch, English, and French Huguenots were drawn to the area for the same reasons the Lenape found appealing—the rich, fertile soil and the navigable river. The Dutch also realized they could establish their own church, the Dutch Reformed Church, and live in freedom. These opportunities played a major role in the establishment of the town of Raritan. Raritan became a trading center for neighboring farmers.

George Middaugh, one of the first settlers of Raritan, began constructing a tavern in 1734. For many years, the Middaugh Tavern was the meeting place for the early governments of Raritan and neighboring Bridgewater, a gathering spot for colonists, and a stagecoach stop between New York and Philadelphia. The tavern remains one of the oldest buildings in town.

During the American Revolution, while George Washington wintered at the Wallace House in nearby Somerville, the Marquis de Lafayette enjoyed the hospitality of Andreas Coejeman. Considered the most opulent home in Raritan, the Coejeman House had hearths of fine Egyptian marble and mantels of carved mahogany.

After the Revolutionary War, Alexander Hamilton visited Raritan with the idea of constructing a series of canals. The town fathers thought the idea was ludicrous, but the seed was planted, and a waterpower canal was dug from Bradley Gardens east to Raritan in 1840. This canal proved to be a boon to the town, and industries sprang up along the waterway, where they could harness the waterpower and also be close to the railroad.

One night, in 1848, a fire broke out in the northwest corner of the small village. Unfortunately, the bucket brigade was ineffective and the village lost two houses and one store. As a result of that fire, a "gooseneck" fire engine was purchased, and Lafayette No. 1, the first organized fire company in Somerset County, was born. In later years, the company was reorganized and became Relief Hose Company No. 2.

By a special act of the New Jersey Legislature, the village officially became the town of Raritan in 1868. Joseph Frelinghuysen, a name long associated with Raritan, was elected president of the board of commissioners and set out to make Raritan attractive to new industry. After a slow start, Raritan saw much growth and development. With large numbers of immigrants coming to America and consequently to Raritan, the population increased.

In 1891, the first police department was established, and in 1892, the town purchased a lot for $475 from Mrs. A. H. Brokaw for the fire department's new engine house.

The Raritan Woolen Mills, established in 1846, was the largest and most famous of Raritan's early industries; the quality of its goods was known throughout the United States. In 1882, its name was changed to the Somerset Manufacturing Company. As many as 400 people were employed there at one time. Workers made uniforms and blankets for Union soldiers during the Civil War and uniforms for the U.S. Army during World War I.

During World War I, many patriotic men of Raritan enlisted to defend their homeland. Those who remained on the home front spent thousands of dollars buying war bonds. This determined war effort became widely known, and officials in Washington, D.C., commissioned the building of a ship to be called the SS *Natirar* (Raritan spelled backwards) in appreciation of the sacrifices made by the citizens of Raritan. Raritan dignitaries launched the SS *Natirar* at Wilmington, Delaware, in 1920.

U.S. Pres. Warren G. Harding often visited his friend Sen. Joseph S. Frelinghuysen and his family and attended the Third Reformed Dutch Church in Raritan. It was not surprising that Harding and Frelinghuysen were playing a round of golf on July 2, 1921, when Sen. Hale Kellogg, a messenger from Washington, D.C., arrived with an important document requiring the president's signature. The Knox-Porter Resolution, also known as the Treaty of Raritan, was signed by President Harding in the library of the Frelinghuysen home in Raritan on that day. The resolution officially ended World War I.

Once again, in 1941, the United States went to war, and hundreds of Raritan's sons and daughters enlisted or were drafted into the service of their country. One of these young men was Marine Gunnery Sgt. John Basilone. Basilone was the first enlisted man to receive the Congressional Medal of Honor during World War II for heroic action on Guadalcanal from October 24 through October 27, 1942. A Japanese regiment of nearly 3,000 men attacked Basilone and his platoon, and Basilone wiped out the entire regiment almost single-handedly. Rather than spend the rest of the war traveling throughout the United States encouraging people to buy war bonds, he elected to return to active duty. On February 19, 1945, Basilone was killed in action in the assault on Iwo Jima. He was awarded the Navy Cross posthumously for his bravery during that battle. A grateful and proud town erected a statue in Basilone's memory in 1948 and has honored him with a parade since 1981.

Although many years have passed since the first settlers set foot in this area, Raritan still retains its small town charm and appeal. Walking along Somerset Street, one can still see original Colonial homes, stores, and churches, and three of the four original homes are still in use today. For those of you who remember the Raritan of yesterday, enjoy this walk down memory lane. We all must treasure the images of the past and remember to capture the images of today. This is the way to preserve our heritage and culture for future generations.

One

Transportation, Waterpower, and Industry

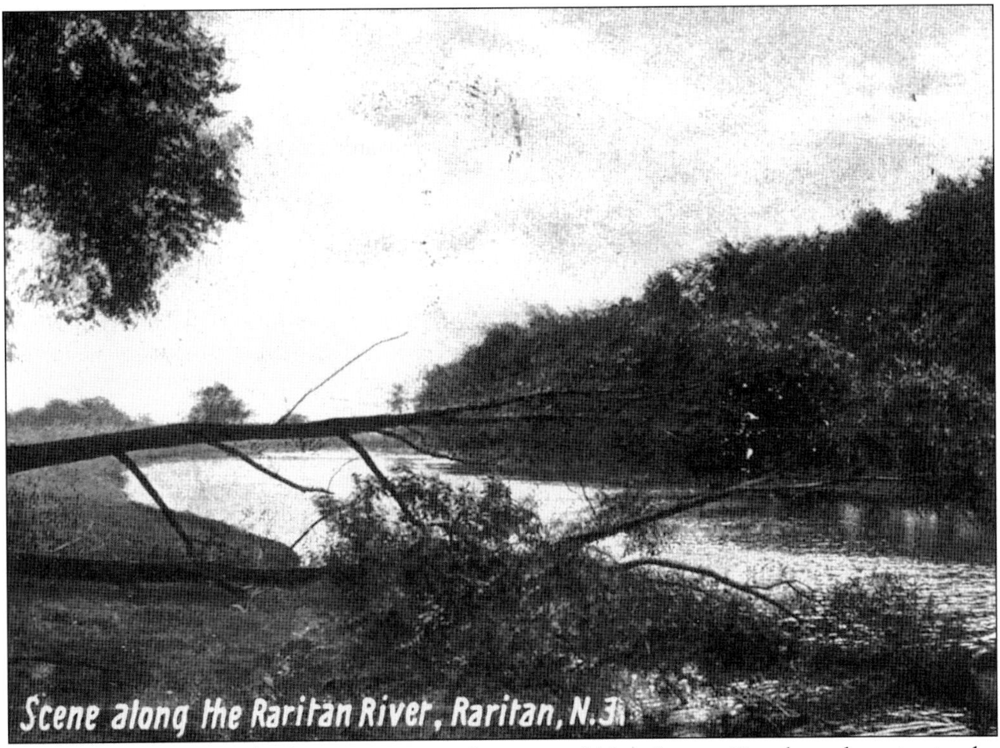

The Raritan River is the longest river in the state of New Jersey. Two branches rise in the northern highlands of the state to form the Raritan River, which then flows southeast for 75 miles into the Raritan Bay. (Courtesy of Frank Tropiano.)

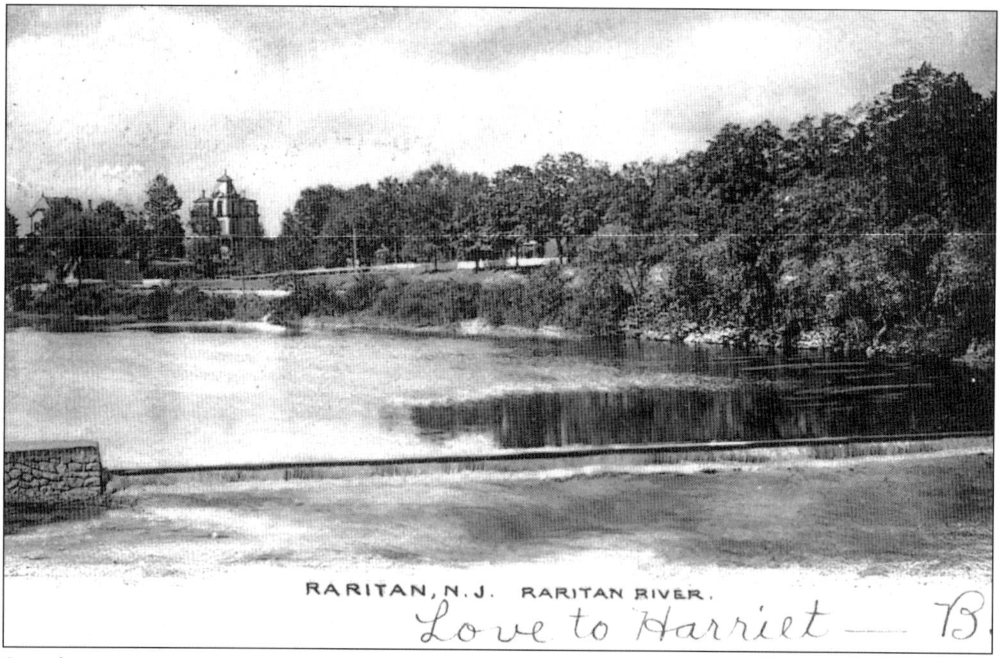

Stately mansions were built along the Old York Road overlooking the Raritan River in the 1800s. The Van Sickle home seen in the background of this photograph was originally owned by R.D. Kenyon and was purchased by the Van Sickles in 1915. (Courtesy of Barbara Navatto.)

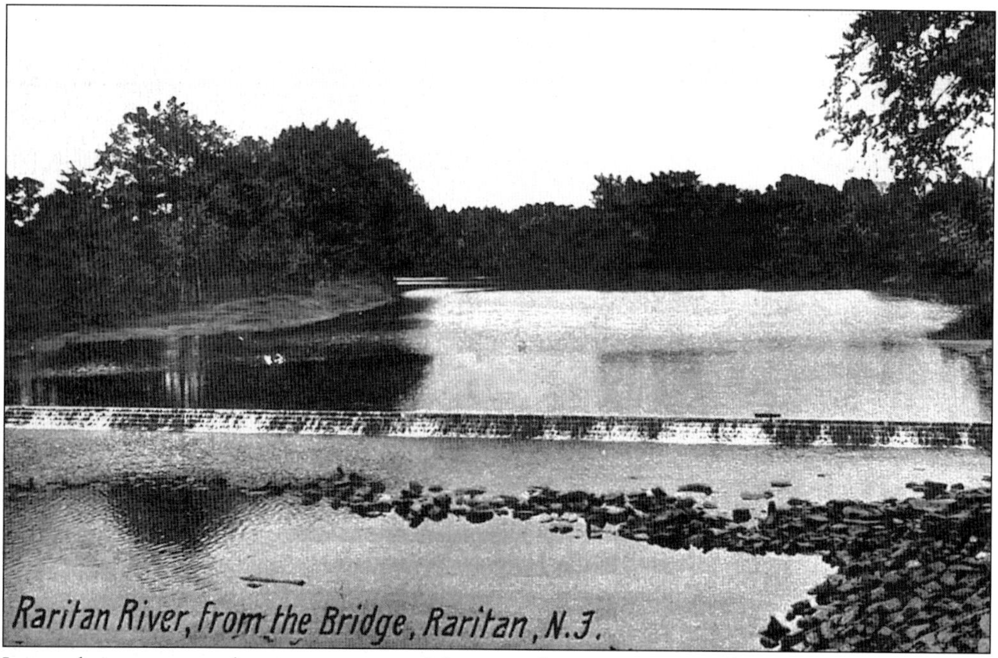

Long, lazy summer days were spent fishing and swimming in the Raritan River. This scene taken from the Nevius Street Bridge looks west toward Bradley Gardens. (Courtesy of Barbara Navatto.)

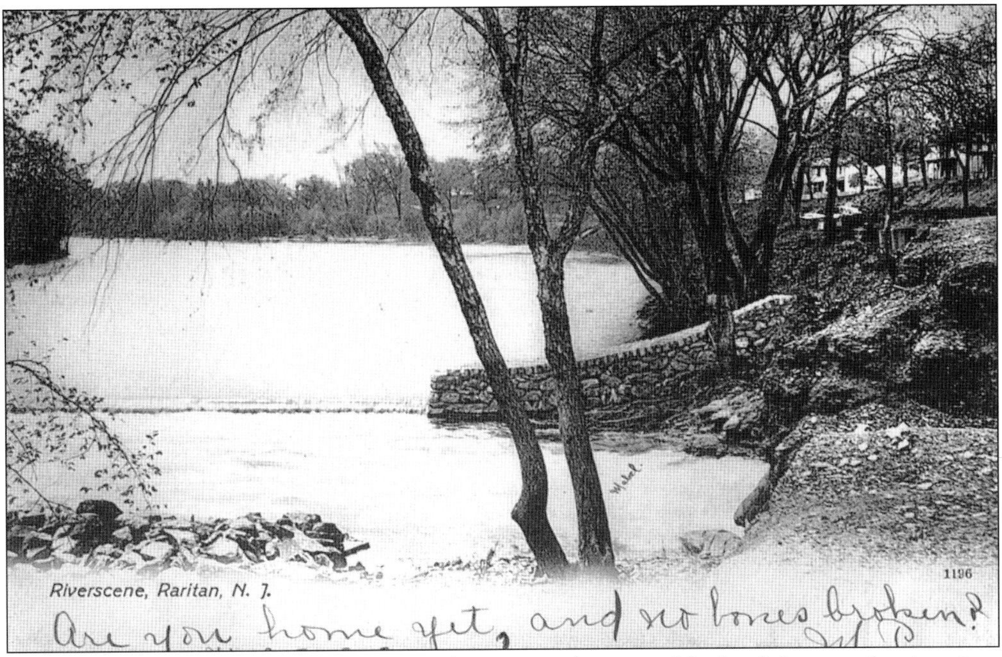

A stone jetty extends into the river, making it easily accessible for fishing and swimming. (Courtesy of Barbara Navatto.)

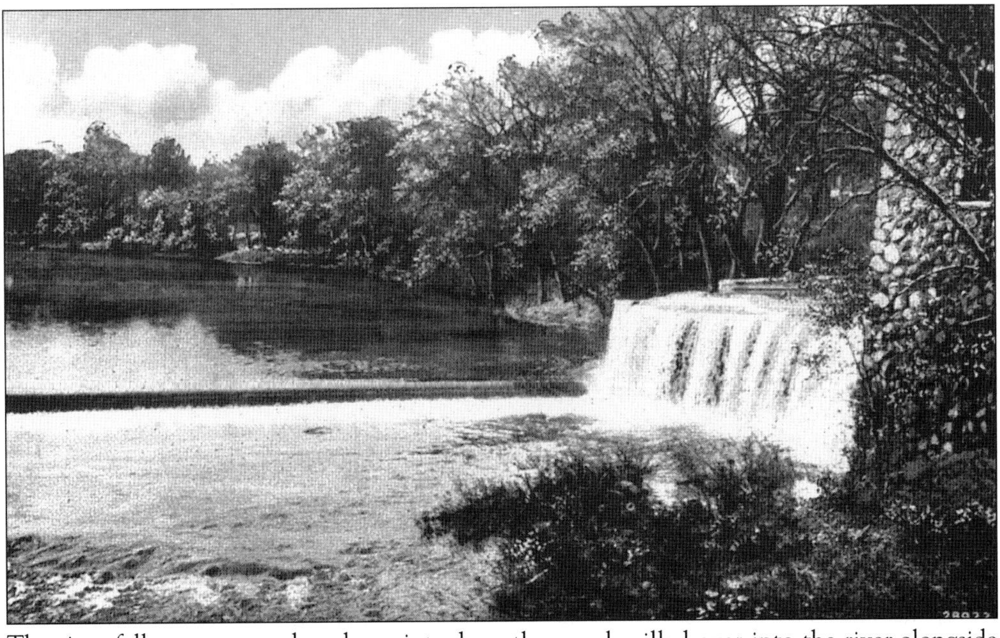

The river falls were created at the point where the canal spilled over into the river alongside the Duke Estate Pumping Station.

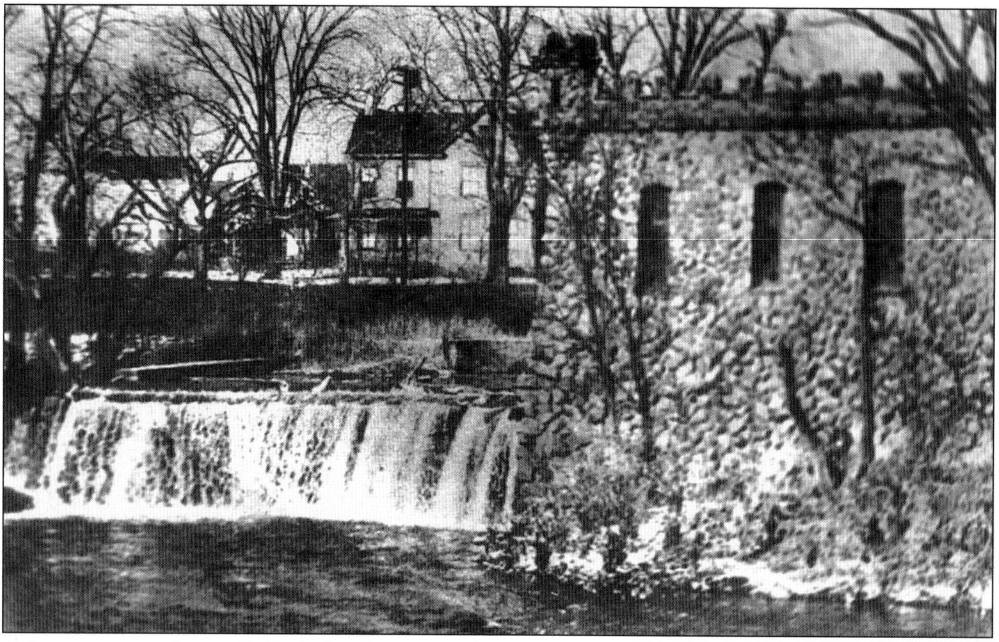

Tobacco tycoon James B. Duke built a magnificent estate across the river from Raritan in 1893. This stone pumping station provided water from the river to fill the many man-made lakes, cascades, fountains, and streams used in the landscaping of his estate.

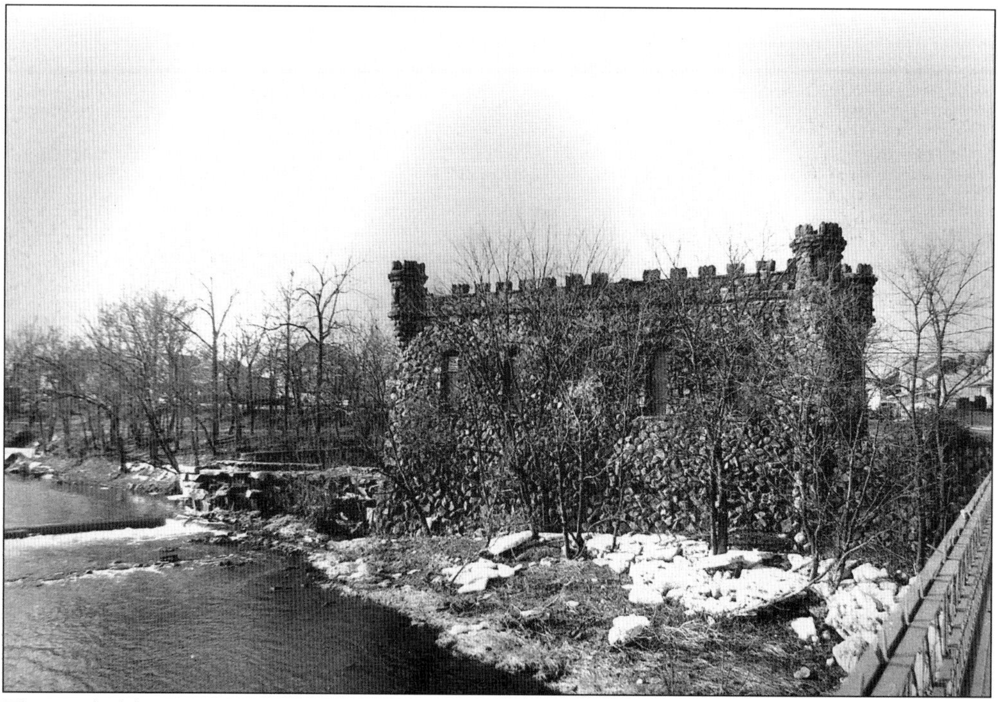

The castle-like structure remains a fascinating architectural treasure to this day.

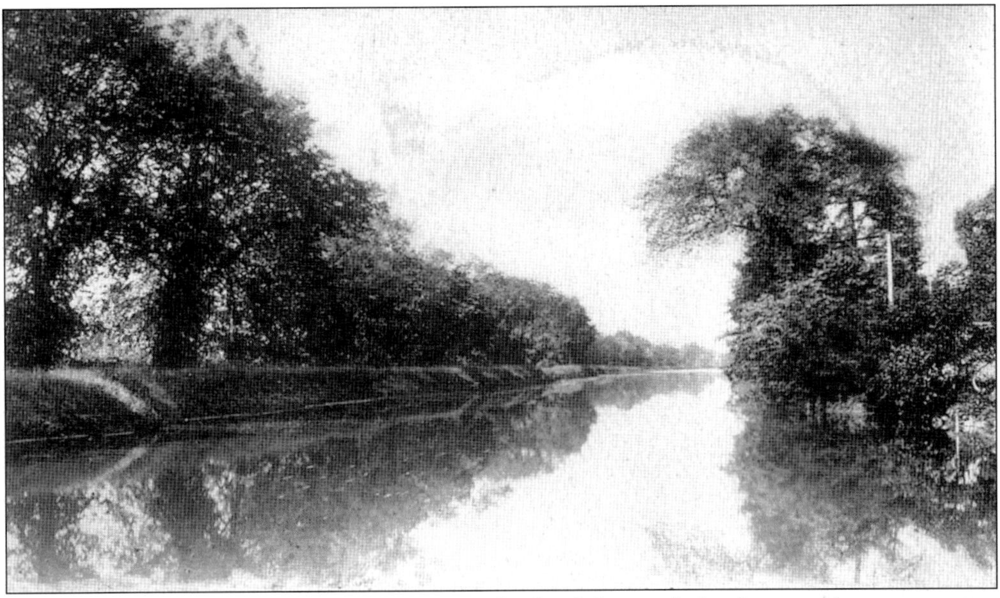

In 1836, a group of local businessmen proposed a feasibility study be done on the construction of a raceway that would use the flow of the Raritan River to power industry. It was discovered that the natural curve of the river outside the village of Raritan would make it possible to build a canal in place of the raceway to supply the waterpower needed for industrial growth. (Courtesy of Frank Tropiano.)

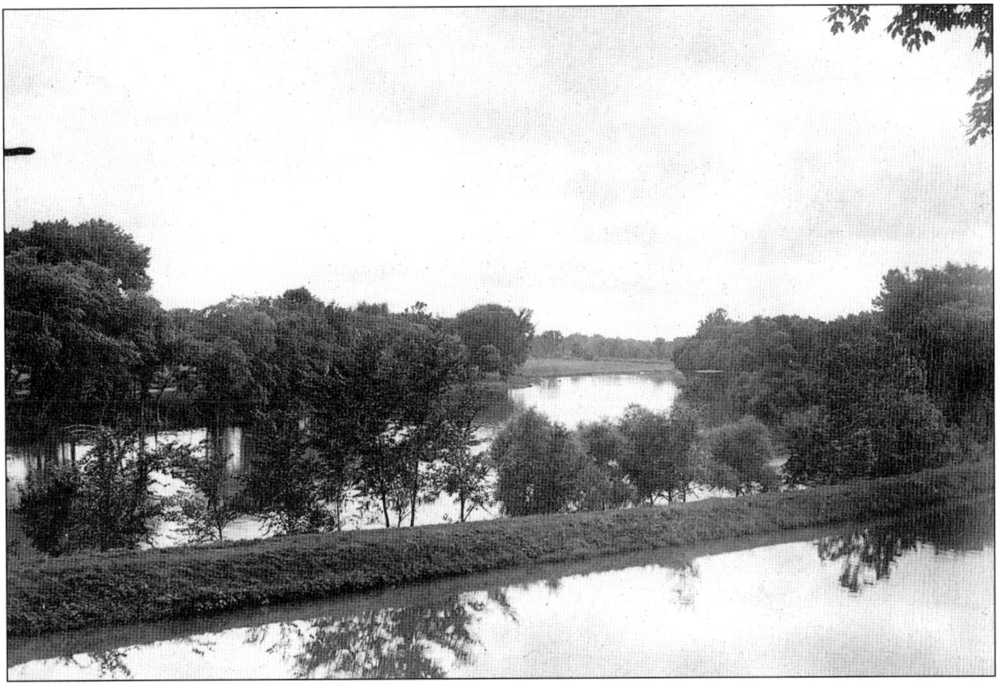

The Raritan Waterpower Canal was dug by hand in the 1840s. Irish, German, Italian, French, Hungarian, Bohemian, and Chinese workers were brought in to do the excavating. The canal ran parallel to the river and Old York Road, approximately three miles from Bradley Gardens through Raritan. (Courtesy of Linda Barth.)

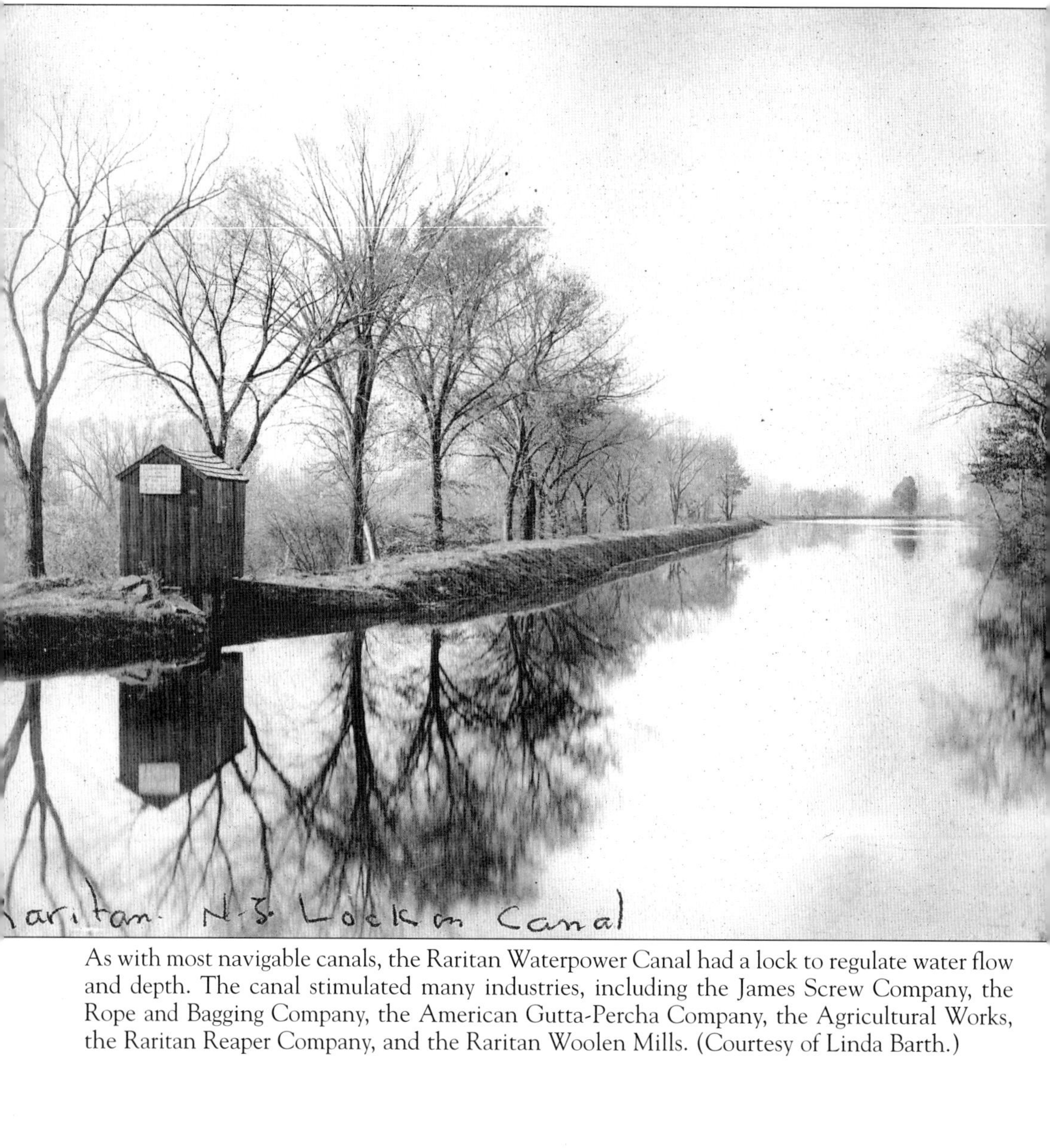

As with most navigable canals, the Raritan Waterpower Canal had a lock to regulate water flow and depth. The canal stimulated many industries, including the James Screw Company, the Rope and Bagging Company, the American Gutta-Percha Company, the Agricultural Works, the Raritan Reaper Company, and the Raritan Woolen Mills. (Courtesy of Linda Barth.)

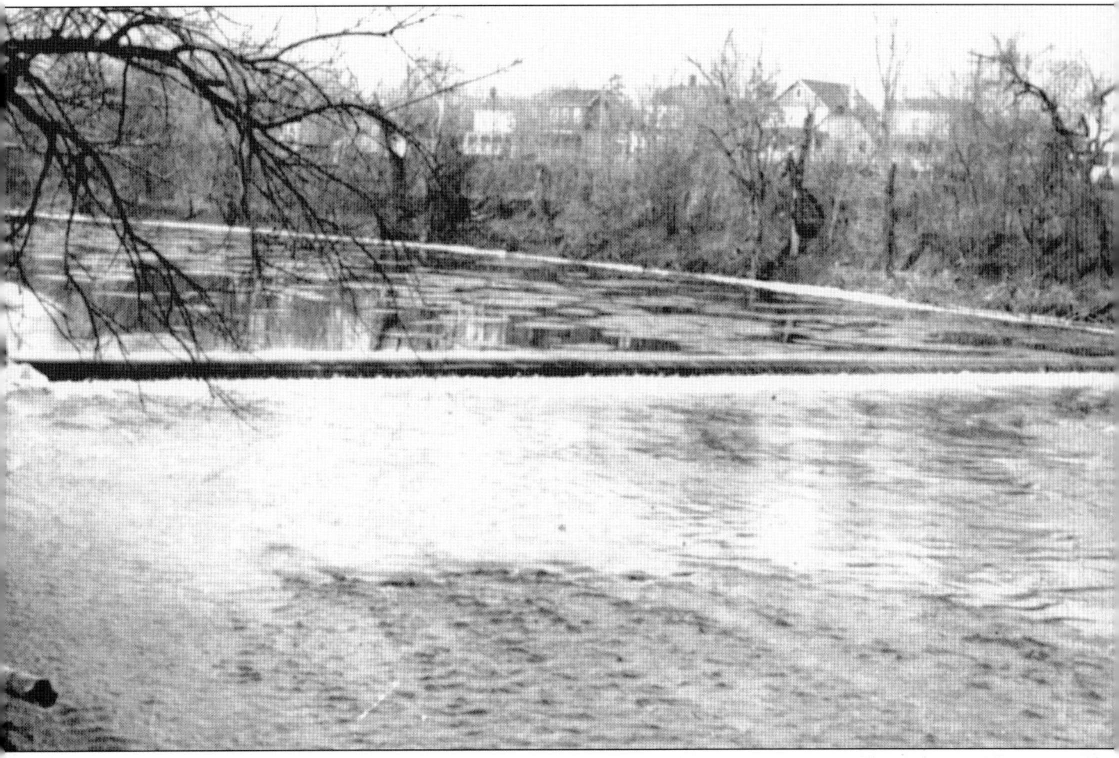

The tranquil and calm Raritan River has many excellent fishing spots. Young boys have often used it as a favorite swimming hole as well. (Courtesy of Barbara Navatto.)

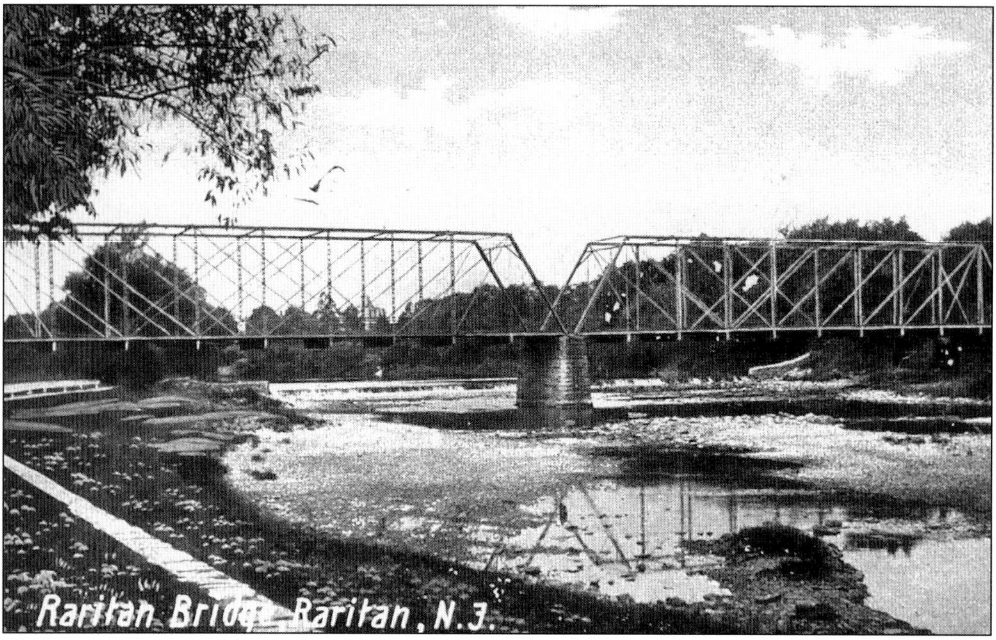

The Nevius Street Bridge is the oldest actively used metal truss bridge in Somerset County. The bridge was built by the Wrought Iron Bridge Company of Canton, Ohio, and spans the river between Raritan and Hillsborough Township. (Courtesy of Barbara Navatto.)

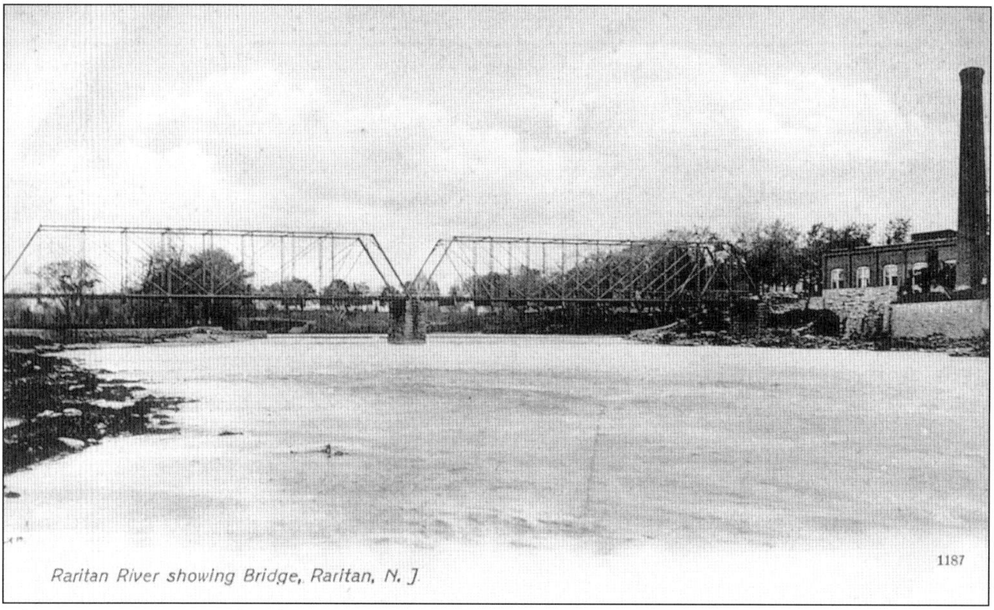

The pumping station for the Raritan Waterpower Canal can be seen on the far right of this picture. The Nevius Street Bridge has endured many floods that covered the roadbed over the years, but none as bad as Hurricane Floyd in 1999. (Courtesy of Barbara Navatto.)

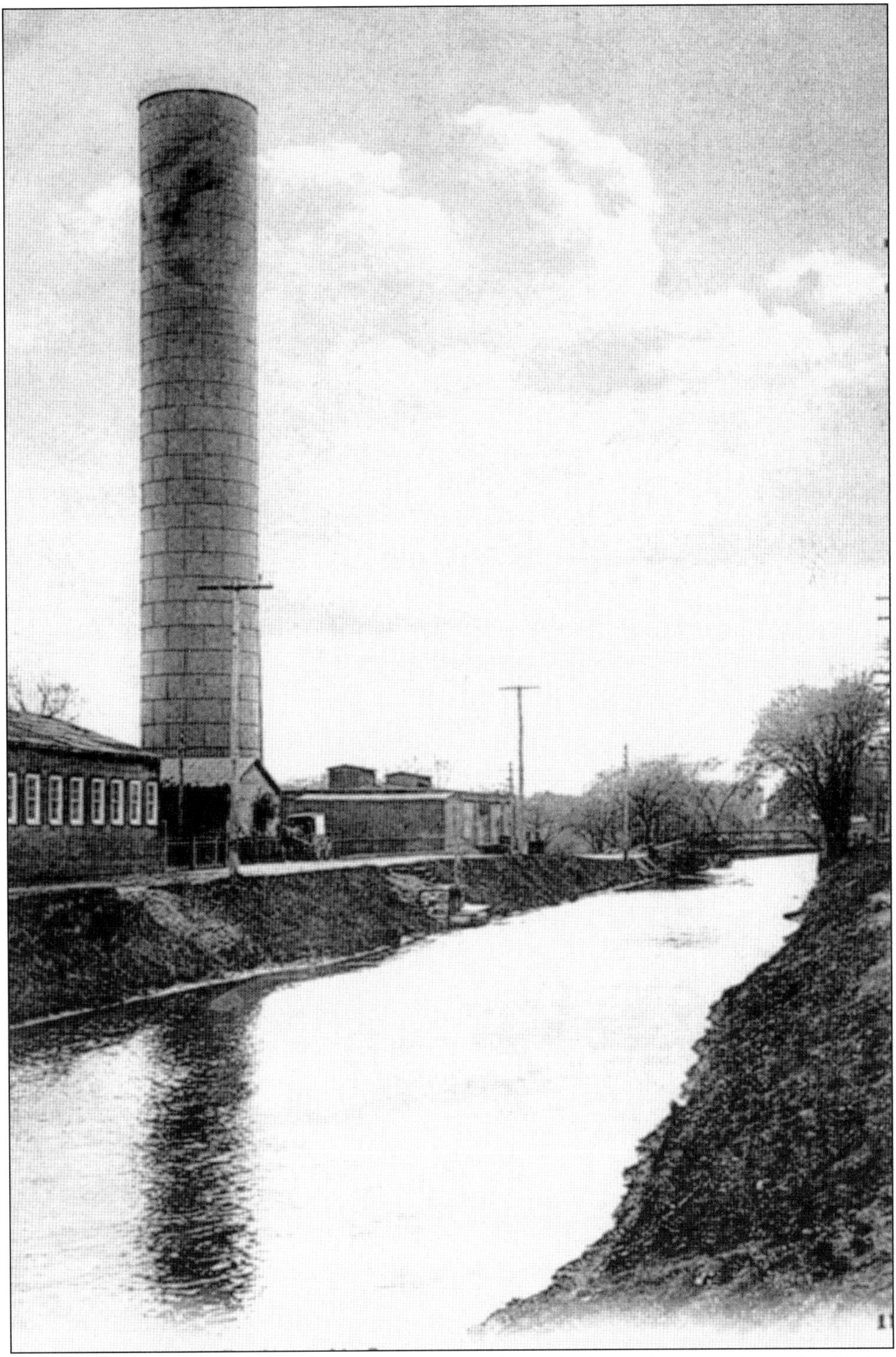

Seen here is an example of one of the many industrial plants located along the Raritan Waterpower Canal. (Courtesy of Barbara Navatto.)

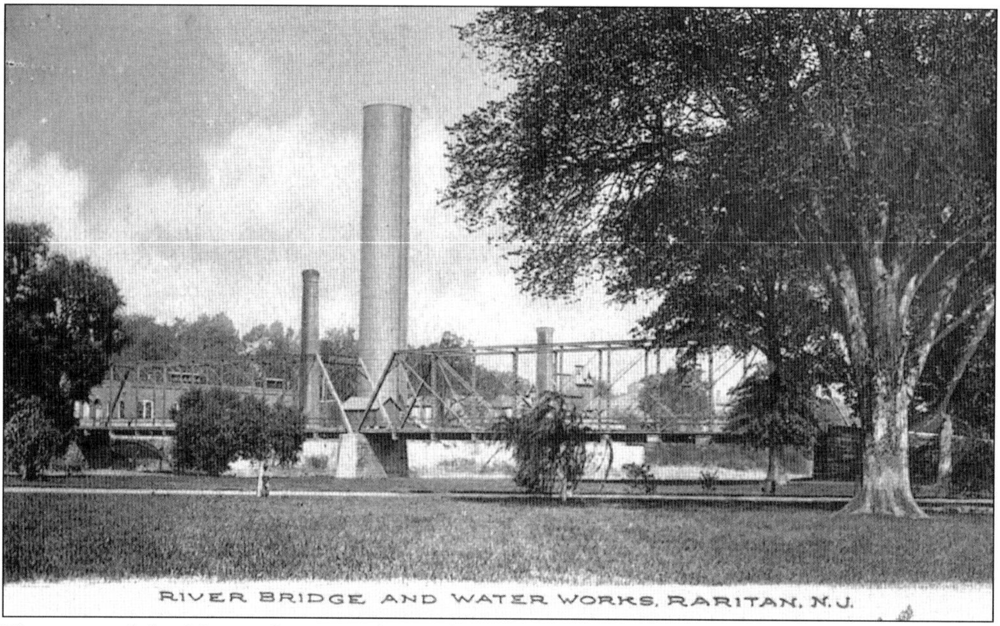

This view of the Nevius Street Bridge and Raritan Waterpower Canal waterworks was taken from the southern bank of the river. (Courtesy of Frank Tropiano.)

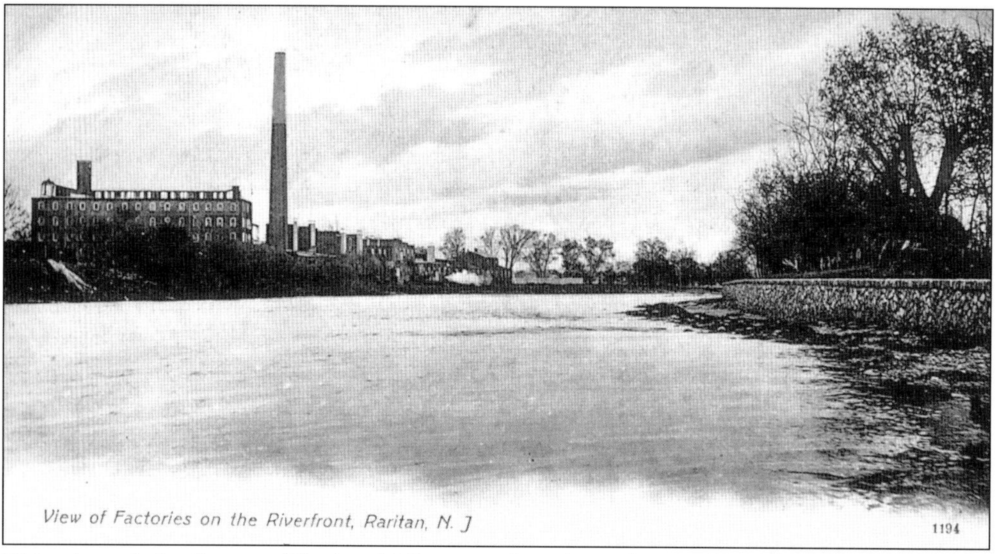

This view of the Raritan Woolen Mills was taken from the southern bank of the river in Hillsborough Township. (Courtesy of Barbara Navatto.)

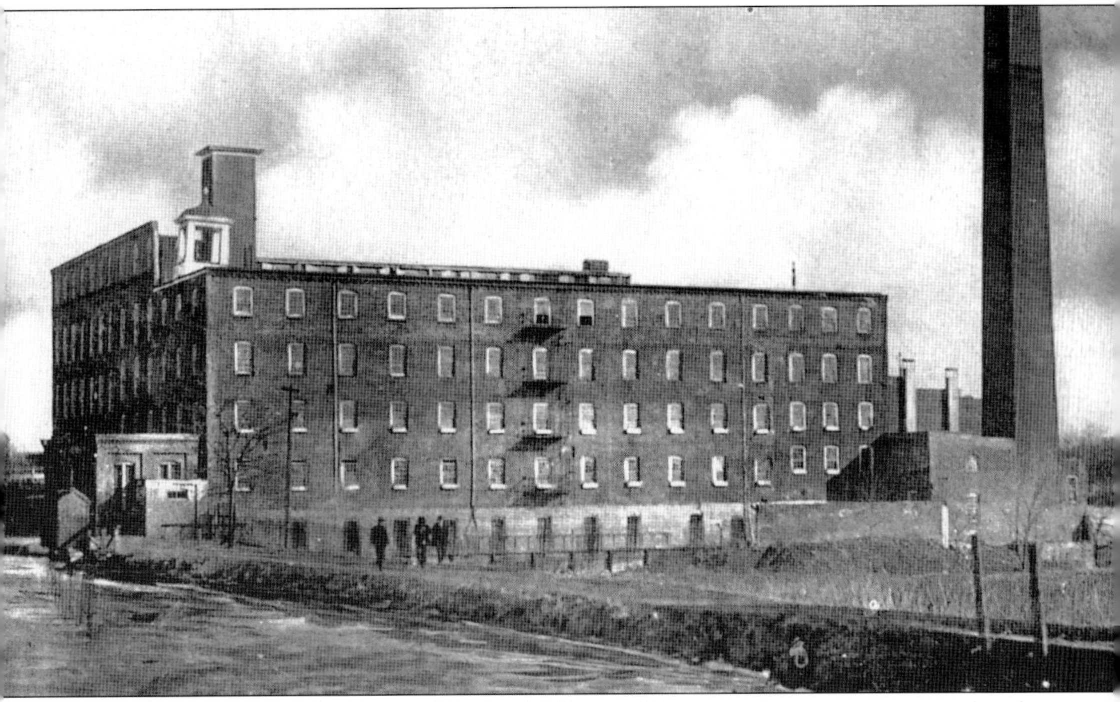

Another building, part of the Raritan Woolen Mills, stood between the waterpower canal and the Raritan River. Although child labor was illegal in the late 19th century, the grandmother of author Jo-Ann Liptak worked here in 1889 at the age of nine. She stood on a box to reach her loom and earned 5¢ a week. (Courtesy of Barbara Navatto.)

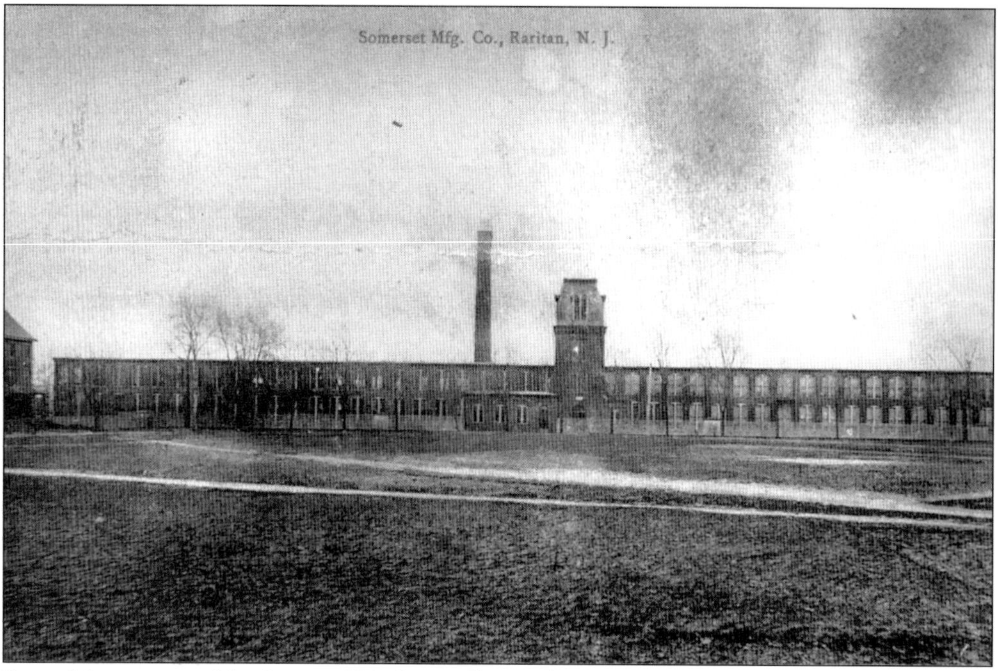

Part of the success of the Raritan Woolen Mills was the opportunity for the workers to live near their place of employment. Employee row housing, seen here in the left of the photograph, was located next to the mill. (Courtesy of Barbara Navatto.)

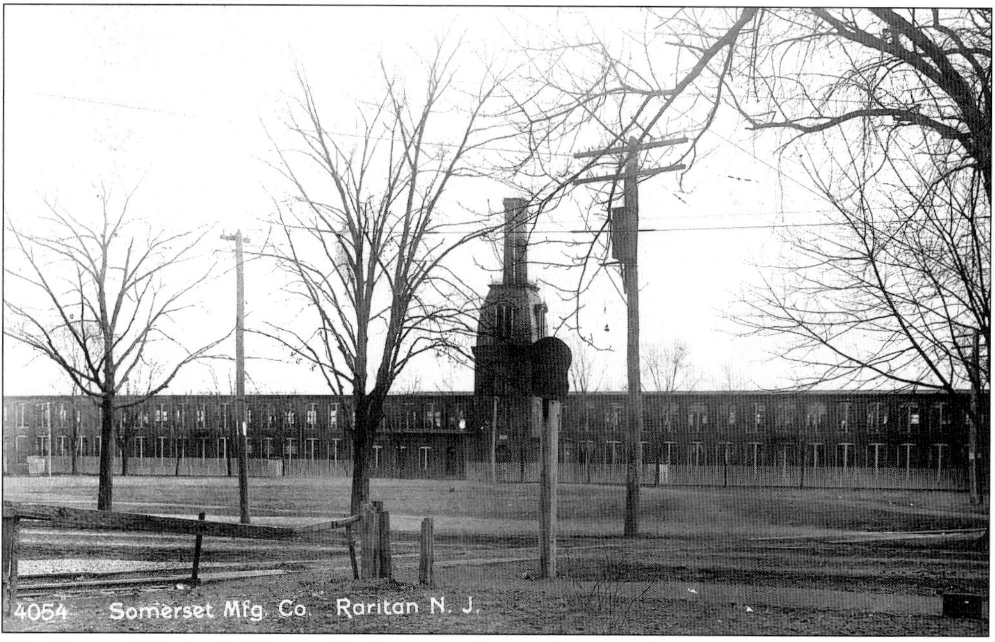

The Raritan Woolen Mills was the largest and most famous of Raritan's early industries. It was known throughout the United States as a manufacturer of the finest woolen goods. In 1882, its name changed to the Somerset Manufacturing Company. At one time, some 400 people worked here. The mill made uniforms and blankets for Union soldiers during the Civil War and uniforms for the U.S. Army during World War I. (Courtesy of William Dudeck.)

This lovely clock was part of the original fixtures found in the Raritan Woolen Mills. Today, the clock hangs on a wall in the Raritan Public Library.

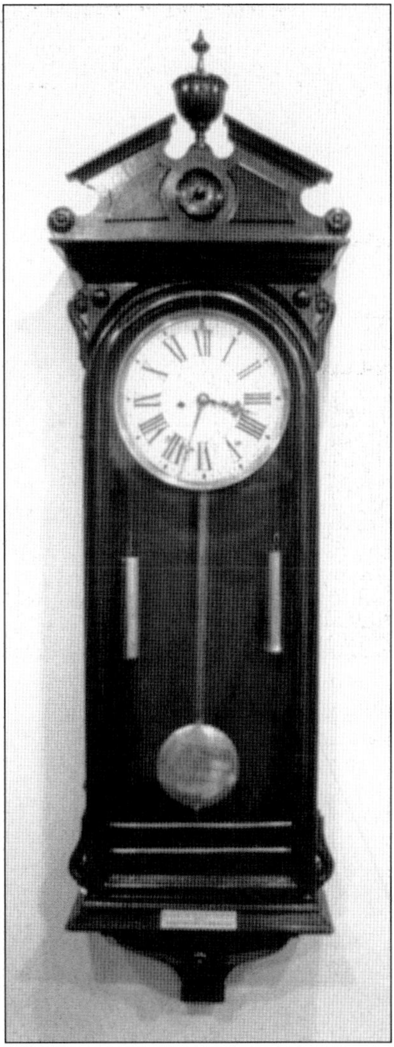

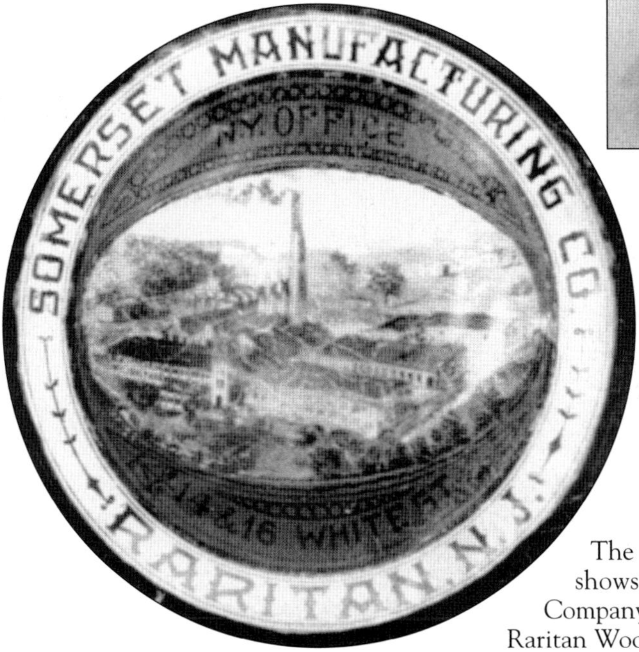

The picture within the paperweight shows the Somerset Manufacturing Company, which was also known as the Raritan Woolen Mills.

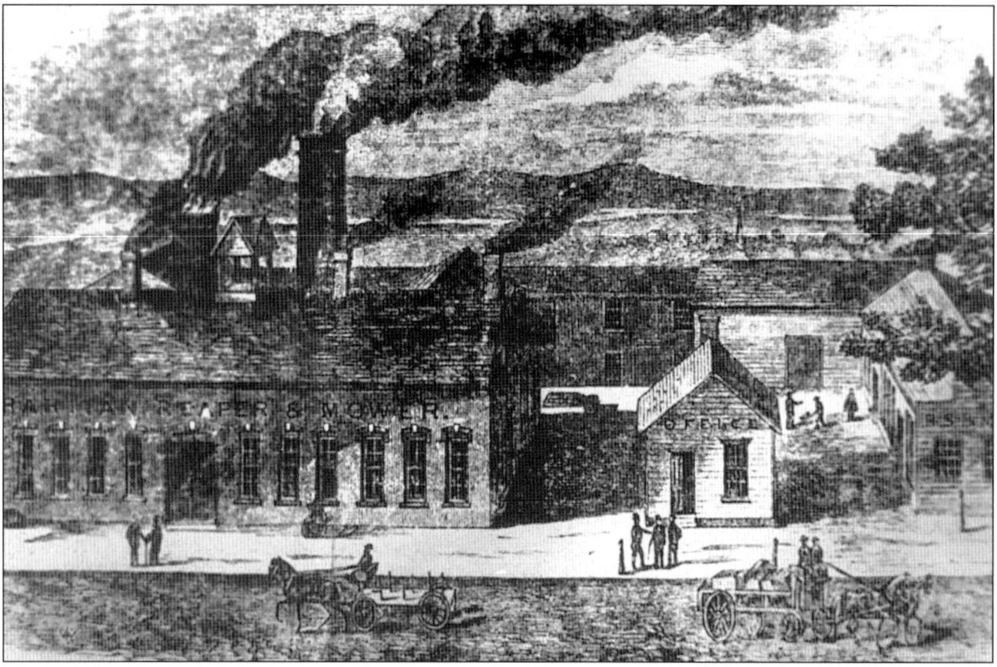

One of Raritan's early industrial companies was the Raritan Reaper and Mower Manufacturing Company. The company manufactured mowers and reapers for area farmers. It was fairly successful, but a better reaper developed by Cyrus McCormick eventually led to the demise of this plant.

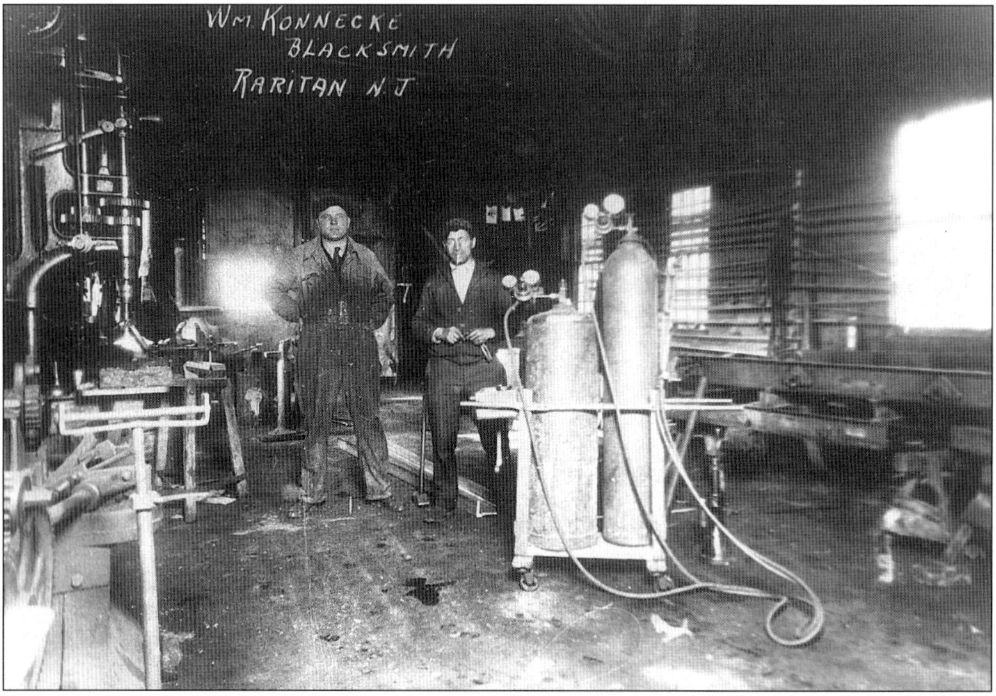

A blacksmith shop was the center of many towns in the 19th and early 20th centuries. Seen here are two busy workers in William Konnecke's blacksmith shop in Raritan.

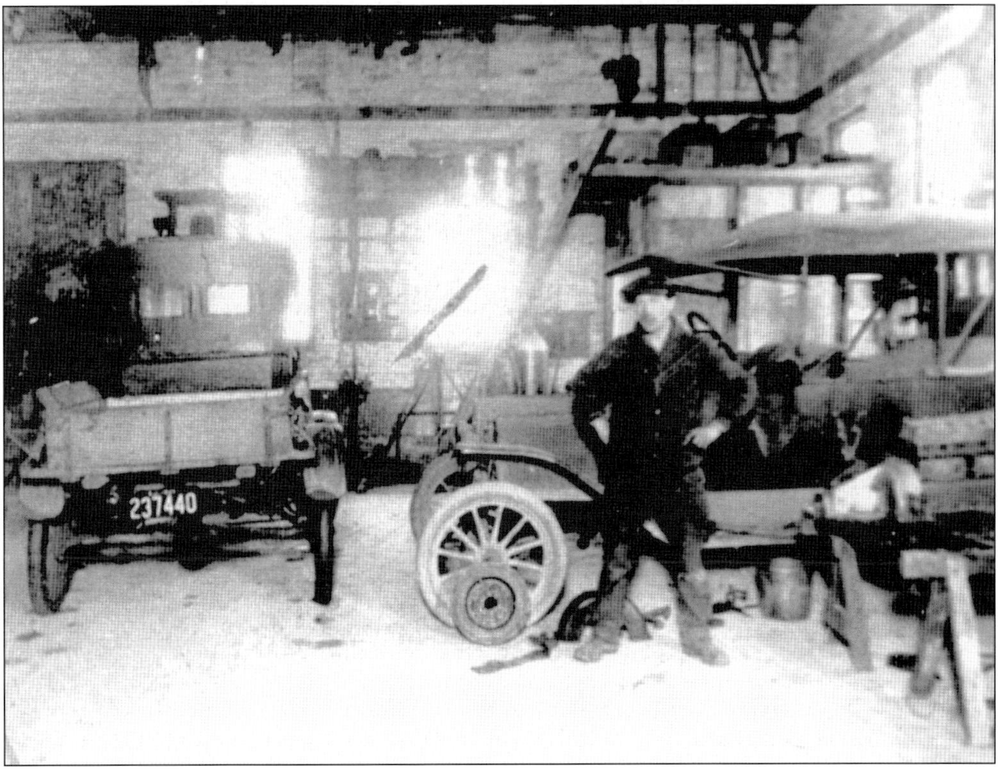

This 1920s auto repair shop was not quite as sophisticated as modern ones are, but it had everything needed to repair the cars of the day.

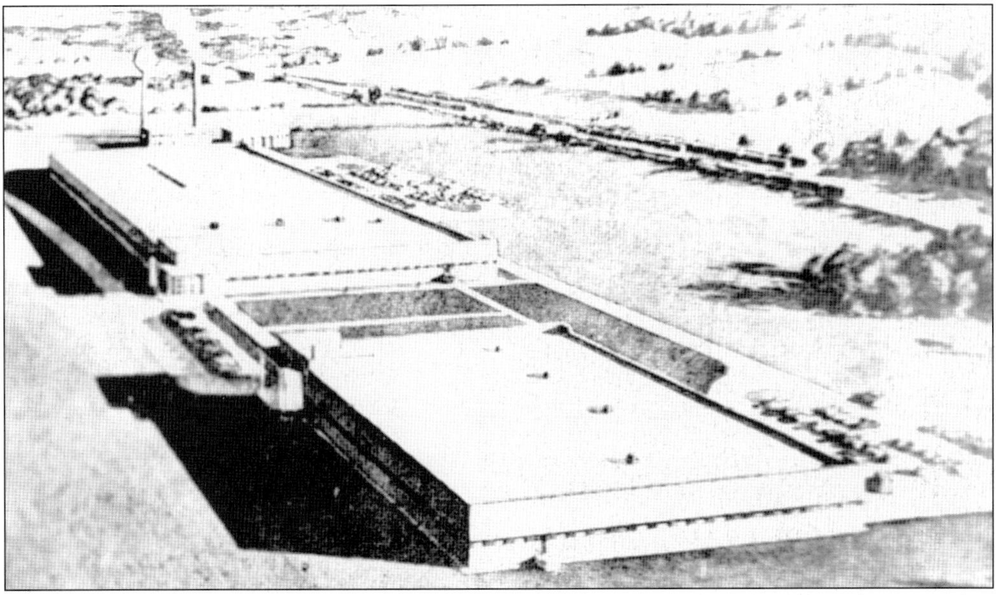

Ortho Pharmaceuticals has been a major employer in Raritan for many years. What started as a one-building facility manufacturing medical tests has grown into a pharmaceutical complex that is a major medical research facility in the United States and a subsidiary of Johnson and Johnson.

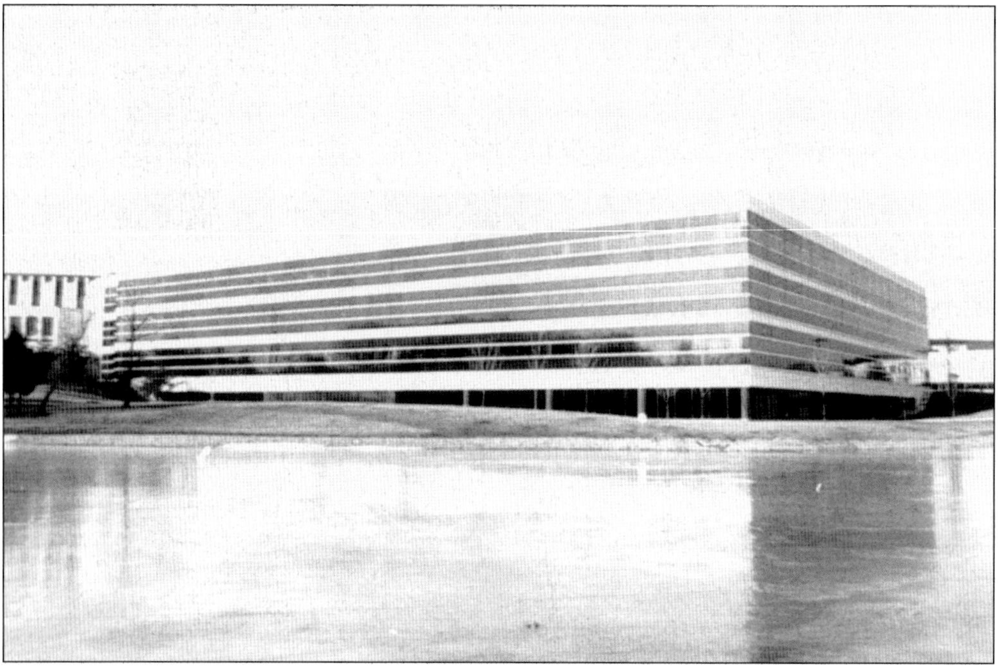

This is one of the many new research buildings dotting the Ortho Pharmaceutical campus.

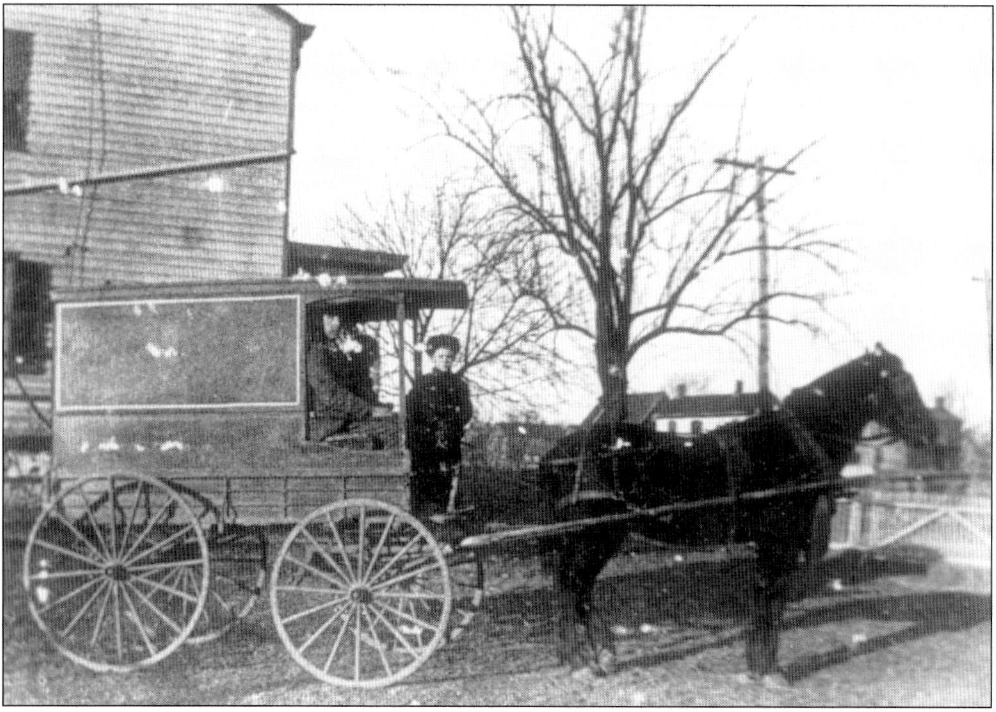

In the early days of Raritan, all deliveries were made by horse and wagon. This young man and his father are ready for their deliveries.

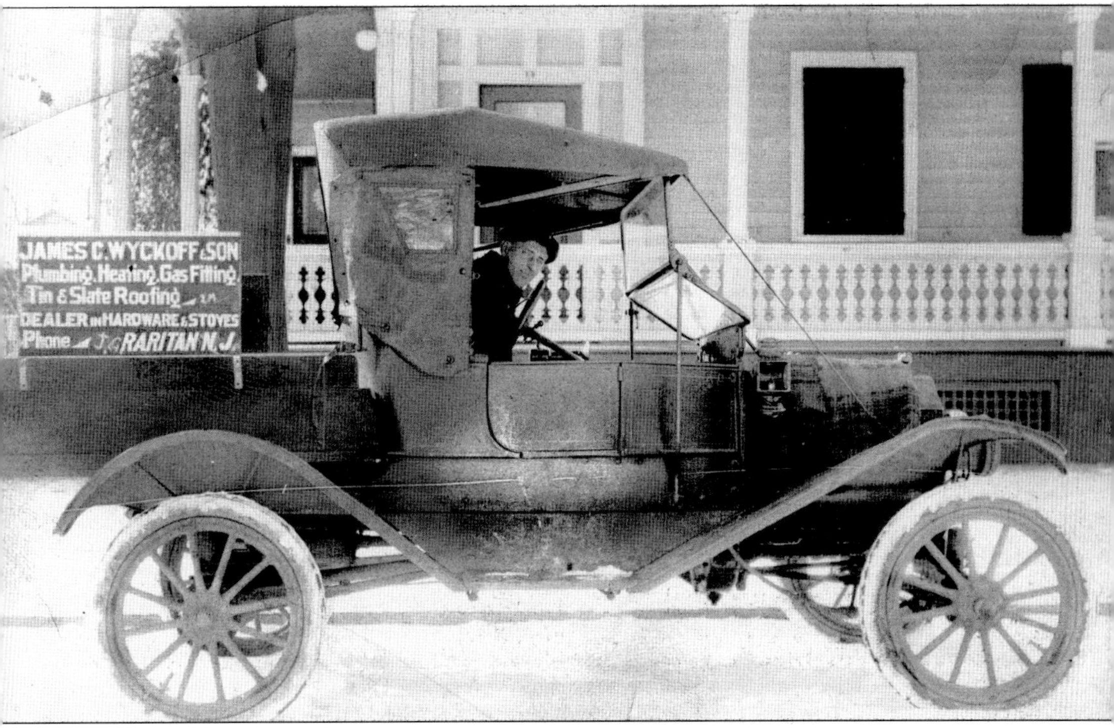

James C. Wyckoff was a busy businessman. His truck sign indicates that he did plumbing, heating, gas filling, and tin and slate roofing, as well as serving as a hardware and stove dealer. (Courtesy of Lilyan Navatto.)

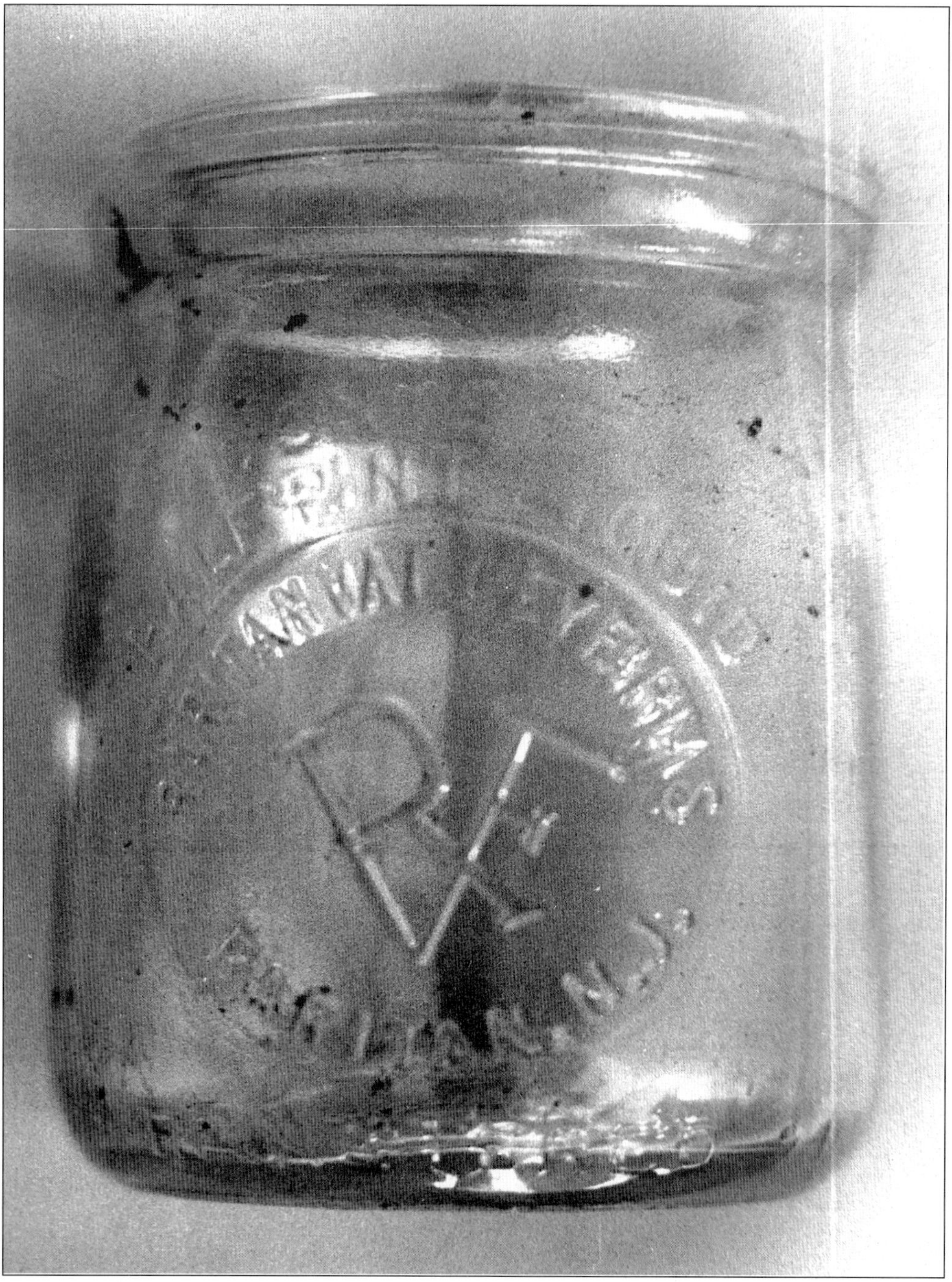

Raritan Valley Dairy was founded in 1907 by Sen. Joseph S. Frelinghuysen. The dairy began as a small producing herd near Raritan and became a leader in the production and processing of certified milk. With the help of Dr. Henry Coit, a Newark child specialist deeply concerned over the fact that children were undernourished for lack of clean, wholesome milk, Frelinghuysen introduced and passed a bill known as the Certified Milk Law of New Jersey. This bill served as a model across the state. Pictured is an example of one of the half-pint bottles of milk served in local schools.

Many small breweries and soda-bottling companies were located in Raritan. This bottle is from the Babey and Daniel Beer Bottlers.

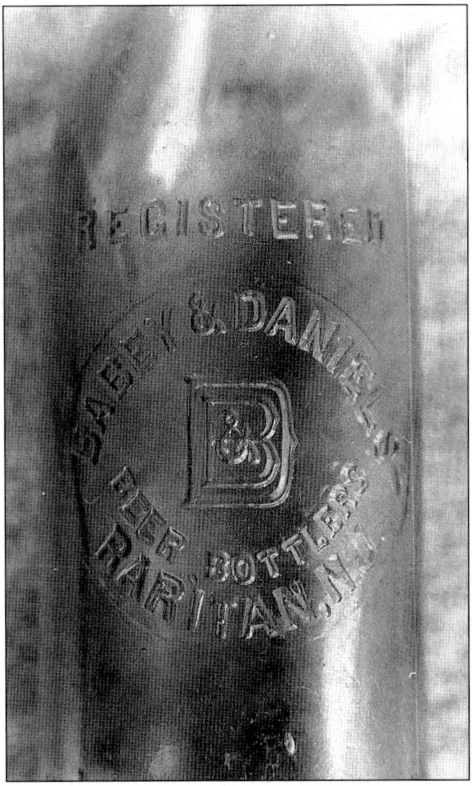

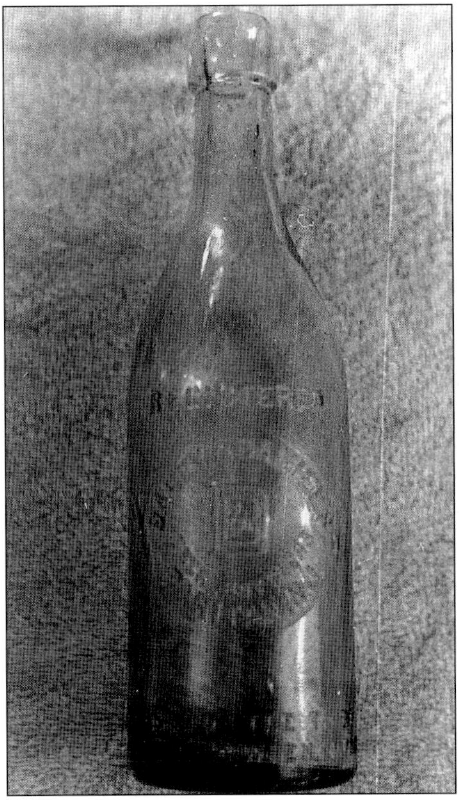

Other bottlers in town were Michael Ruggieri, Michael Tarangelo, A. Stabile and C. Fasoli, and Vena and Tozzi.

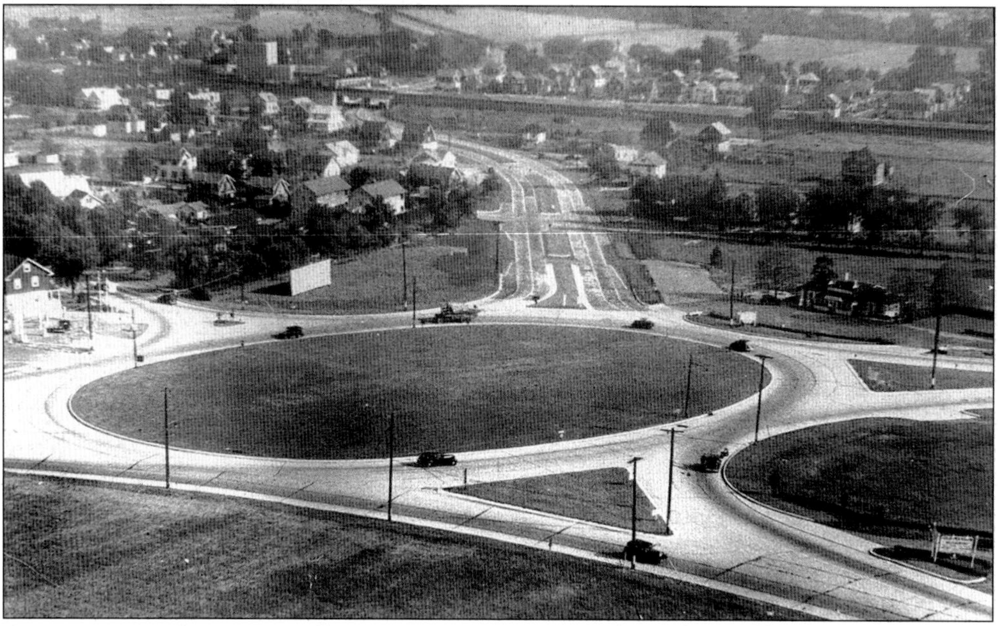

An innovative design in traffic movement was the traffic circle. Although known as the Somerville Circle, this rotary has no part that is located within Somerville's borders. About one-third of the circle is in Raritan, and the rest of it is in Bridgewater Township.

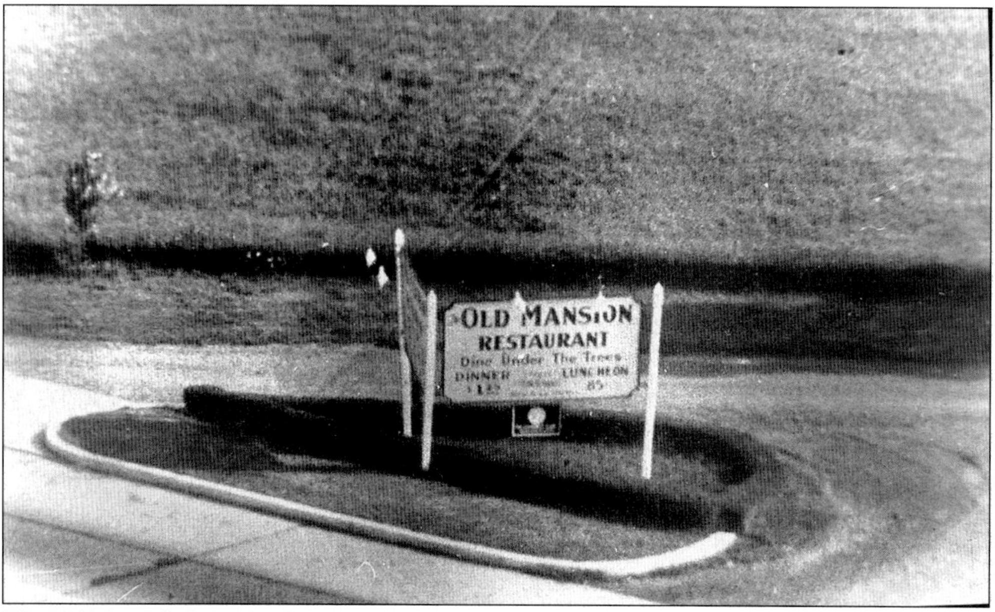

The Hill, Joseph S. Frelinghuysen's estate in Raritan, was sold and became the Old Mansion Restaurant. It was one of two restaurants located on the circle. Lunch was served for 85¢ and dinner was served for $1.25.

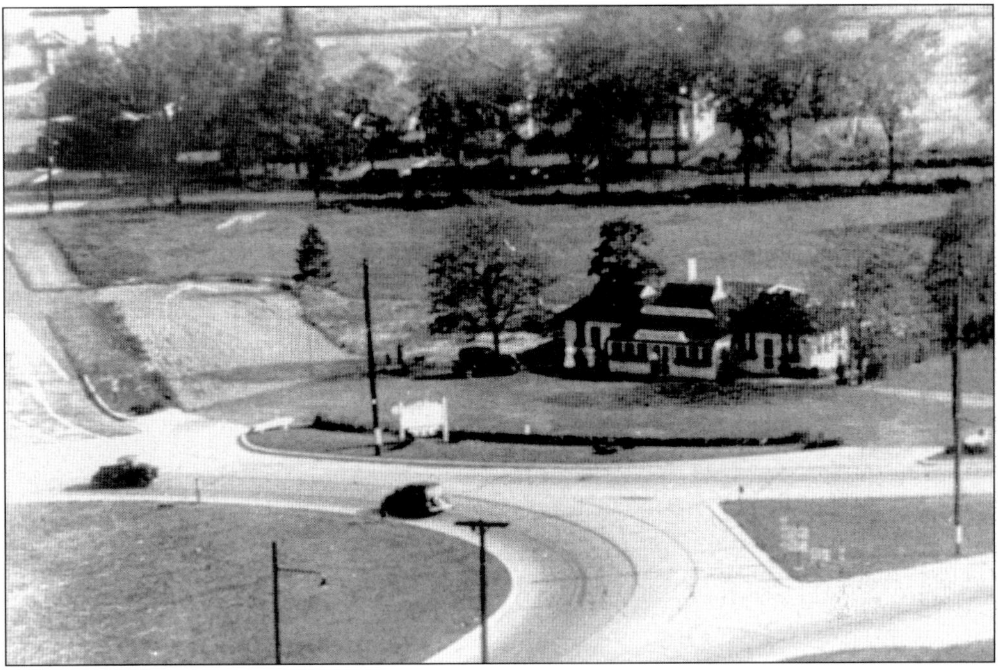

The other restaurant on the circle was the Raritan Valley Inn. This early photograph shows what the inn looked like in the 1930s.

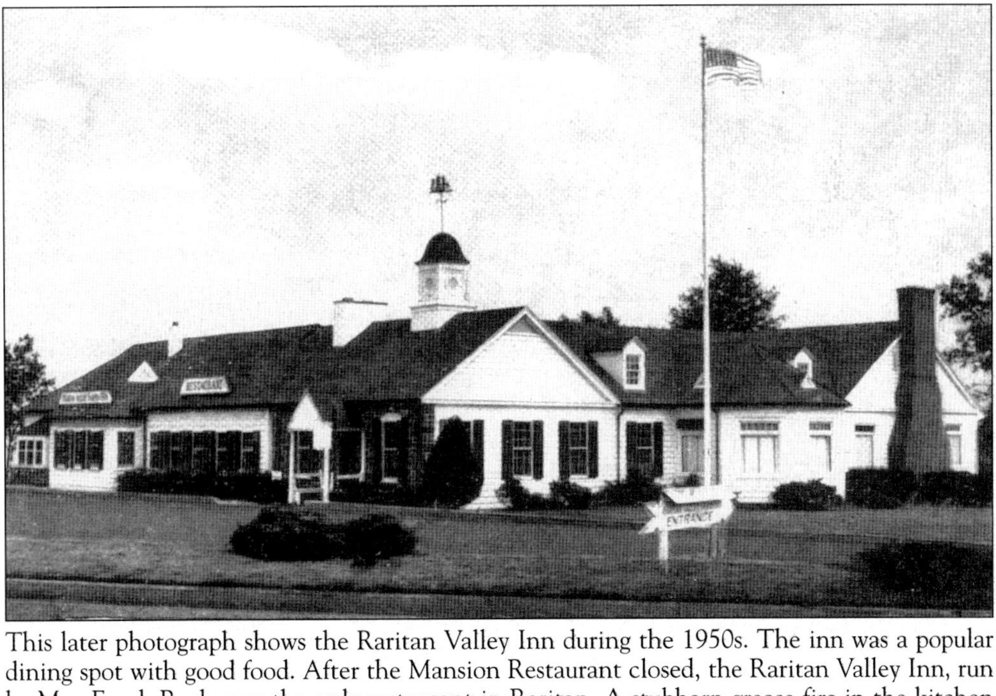

This later photograph shows the Raritan Valley Inn during the 1950s. The inn was a popular dining spot with good food. After the Mansion Restaurant closed, the Raritan Valley Inn, run by Mrs. Frank Buck, was the only restaurant in Raritan. A stubborn grease fire in the kitchen destroyed the structure in 1961—one month before the wedding reception of author M. Frieda Helmstetter was to be held there.

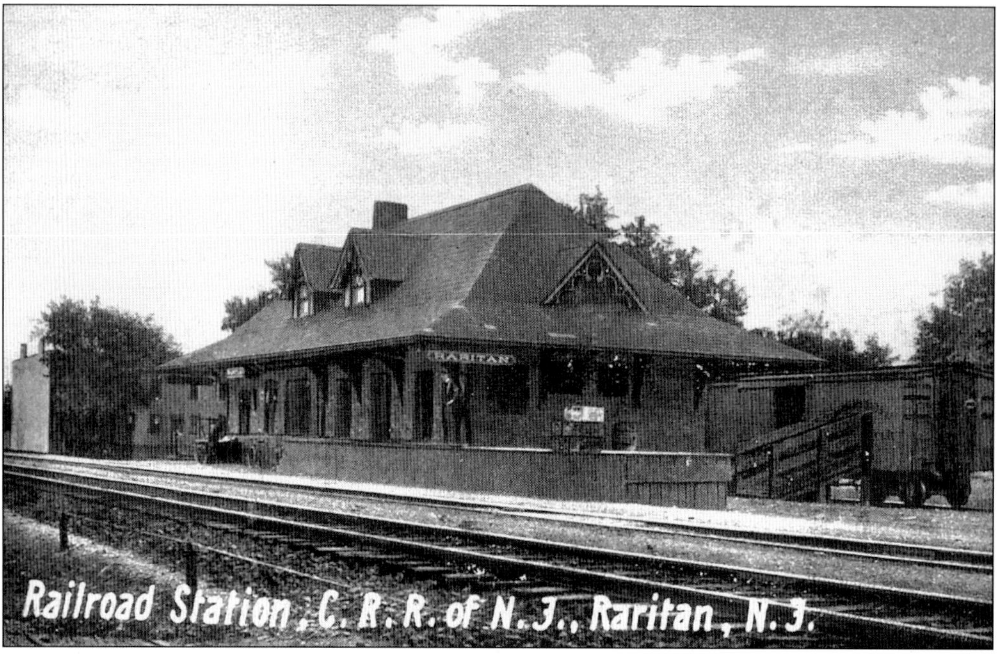

The Central New Jersey Railroad constructed the Raritan train station sometime in the 1890s. This one-and-a-half-story stone building with a hip roof and flared eaves is listed on the National Register of Historic Places. (Courtesy of Barbara Navatto.)

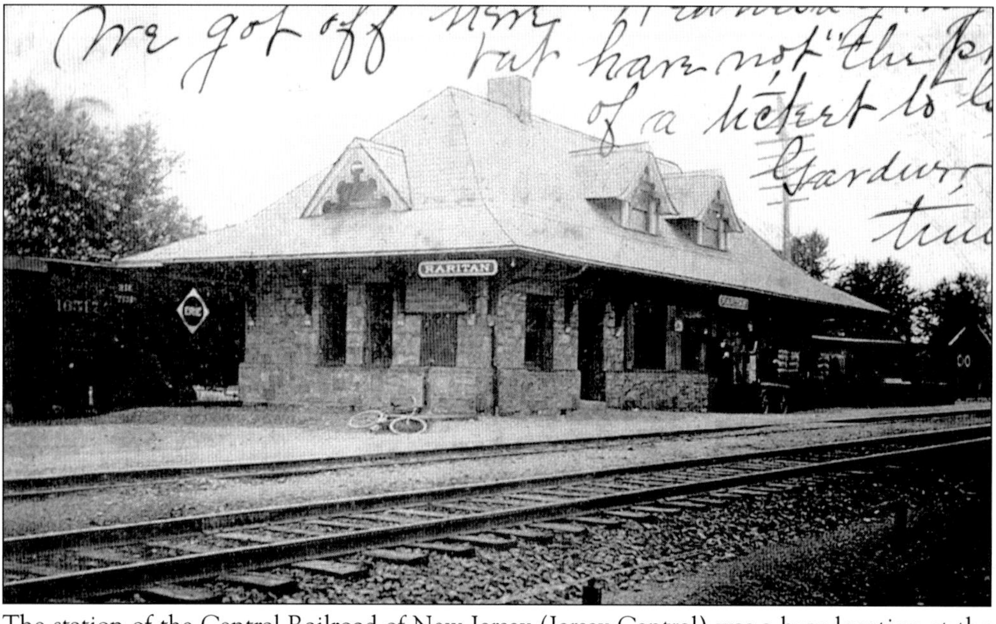

The station of the Central Railroad of New Jersey (Jersey Central) was a busy location at the beginning of the 20th century, handling both passenger and freight trains. Commuters continue to use this station today. (Courtesy of Barbara Navatto.)

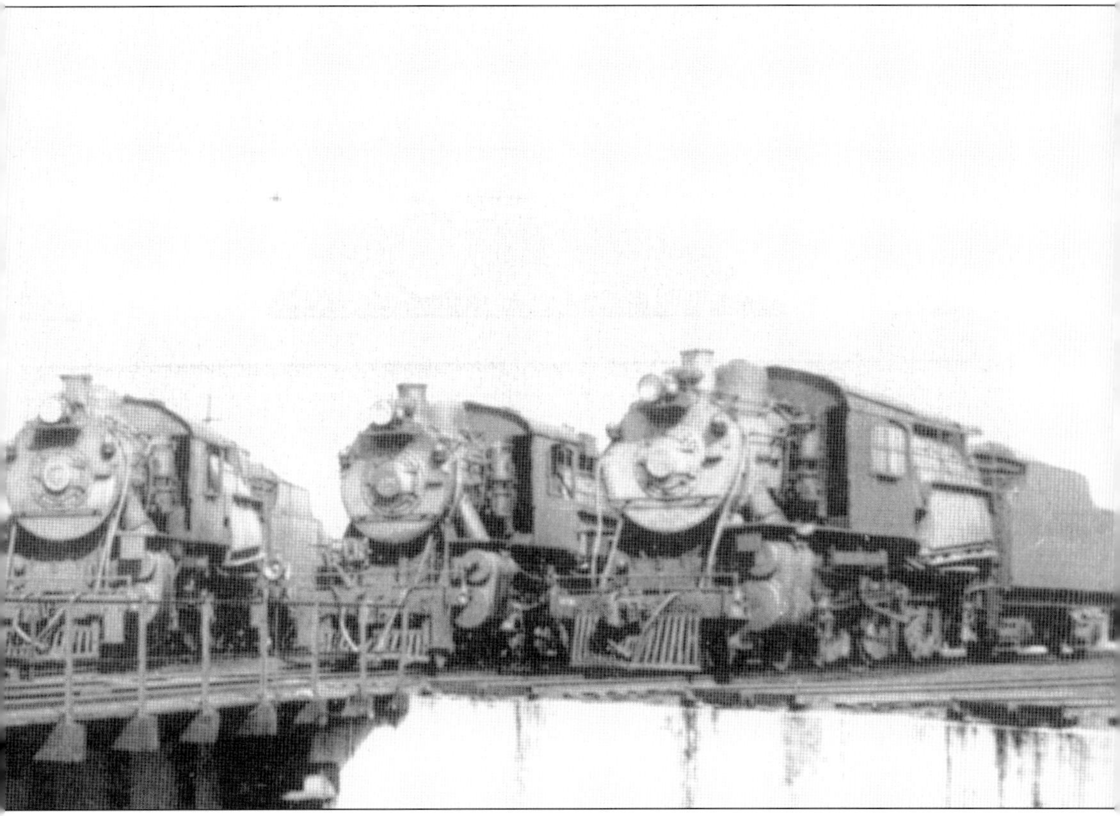

Raritan had a roundhouse, or turntable, for the trains. The Central New Jersey Railroad's roundhouse at Raritan is shown here with a commuter locomotive in the 1930s. (Courtesy of Barbara Navatto.)

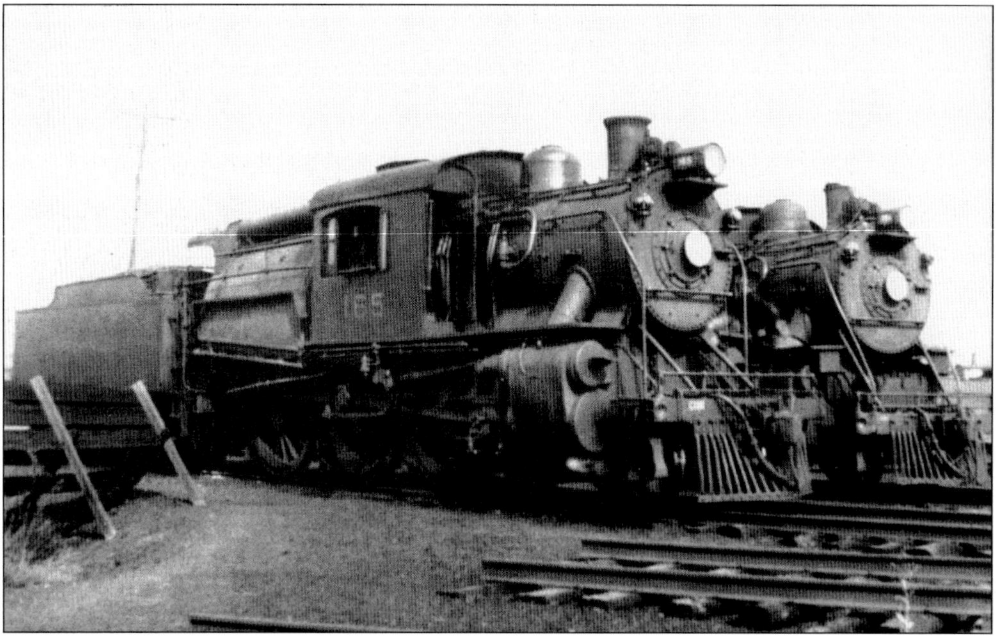

Central New Jersey's 10-wheelers No. 165 and No. 754 are pictured here at the Raritan engine terminal in 1933. (Courtesy of Barbara Navatto.)

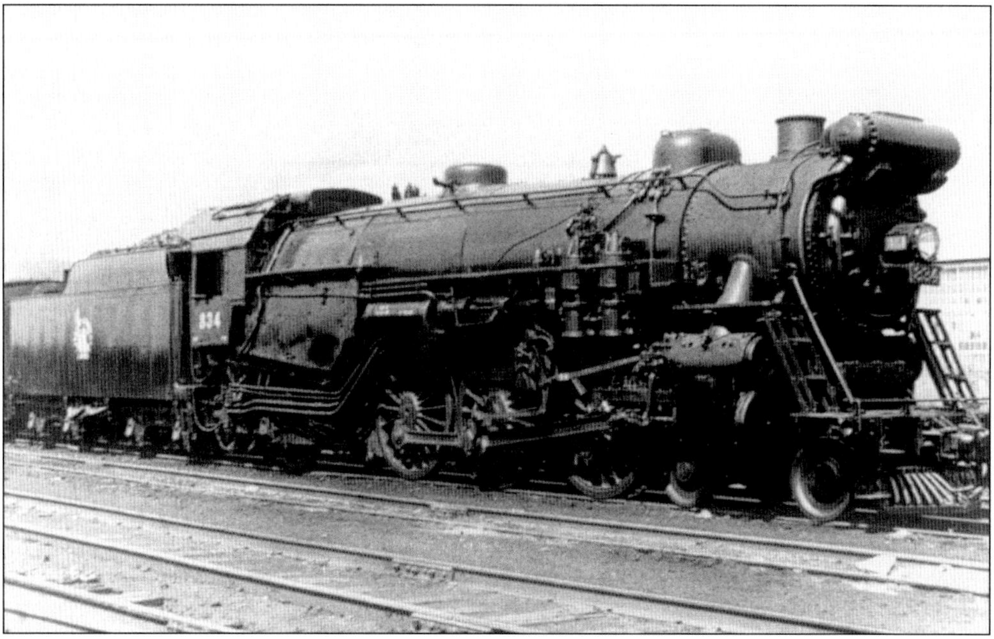

Various steam locomotives, including these two, were housed within the roundhouse in the Central New Jersey Railroad yard.

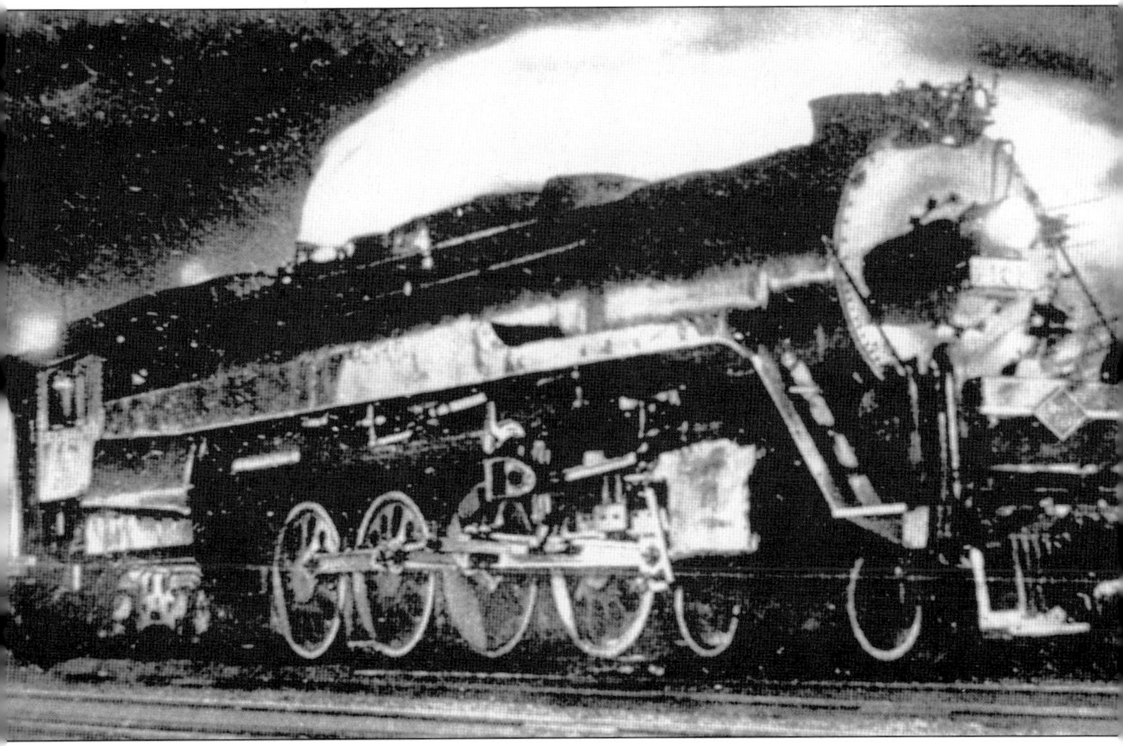
The steam train T-1, 2102 arrives in Raritan on a cold winter night in 1972.

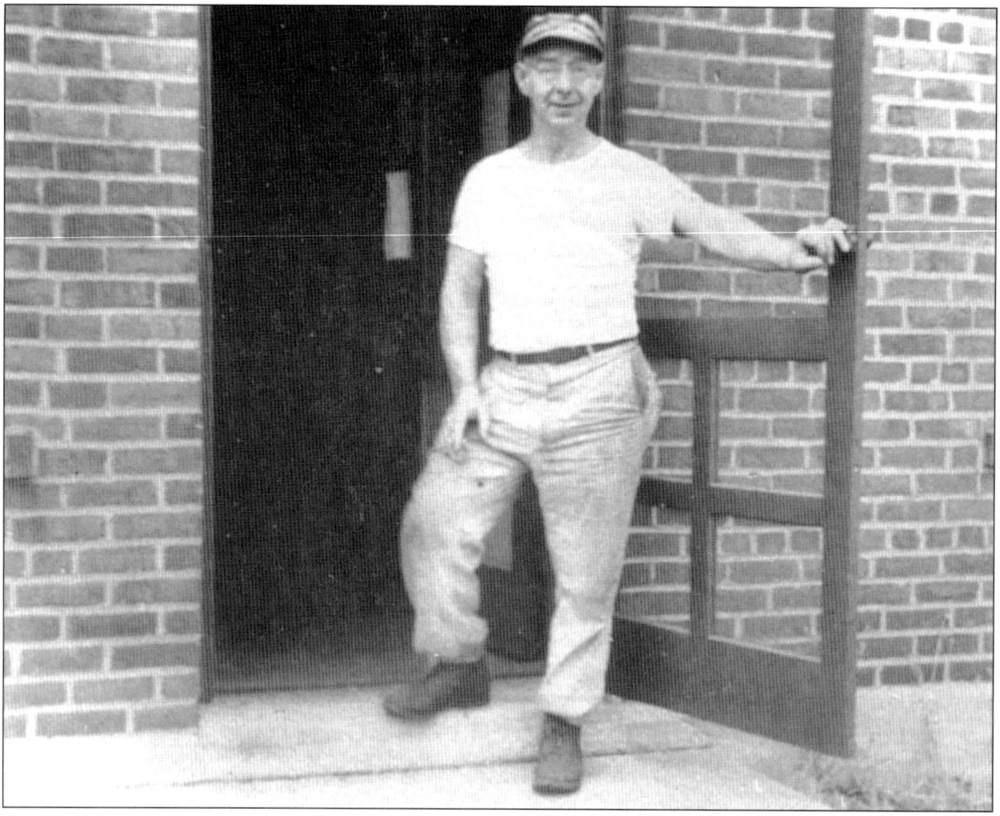

A Jersey Central worker emerges from the control tower building. Many friends and relatives of people living in Raritan came to town from New York City on the fast, convenient trains.

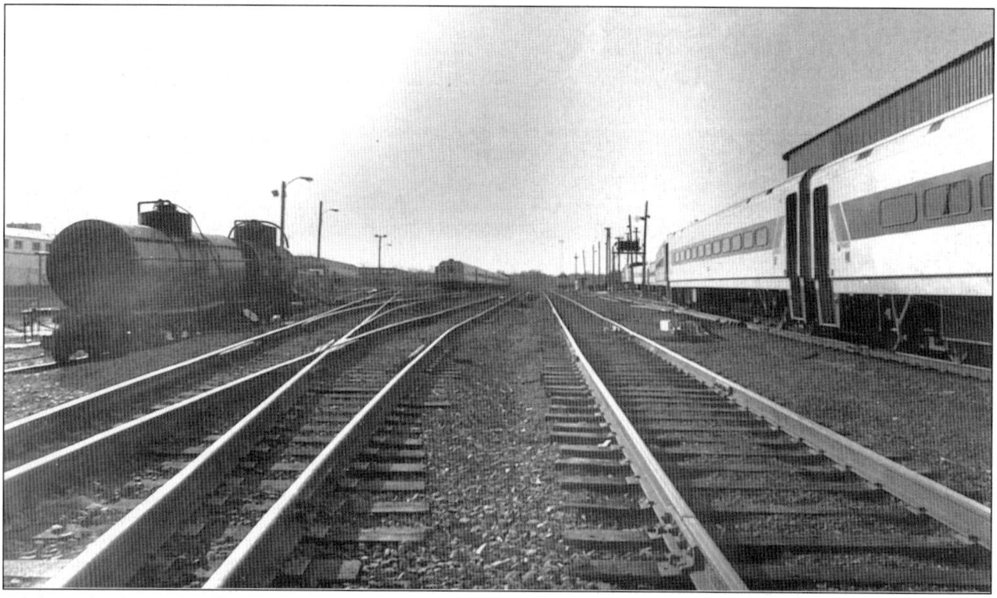

Although the roundhouse and turntable are gone, the Raritan yard is the terminus for many New Jersey Transit trains, with commuter traffic increasing yearly.

Two

Schools, Churches, and Community Organizations

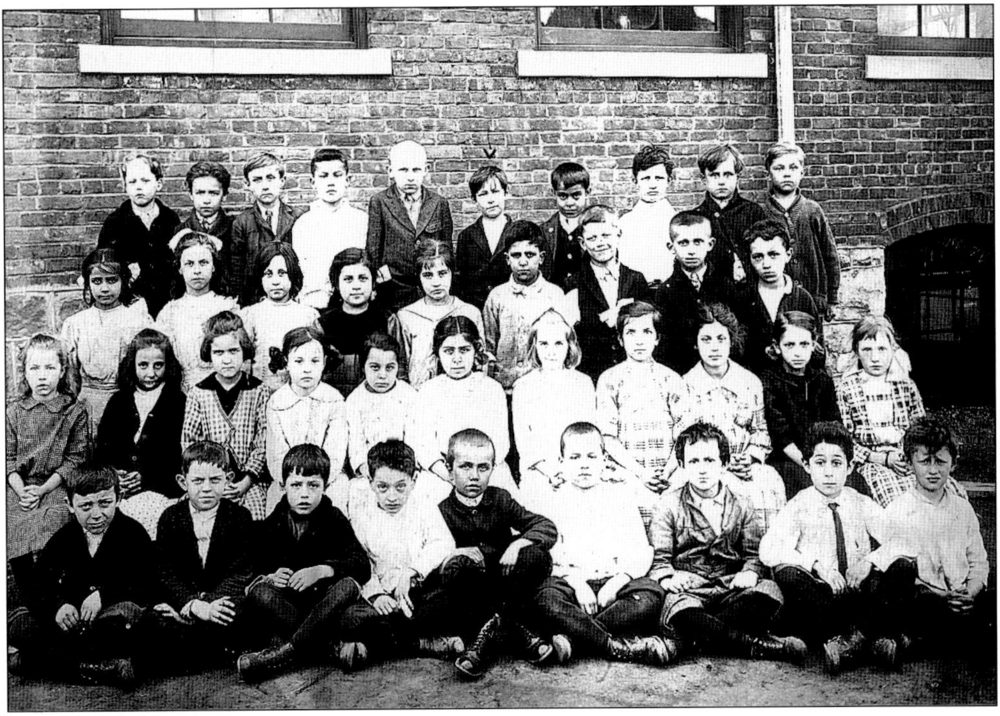

Students pose outside of a Raritan elementary school *c.* 1915.

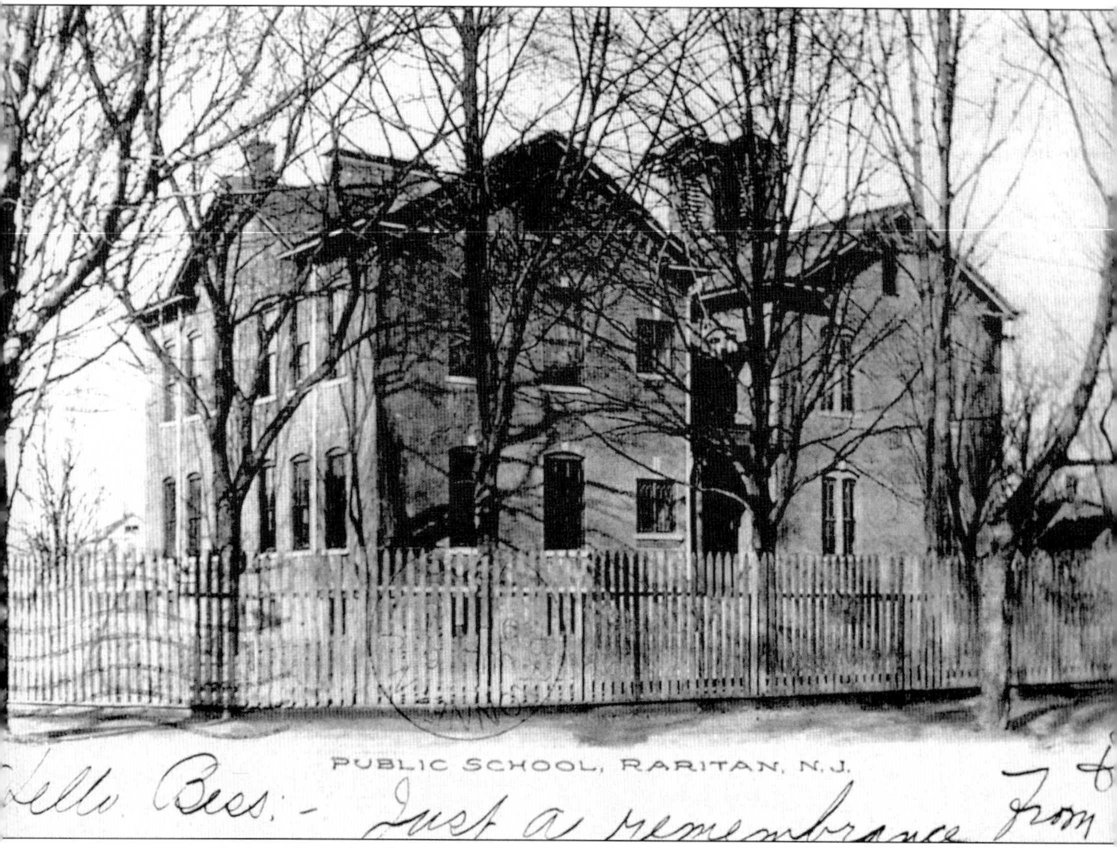

One of the first public schools within the borough of Raritan was known as the Raritan Public School, later called the Raritan Primary School. This photograph shows the original red brick structure with its bell and bell tower. It was constructed *c.* 1870. (Courtesy of Barbara Navatto.)

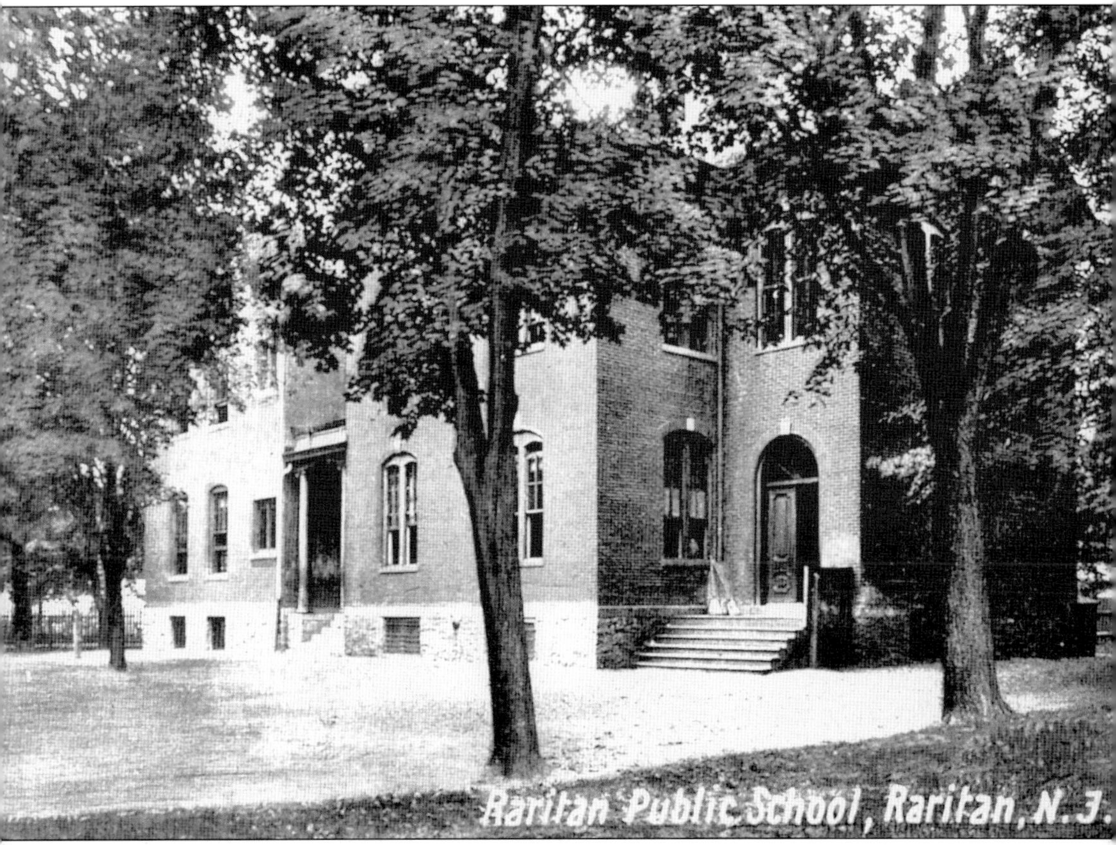

The original school consisted of four rooms and housed grades one through eight. Ten years later, in 1880, two wings of four rooms each were added to accommodate an expanding enrollment. (Courtesy of Barbara Navatto.)

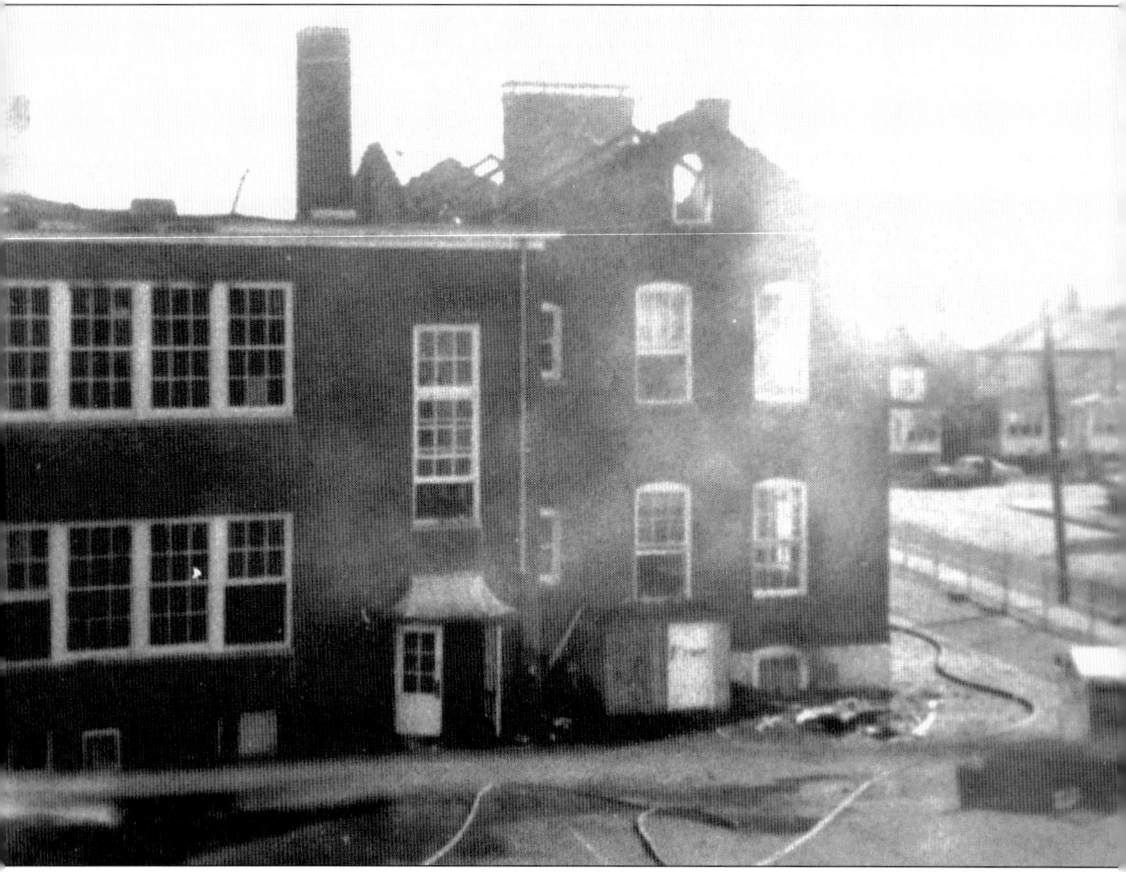

This more recent photograph shows the Raritan Primary School. After the school closed in 1965, the building was used as the Raritan borough municipal building until it was destroyed by fire in 1969.

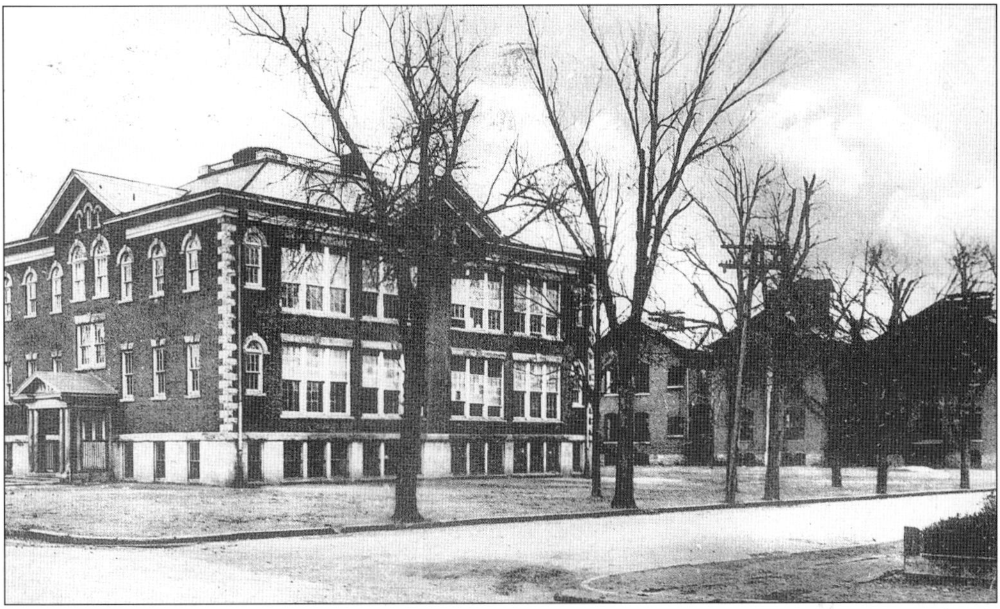

The Raritan Intermediate School was built in 1914 directly behind the Raritan Primary School. It consisted of eight classrooms and housed grades four through eight before the Washington School was built in the 1930s. (Courtesy of Barbara Navatto.)

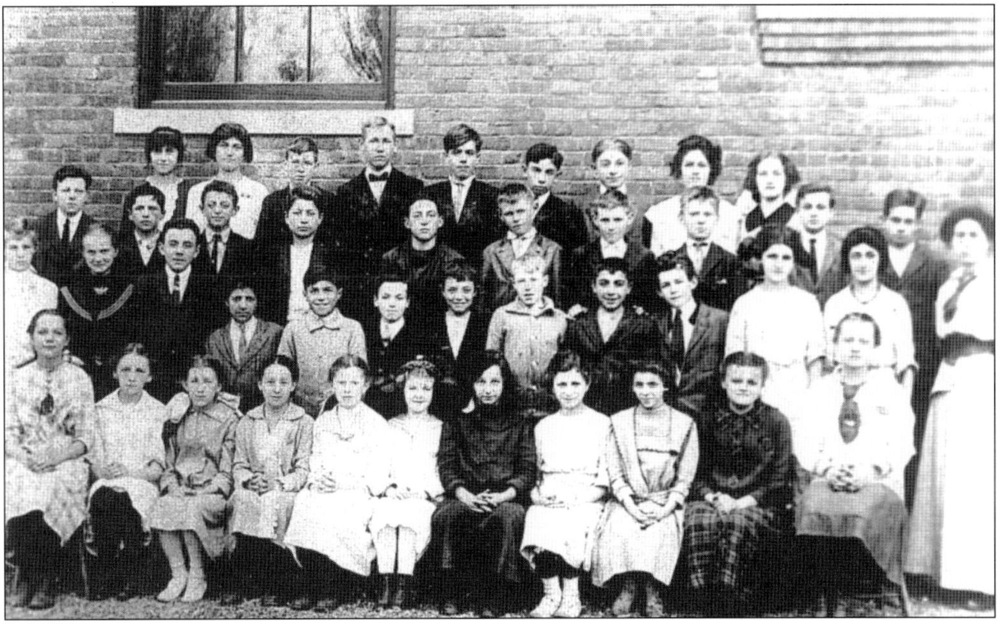

A group of Raritan Intermediate School students and their teacher pose for a class photograph shortly after the school opened in 1914.

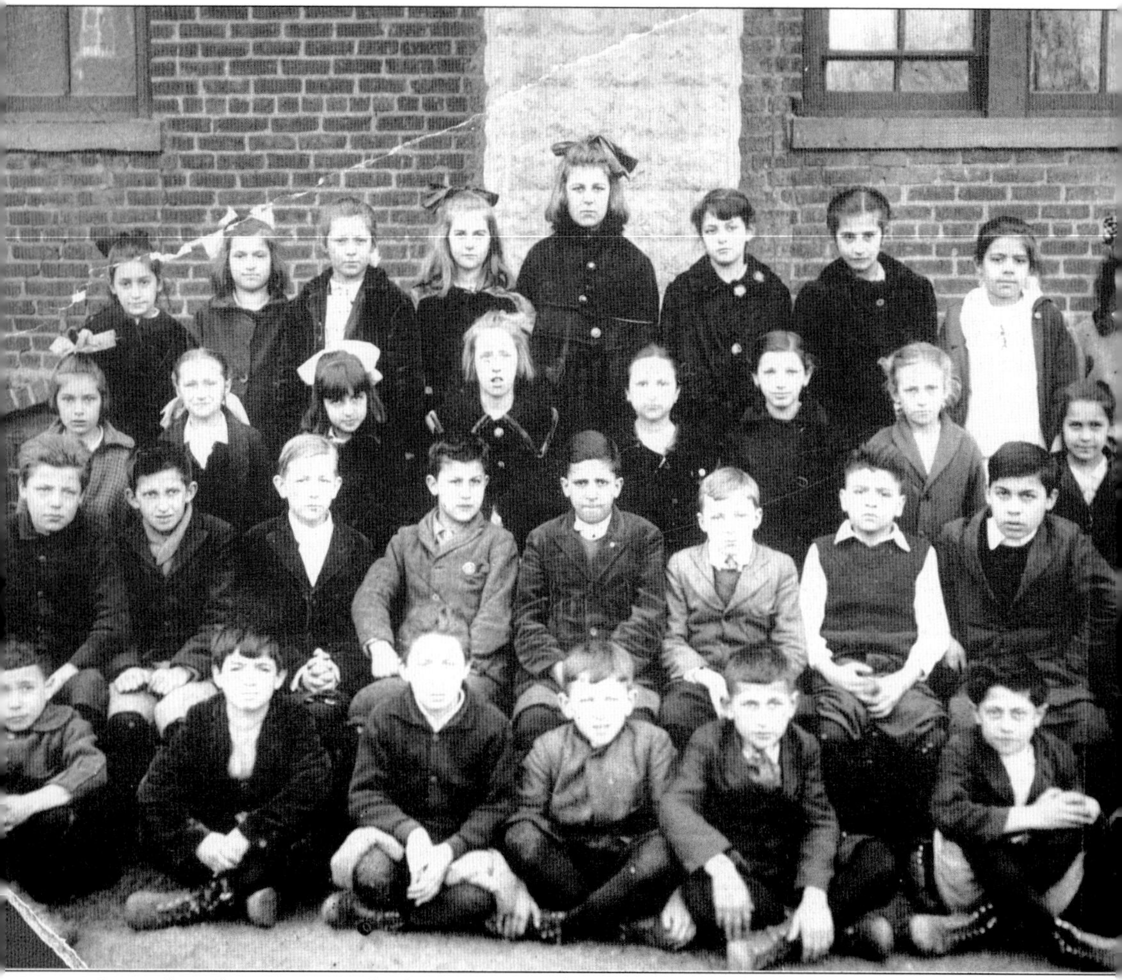

Second-graders pose outside the Raritan Public School *c.* 1916.

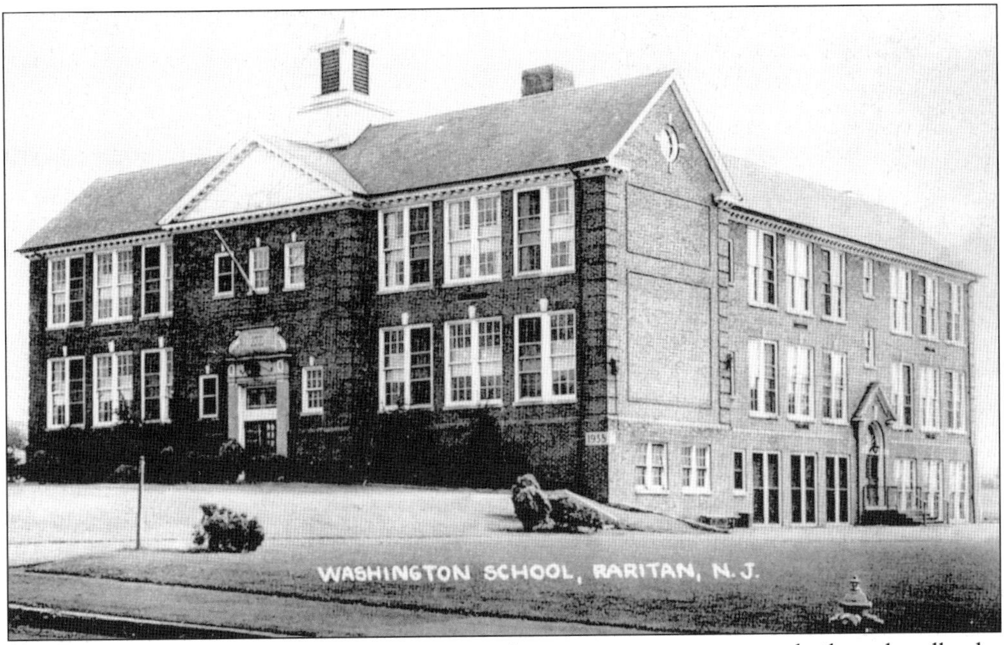

The Washington School, a Works Progress Administration project, was built to handle the growing school-aged population in Raritan. The school held grades six through eight. Its cornerstone was laid in 1935.

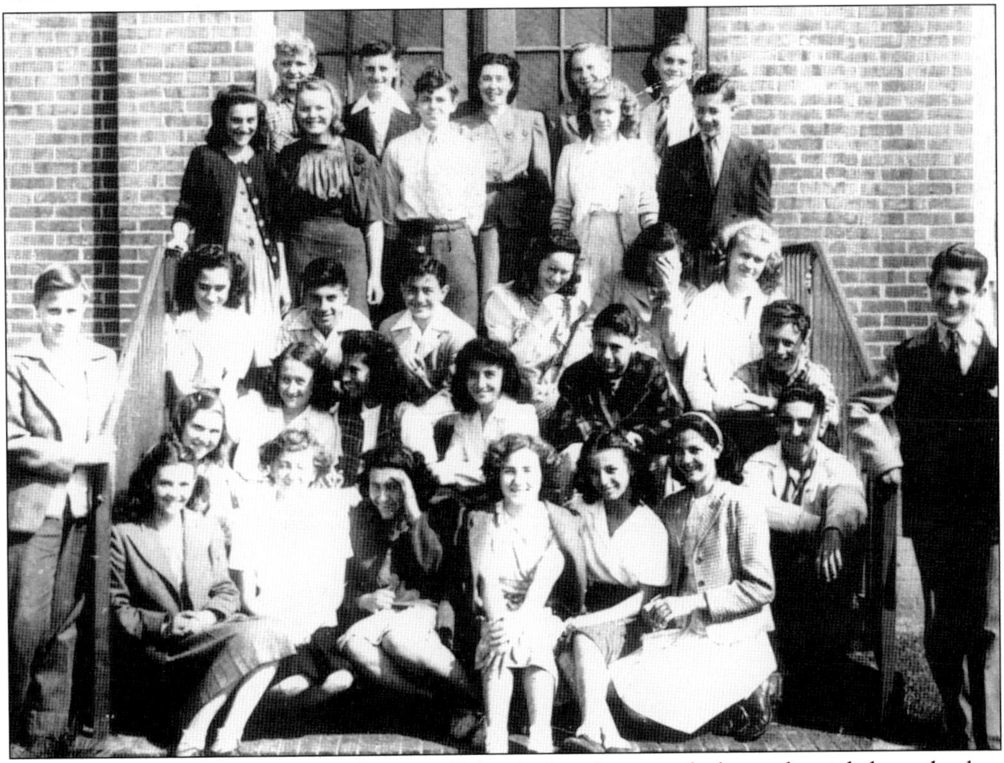

Taken at the side entrance of Washington School, this photograph shows the eighth-grade class of 1945 with teacher Ruth Stugart. (Courtesy of the Raritan Public Library.)

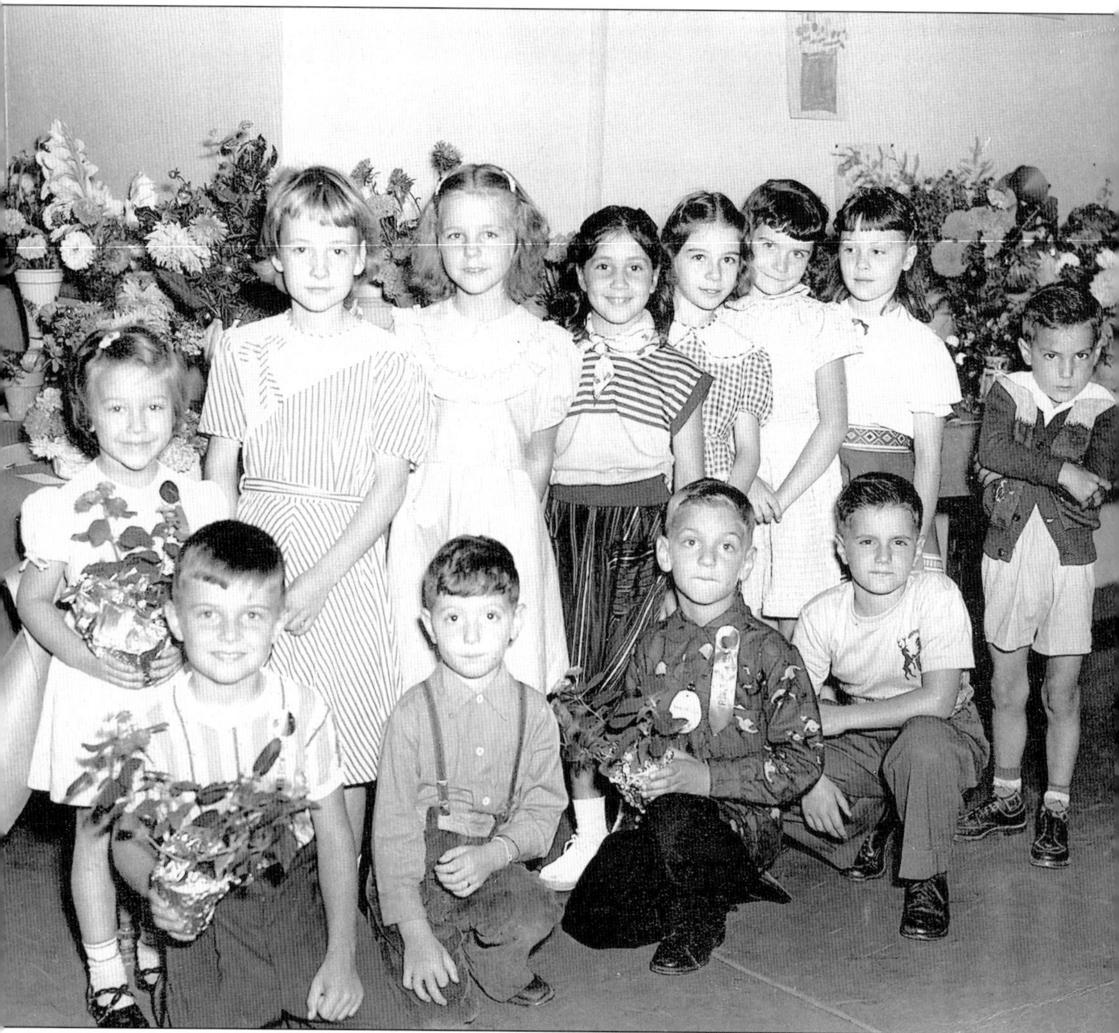

The Raritan Primary School held a flower show every September. The 1951 Flower Show first-prize winners, from left to right, are as follows: (kneeling) Ronald Freund, unidentified, Stephen Koscnick, and Billy Truffarelli; (standing) Jo-Ann Liptak, Stella Gibson, Virginia Rynearson, Jo-Ann Provenzano, Lynne Brelsford, Gloria Garley, Betty Ann Van Note, and John Sian.

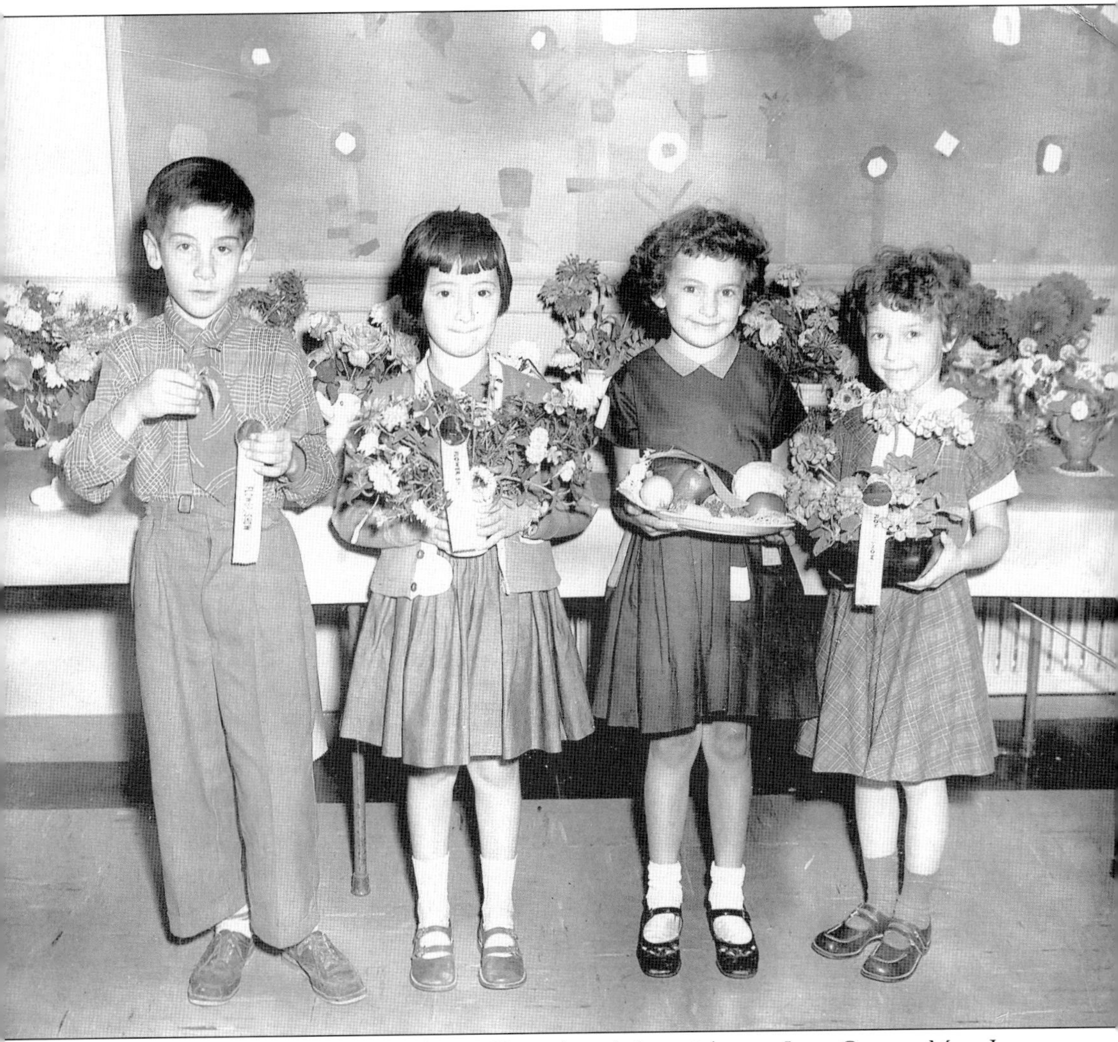

The first-prize winners of the 1953 Flower Show, from left to right, are Jerry Caputo, Mary Jane Strelko, Dorothy Cirello, and Jo-Ann Liptak.

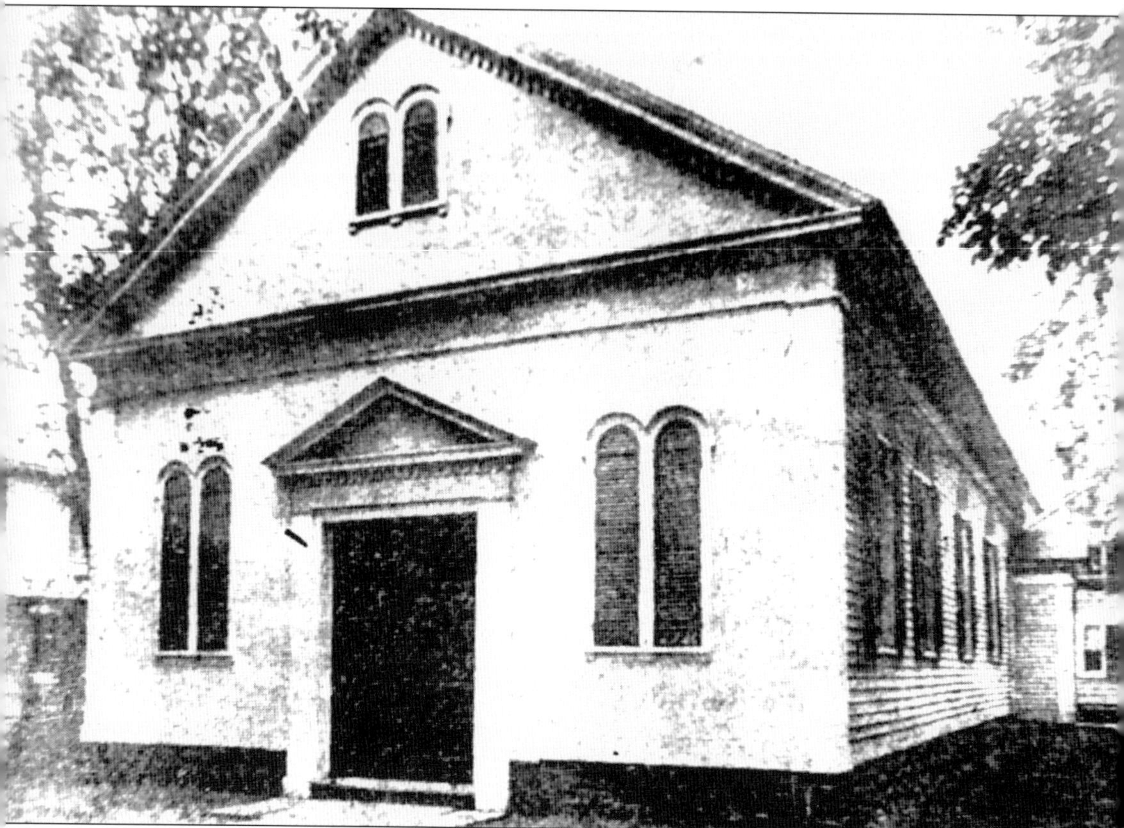

As early as 1841, a small group of people in the community began holding religious services in the village schoolhouse. At the time, there were probably no more than a dozen houses in the village. Prior to the formal organization of the Third Reformed Dutch Church, services were held in the Sunday school building that was erected by the existing Somerville Reformed churches. This building was located on the corner of Doughty and Somerset Streets.

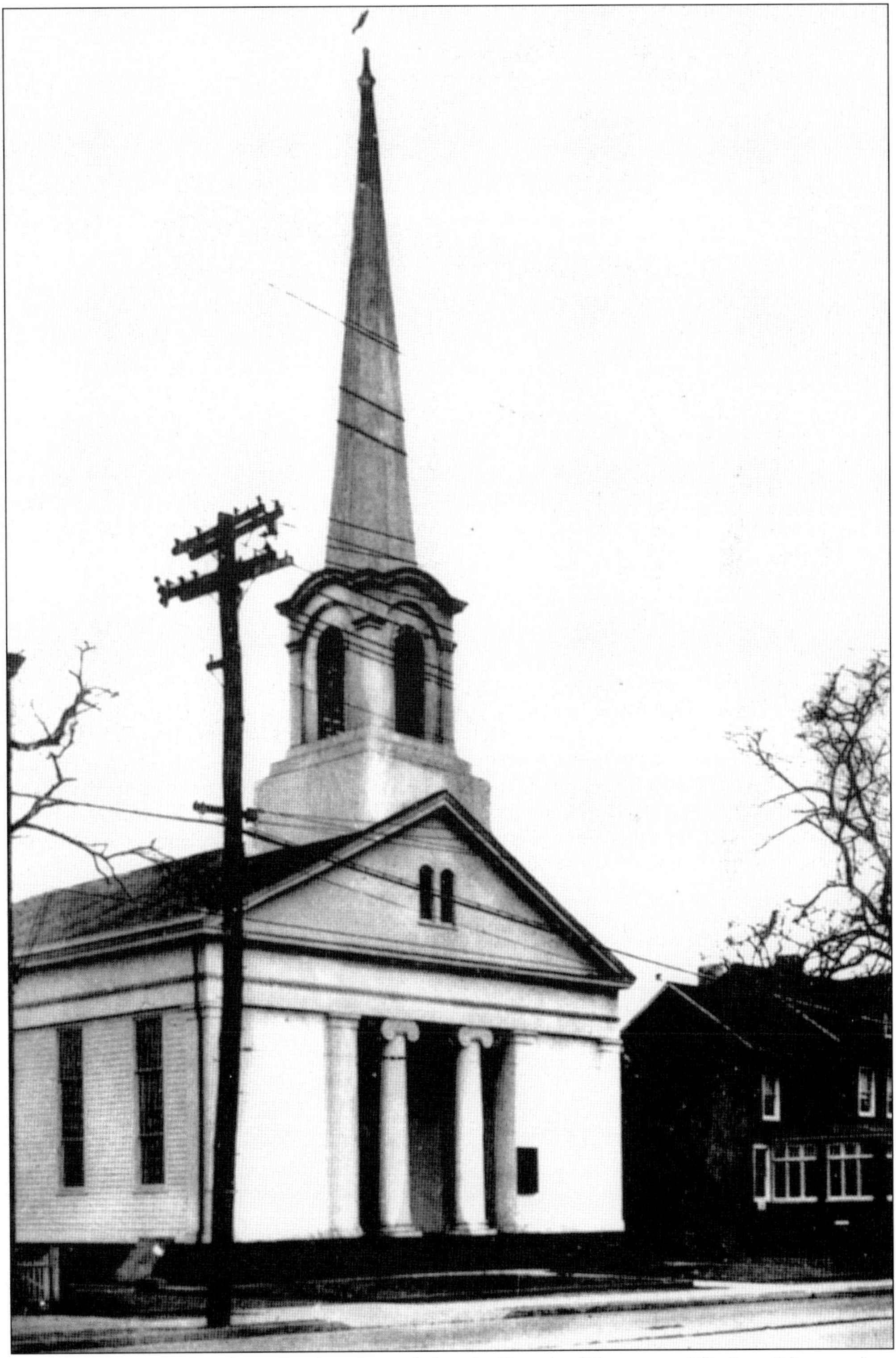
This is a 1920s view of the Third Reformed Dutch Church. (Courtesy of Barbara Navatto.)

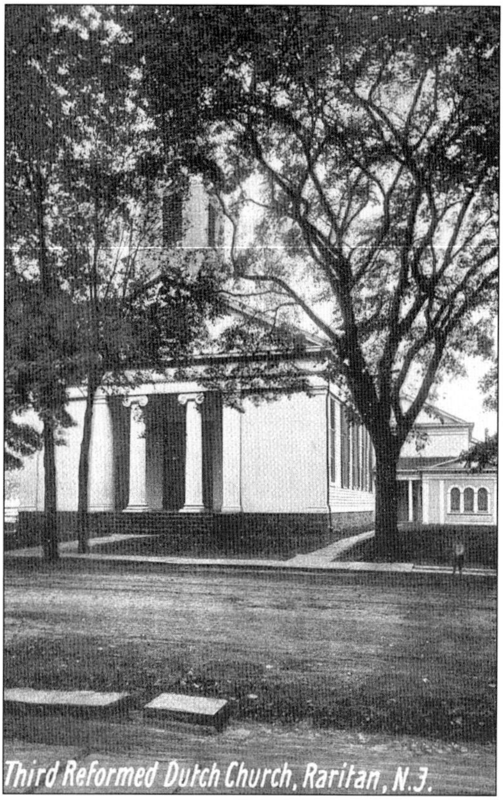

The congregation of the newly organized Third Reformed Dutch Church quickly outgrew its space in the Sunday school building and, in the summer of 1850, purchased three lots from Theodore and Frederick Frelinghuysen for a new church. (Courtesy of Barbara Navatto.)

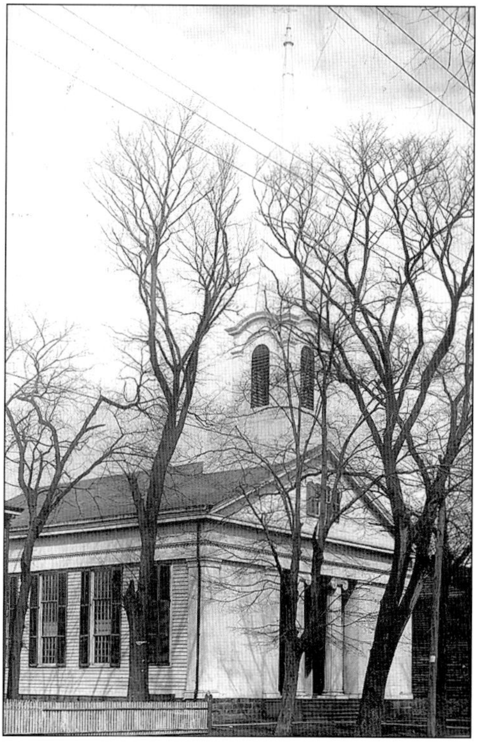

On September 18, 1850, the cornerstone of the new church was laid, and on July 30, 1851, the church was dedicated. A new steeple was added in 1931 after the pointed one pictured here was toppled in a windstorm. (Courtesy of Barbara Navatto.)

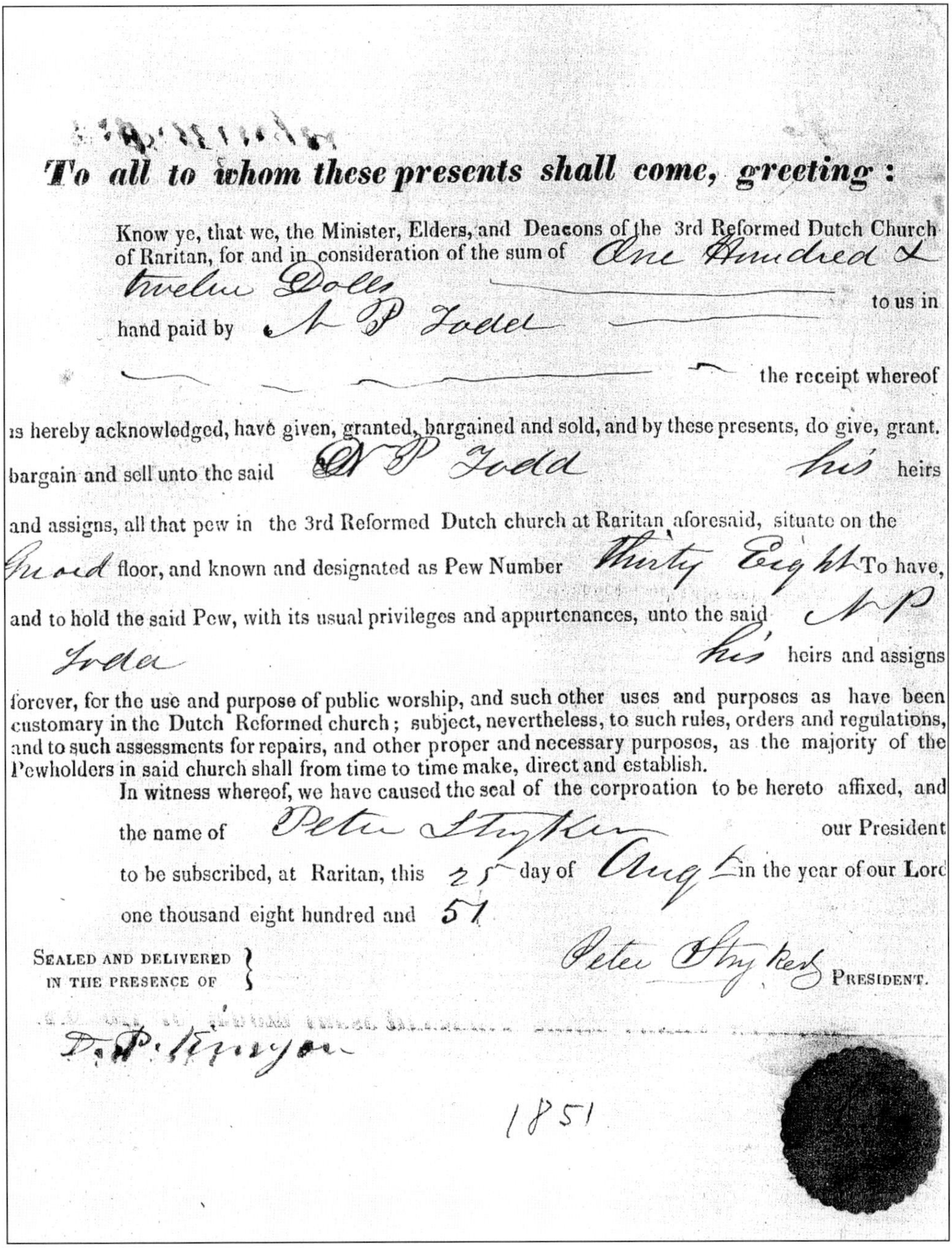

To all to whom these presents shall come, greeting:

Know ye, that we, the Minister, Elders, and Deacons of the 3rd Reformed Dutch Church of Raritan, for and in consideration of the sum of One Hundred & twelve Dolls ——— to us in hand paid by N P Todd ——— the receipt whereof is hereby acknowledged, have given, granted, bargained and sold, and by these presents, do give, grant, bargain and sell unto the said N P Todd his heirs and assigns, all that pew in the 3rd Reformed Dutch church at Raritan aforesaid, situate on the Ground floor, and known and designated as Pew Number Thirty Eight To have, and to hold the said Pew, with its usual privileges and appurtenances, unto the said N P Todd his heirs and assigns forever, for the use and purpose of public worship, and such other uses and purposes as have been customary in the Dutch Reformed church; subject, nevertheless, to such rules, orders and regulations, and to such assessments for repairs, and other proper and necessary purposes, as the majority of the Pewholders in said church shall from time to time make, direct and establish.

In witness whereof, we have caused the seal of the corproation to be hereto affixed, and the name of Peter Stryker our President to be subscribed, at Raritan, this 25 day of Aug in the year of our Lord one thousand eight hundred and 51

SEALED AND DELIVERED IN THE PRESENCE OF } Peter Stryker PRESIDENT.

D. P. Kinyon

1851

Shown is an original deed from the Third Reformed Dutch Church, dated August 25, 1851. This deed was purchased by W.P. Todd for $112 and entitled him and his heirs to pew No. 38 on the main floor of the sanctuary.

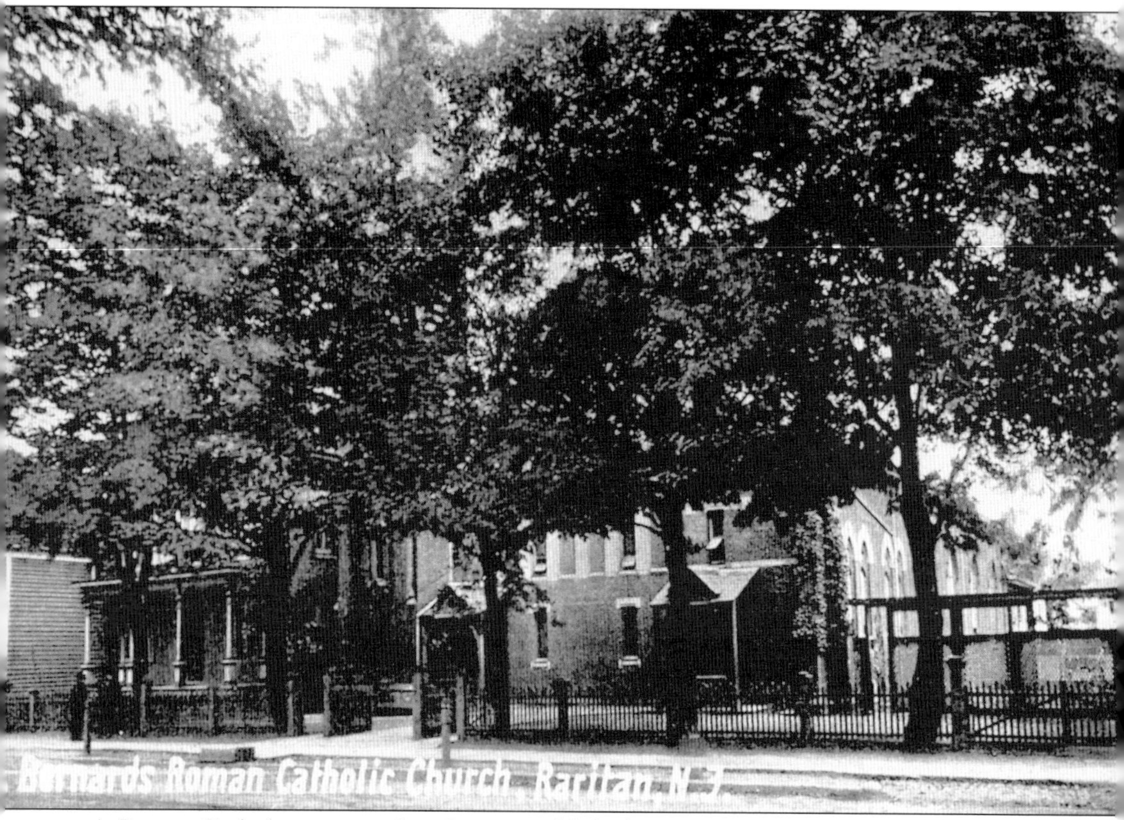

A Roman Catholic mission church was established in Raritan in 1843. It eventually became St. Bernard's Roman Catholic Church, the oldest Roman Catholic parish in Somerset County. The first recorded baptism was in 1854. (Courtesy of Barbara Navatto.)

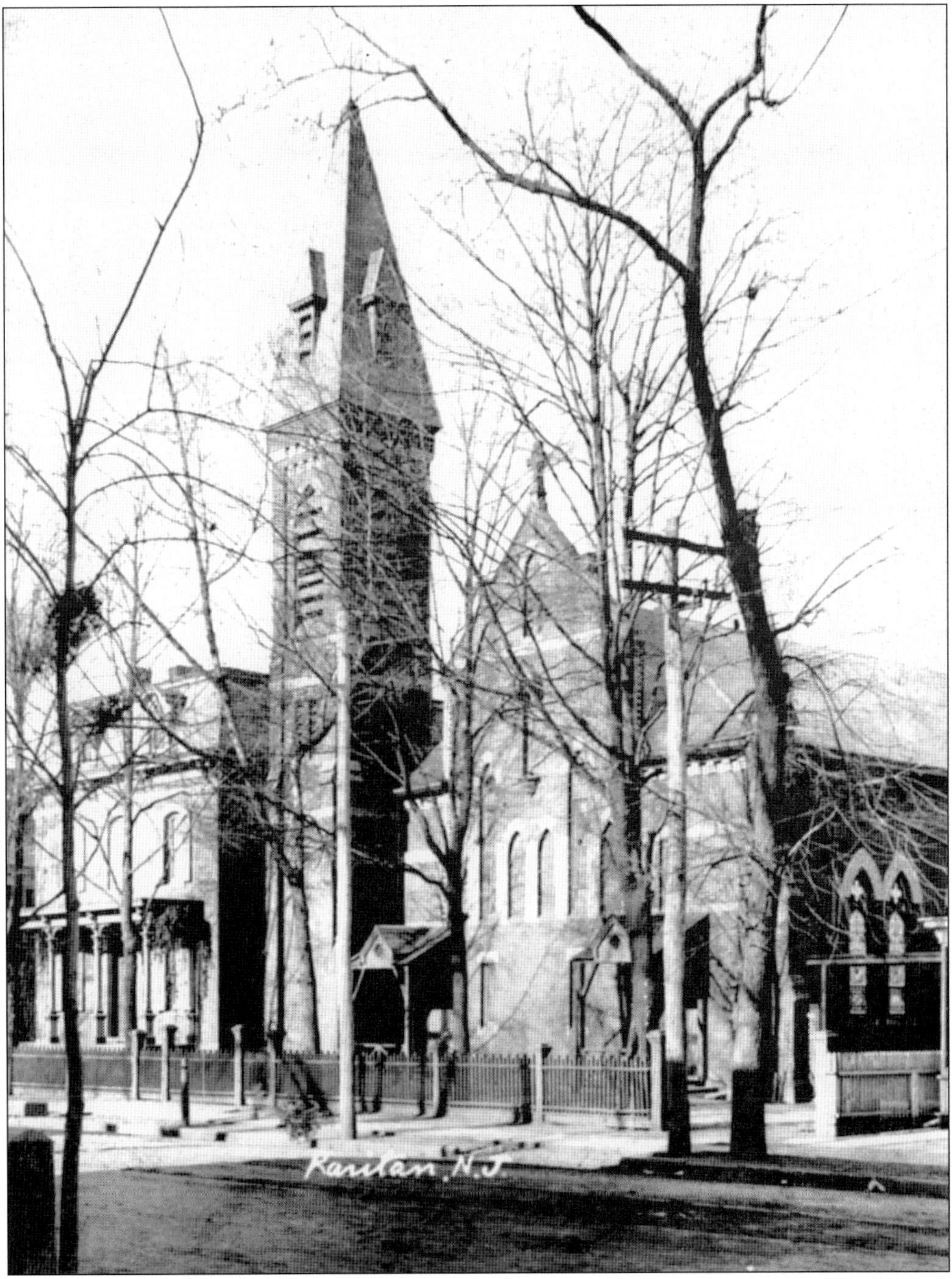

In 1876, Fr. Joseph J. Zimmer was assigned as pastor of St. Bernard's. A plot of land for a cemetery was purchased in 1876, and a new brick rectory was erected in 1881. In 1889, a parochial school was erected. It was staffed by the Sisters of Mercy, who taught there for many years. (Courtesy of Barbara Navatto.)

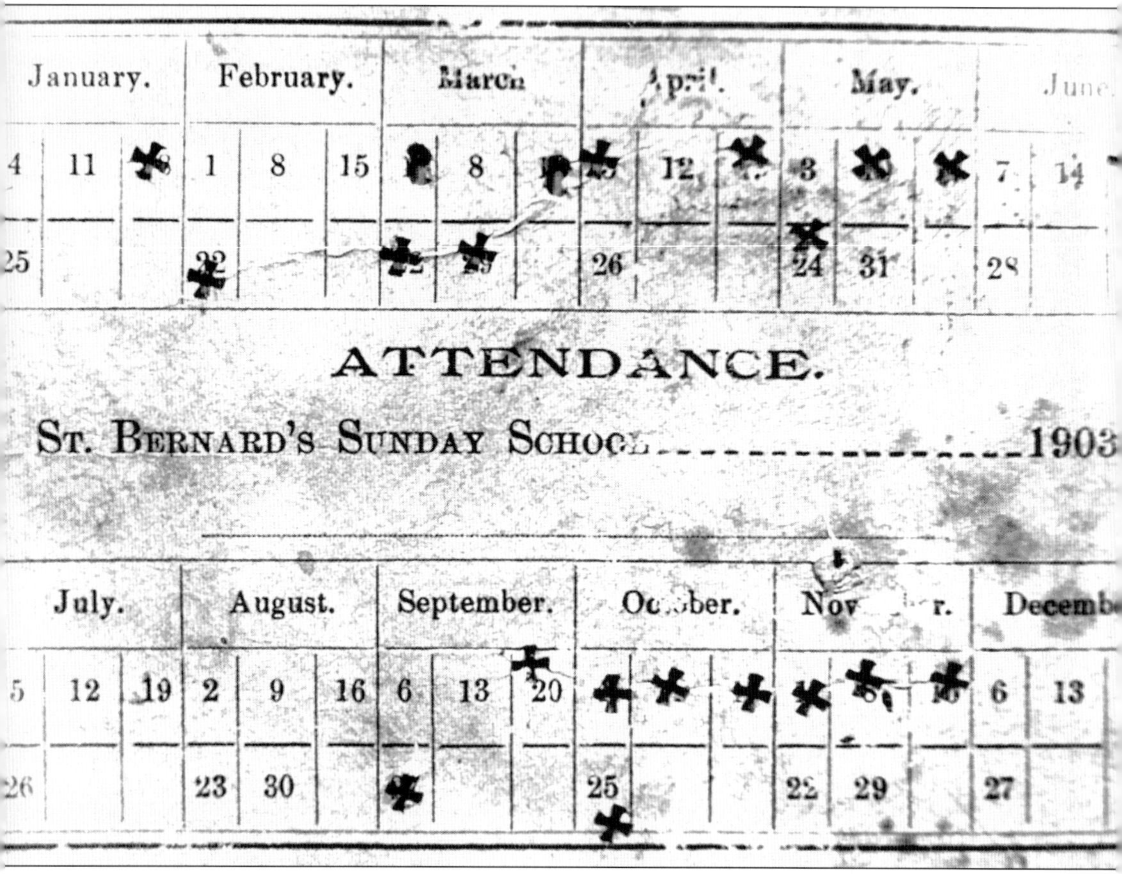

January. | February. | March | April. | May. | June

ATTENDANCE.

ST. BERNARD'S SUNDAY SCHOOL 1903

July. | August. | September. | October. | November. | December

Sunday school attendance records in St. Bernard's parish were kept on personal attendance cards. This one is from 1903.

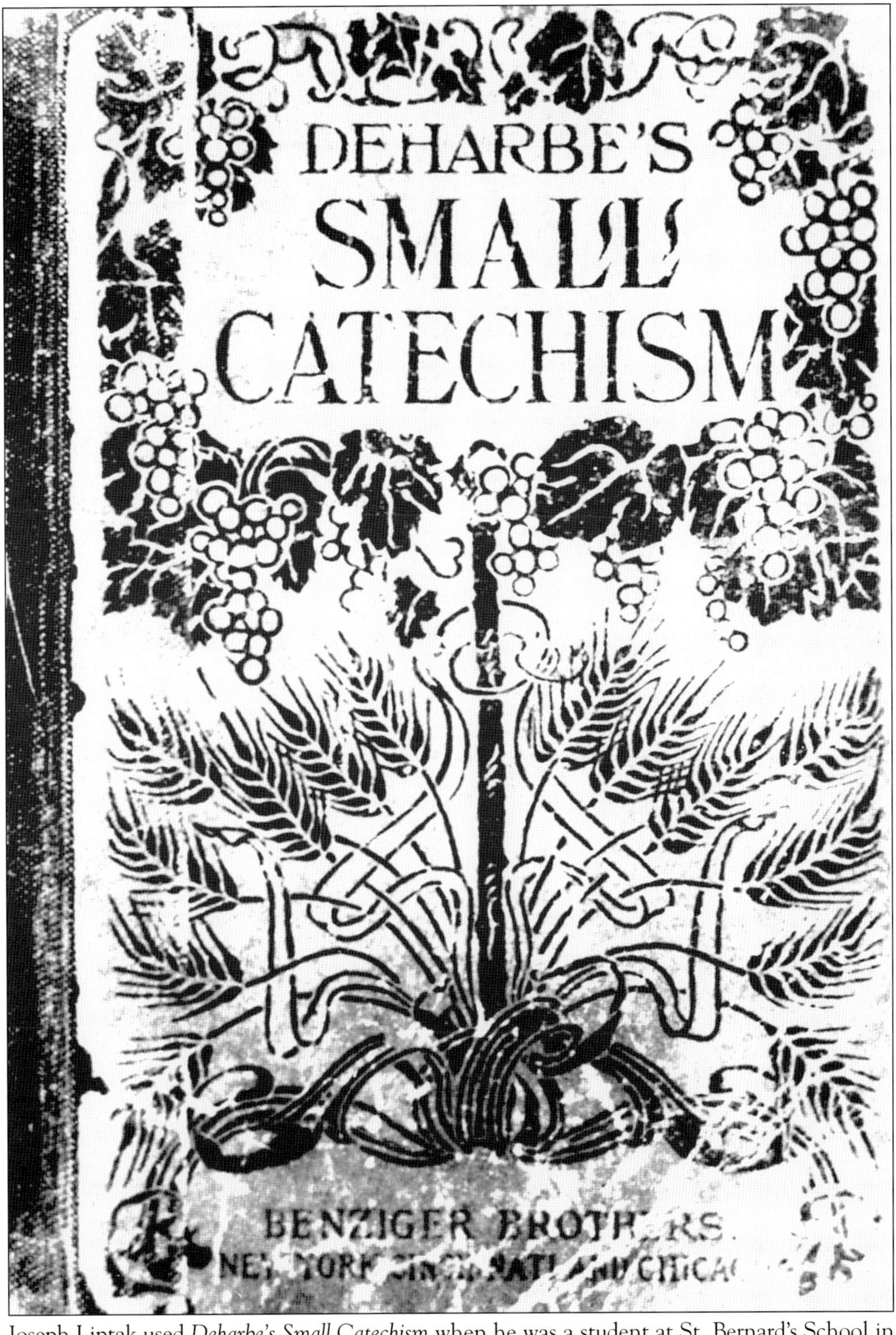

Joseph Liptak used *Deharbe's Small Catechism* when he was a student at St. Bernard's School in 1915. The copyright on the book is 1882.

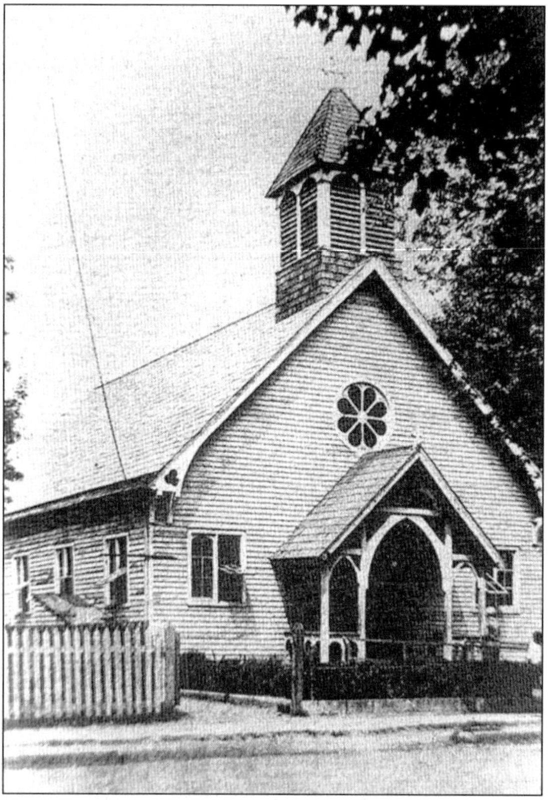

The Catholic Church of St. Ann was incorporated on April 17, 1903. Alfonso Santoro and Tommaso Andreatto met in accordance with the law of the state of New Jersey and signed incorporation papers for the church. This small wooden structure, built in 1906, was the first church.

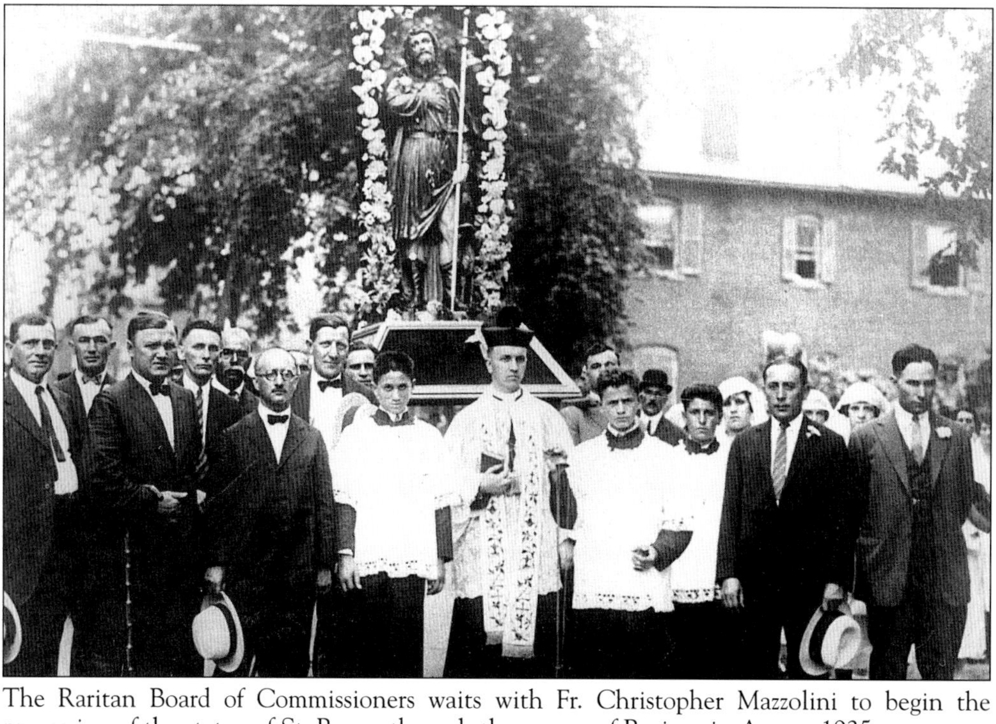

The Raritan Board of Commissioners waits with Fr. Christopher Mazzolini to begin the procession of the statue of St. Rocco through the streets of Raritan in August 1925.

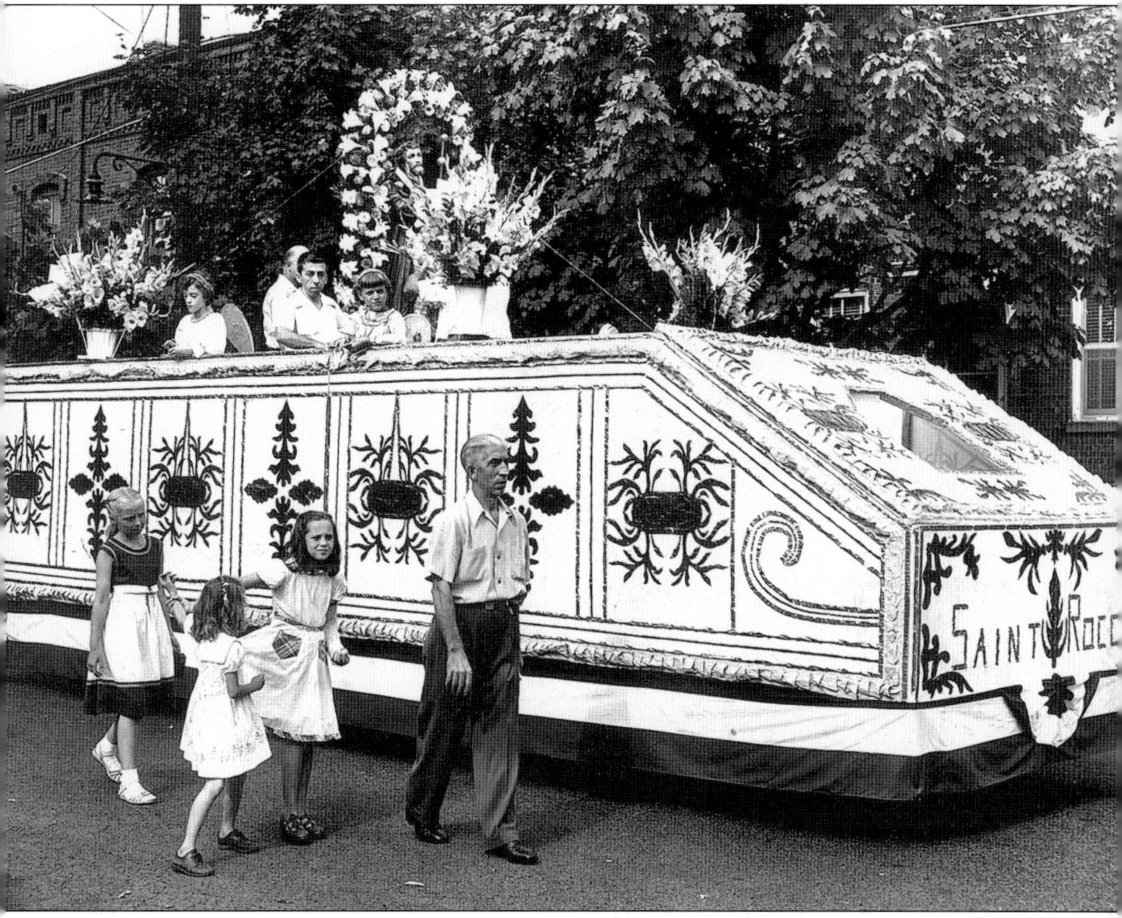

Every August, people came by foot, train, and trolley from New York, Pennsylvania, and other parts of New Jersey for the Feast of St. Rocco. The Italian community of St. Ann's Roman Catholic Church celebrated the Feast of St. Rocco with a procession of various religious organizations from the church through the streets of the town. This float bearing the statue of St. Rocco moves along First Avenue. In those days, ornamental lighting illuminated the streets at night. Booths where Italian delicacies were sold lined the street, and strolling bands of musicians serenaded everyone. All approaching roads were jammed with traffic before and after the fireworks display—the climax of the celebration. (Courtesy of the Raritan Public Library.)

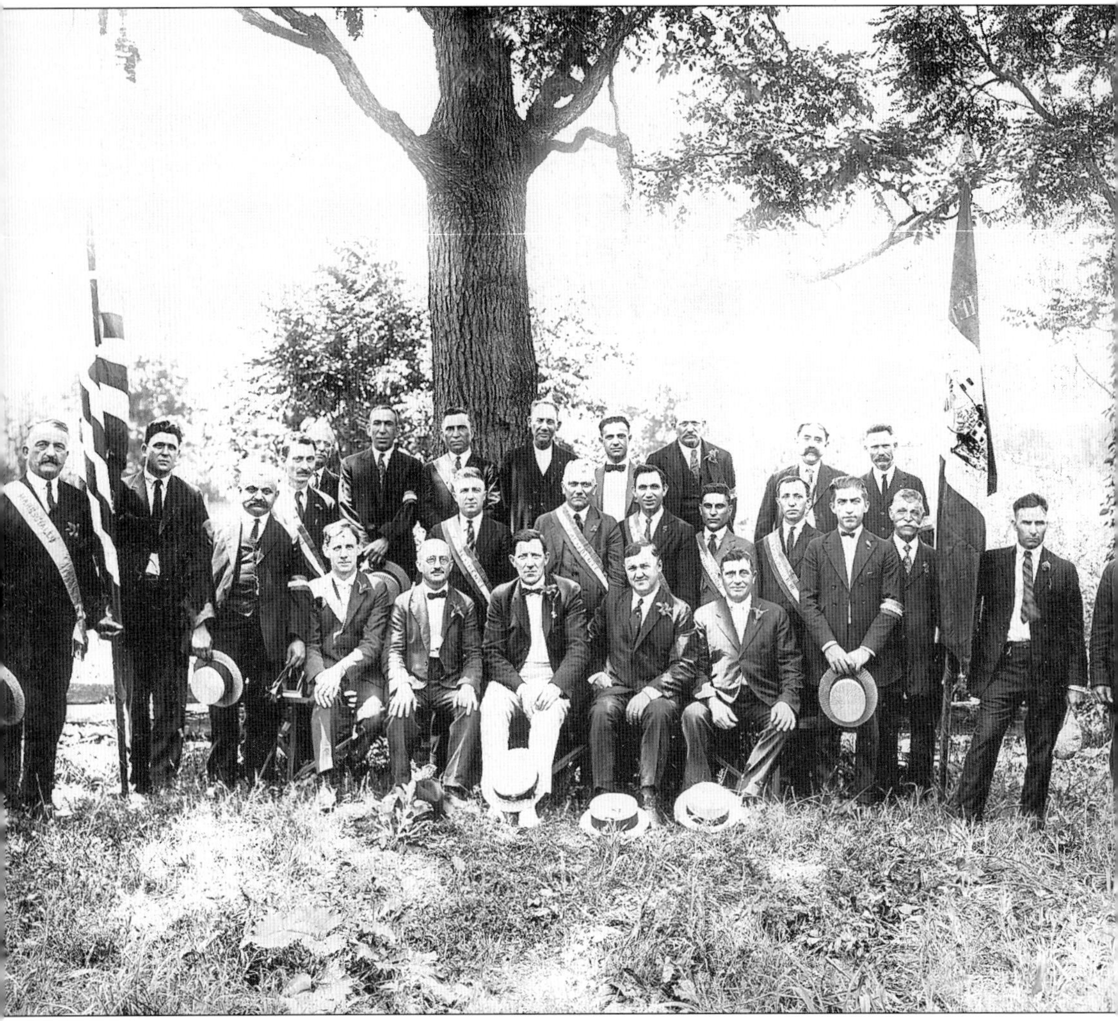

The St. Rocco Society was a social organization made up of Italian immigrants who came together to help one another and serve as a support system for new Italian immigrants living in Raritan. From left to right are the following: (front row, seated) Jere Burke, Joseph Navatto Sr., P. Findley Wykcoff, Charles Mattoe, and Frank Leibold; (middle row, standing) James Angelone, three unidentified men, ? Matteis, ? Angelone, and ? Tarangelo; (back row, standing) ? Rick, unidentified, ? Palmerie, Terry Minetti, unidentified, Frank Esposito, and unidentified; (holding the flags) ? Gaburo, and Angelo D'Ambola, and ? Damici, and Frank ?. (Courtesy of the Raritan Public Library.)

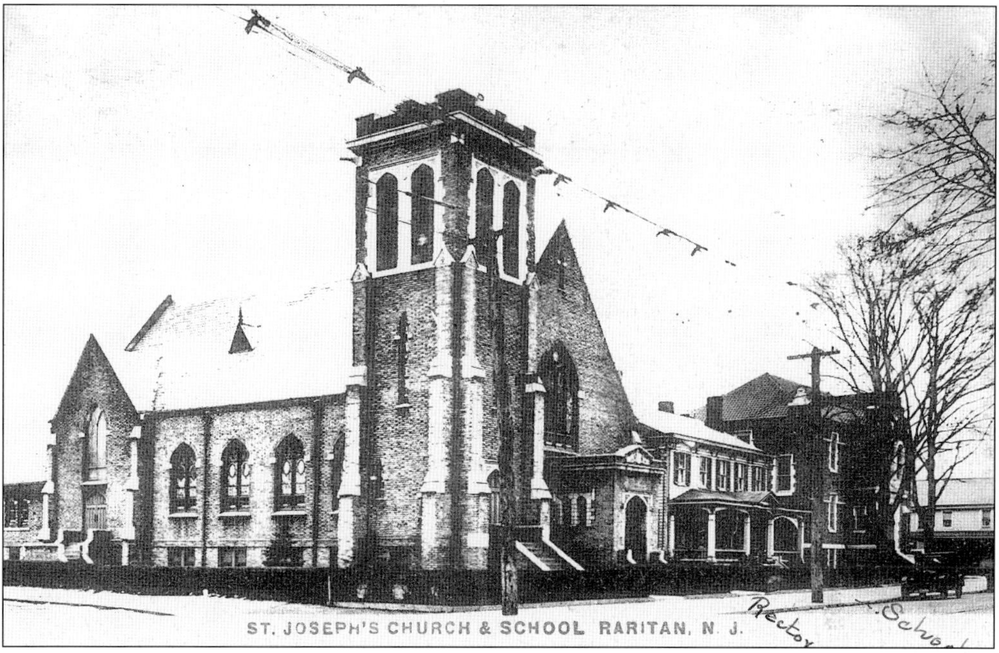

Political oppression, tyranny, and poverty brought many Slovaks to America. Slovaks from Abouj, Saris, Zemplin, and Spis came to Raritan to work in the Raritan Woolen Mills, at the Duke estate and on the railroad. A deeply religious people, the Slovaks wanted to establish a church of their own where they could worship in their own language. The Church Society was formed with Joseph Loska, Albert Fialka, Michael J. Petras, Charles Mattoe, and Paul Pastor as members. The Church Society bought a piece of property on Codington Street from Ella Dalley to use as their first place of worship. The parish grew, and in September 1914, the DeHart property on Somerset Street was purchased for $9,000. The new St. Joseph's Church was built and dedicated on November 30, 1915. The former DeHart home became the rectory, and St. Joseph's Parochial School was constructed in 1926. (Courtesy of Barbara Navatto.)

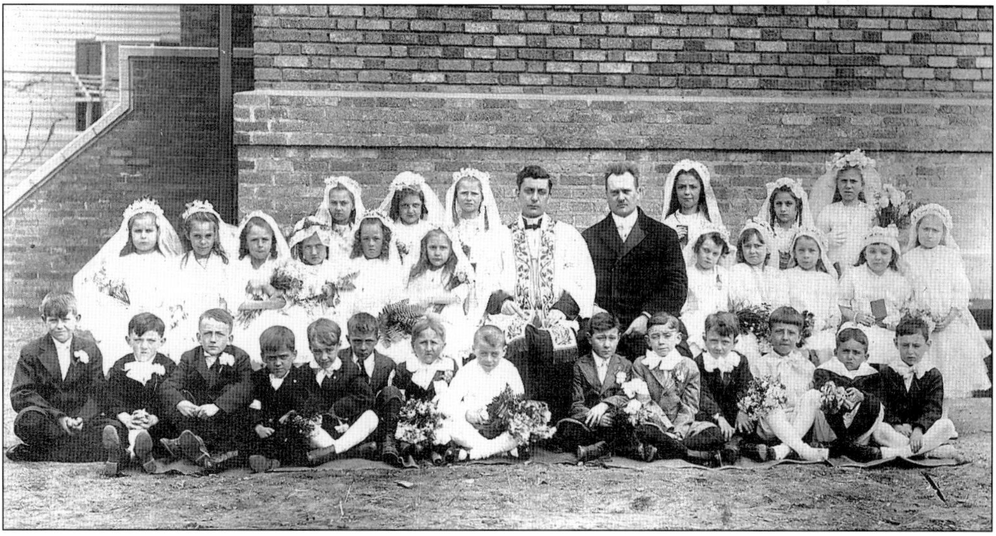

Outside the new St. Joseph's Church, the 1915 First Holy Communion class poses with Fr. Joseph Ketter .

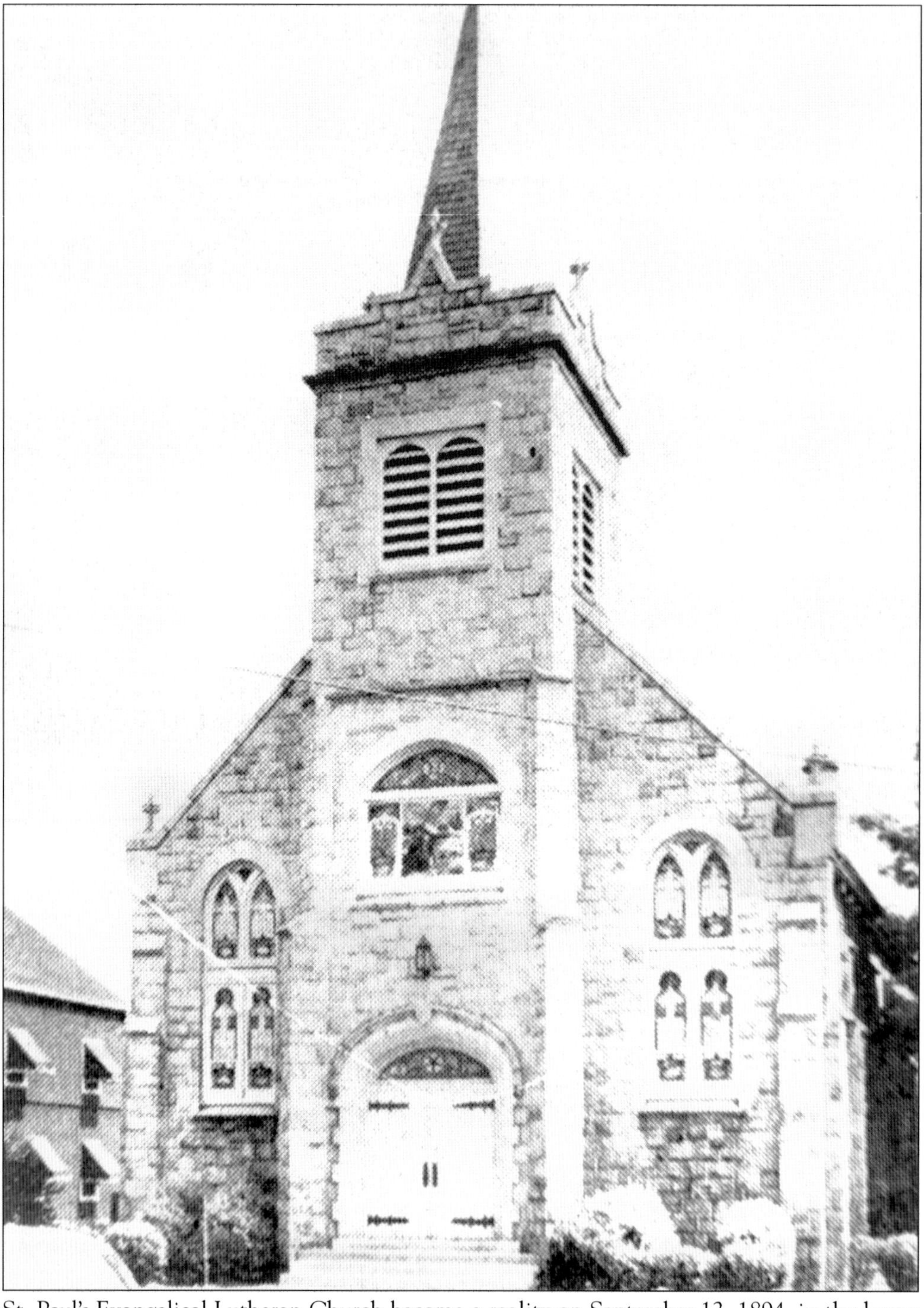

St. Paul's Evangelical Lutheran Church became a reality on September 12, 1894, in the home of George Kovac. The cornerstone for the current church was set in place on July 27, 1924, but previously the congregation worshiped in the Dutch Reformed Sunday school chapel. The Sunday school building, located at the corner of Somerset and Doughty Streets, was purchased and demolished to make way for the present church.

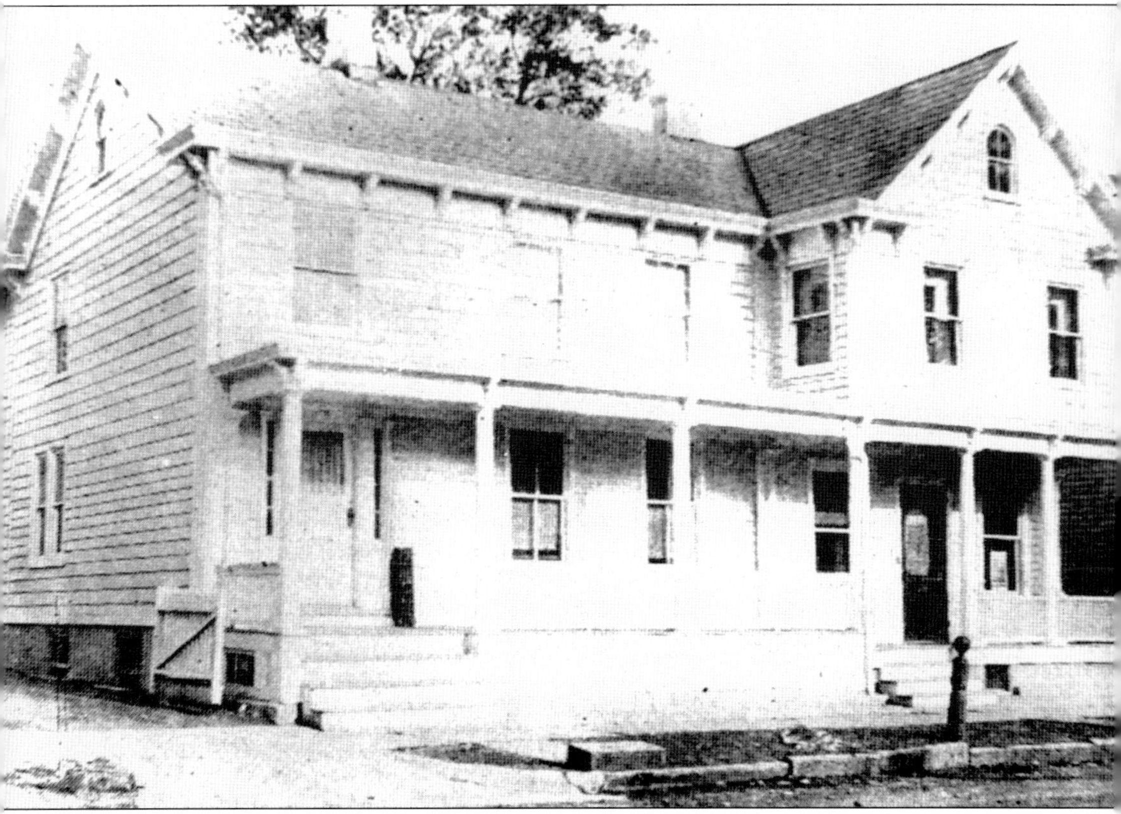

The parsonage was located directly behind St. Paul's for many years. This building was demolished to make way for a much-needed church parking lot. A new parsonage was built in another location in town.

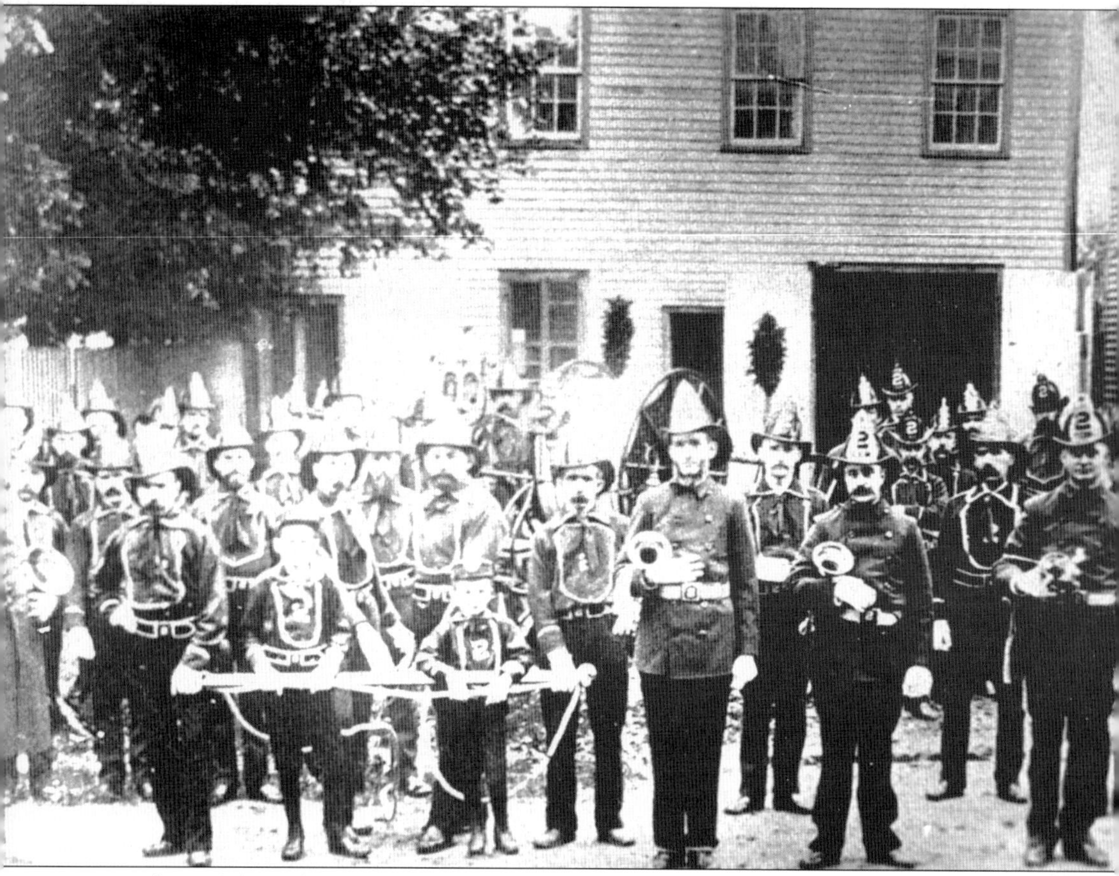

Members of the Relief Hose Company No. 2 pose for a picture in 1889. Chief Job C. Kenyon can be seen on the far left.

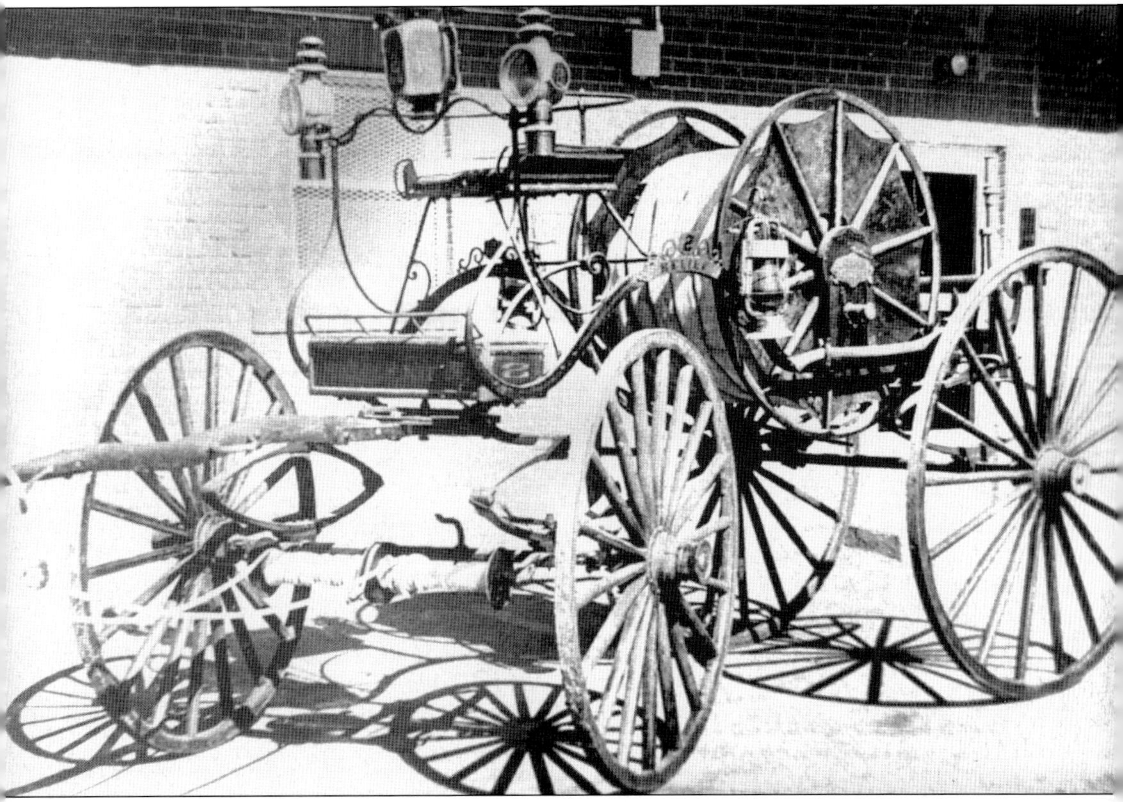

This 1874 Leverich hose wagon, capable of being pulled either by people or horses, went into service when fire hydrants were installed in town. It is currently part of the fire department's museum collection.

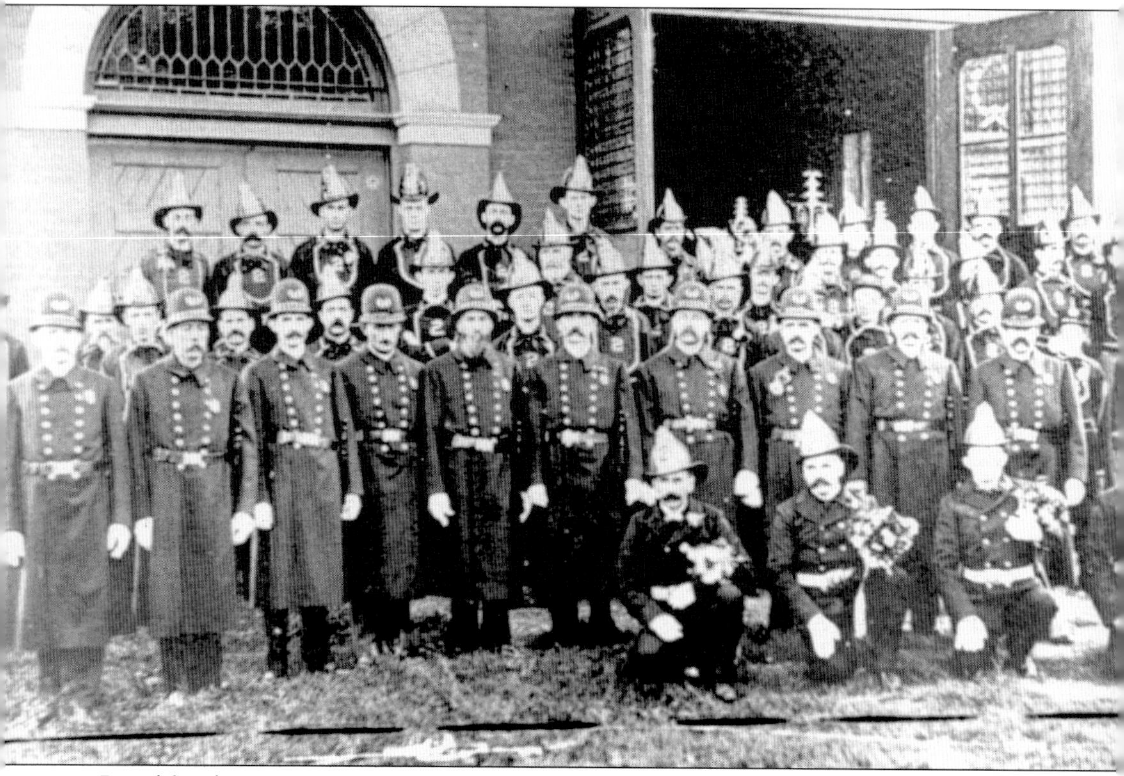

Proud fire department members under the leadership of Fire Chief Eugene Dilts pose in front of the Anderson Street firehouse in 1903.

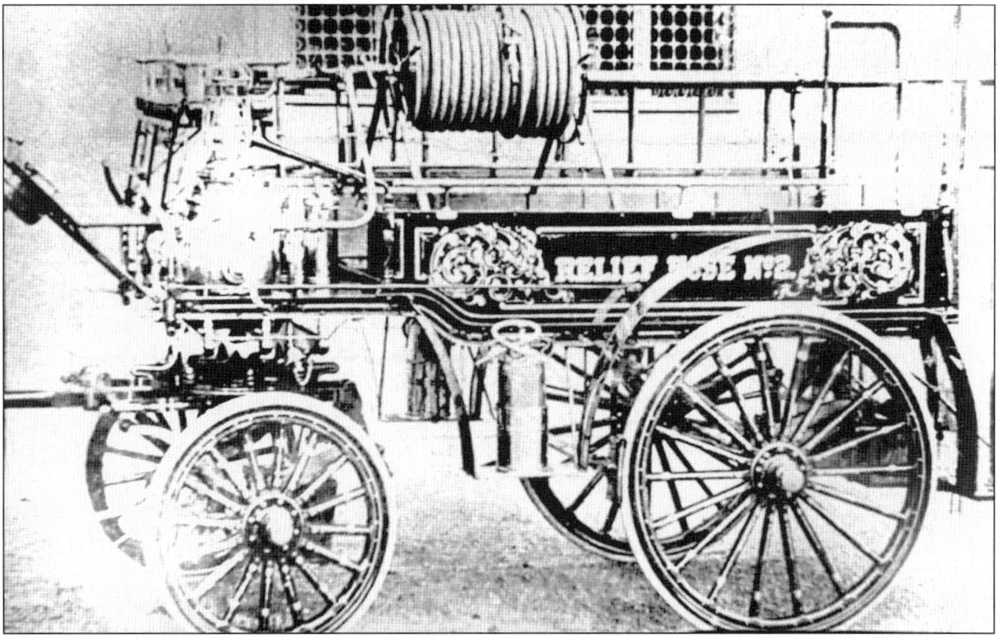

The department acquired this Holloway combination chemical engine and hose wagon in September 1904.

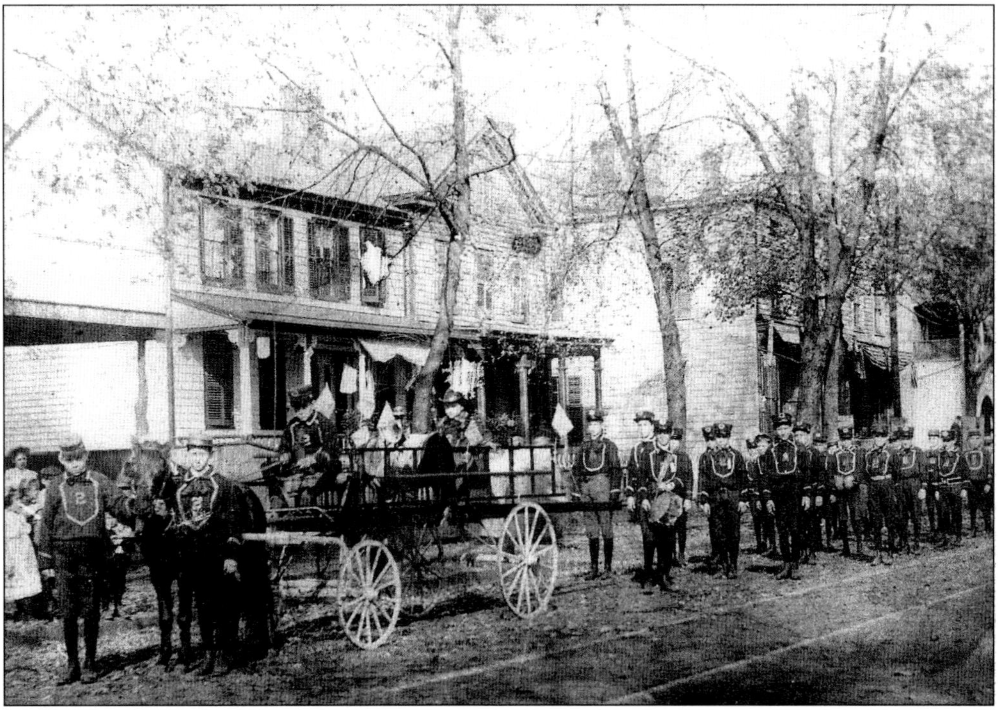

This *c.* 1904 photograph shows the Juvenile Hook and Ladder unit and its pony-drawn apparatus. (Courtesy of Frank Tropiano.)

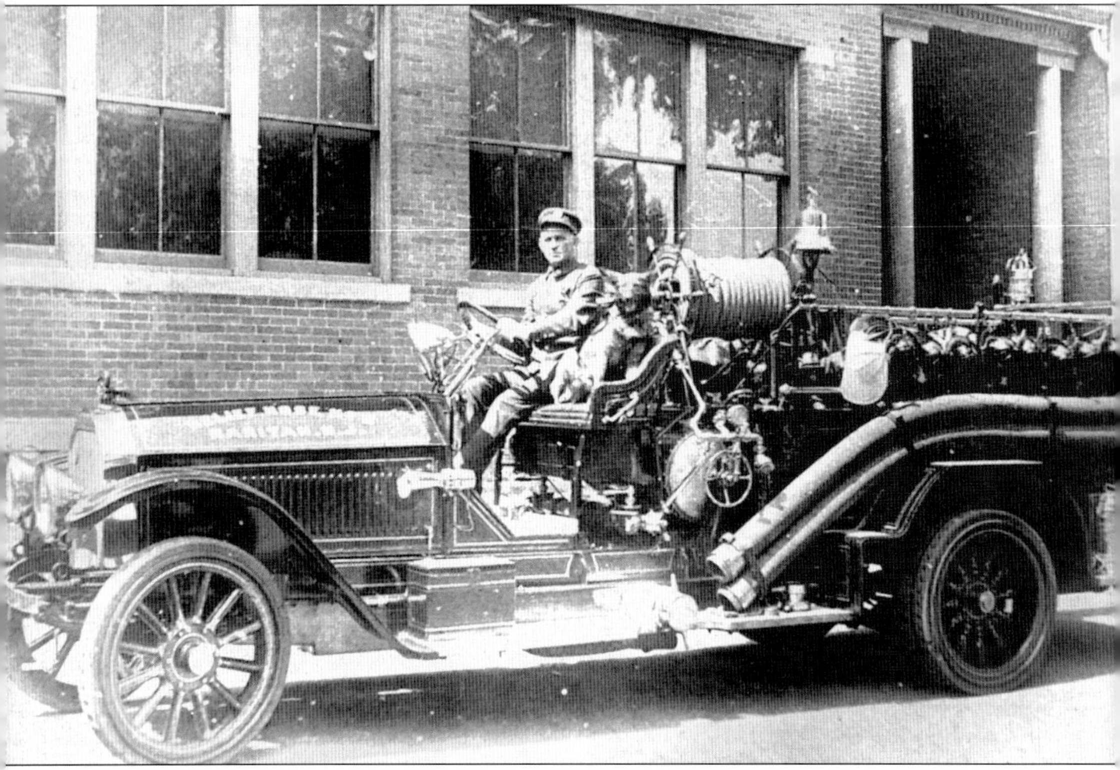

Edward "Busky" Diesbusky, head driver, is seated on a 1922 American LaFrance pumper, the Relief Hose Company's first motorized vehicle. The pumper is now part of the fire department's museum.

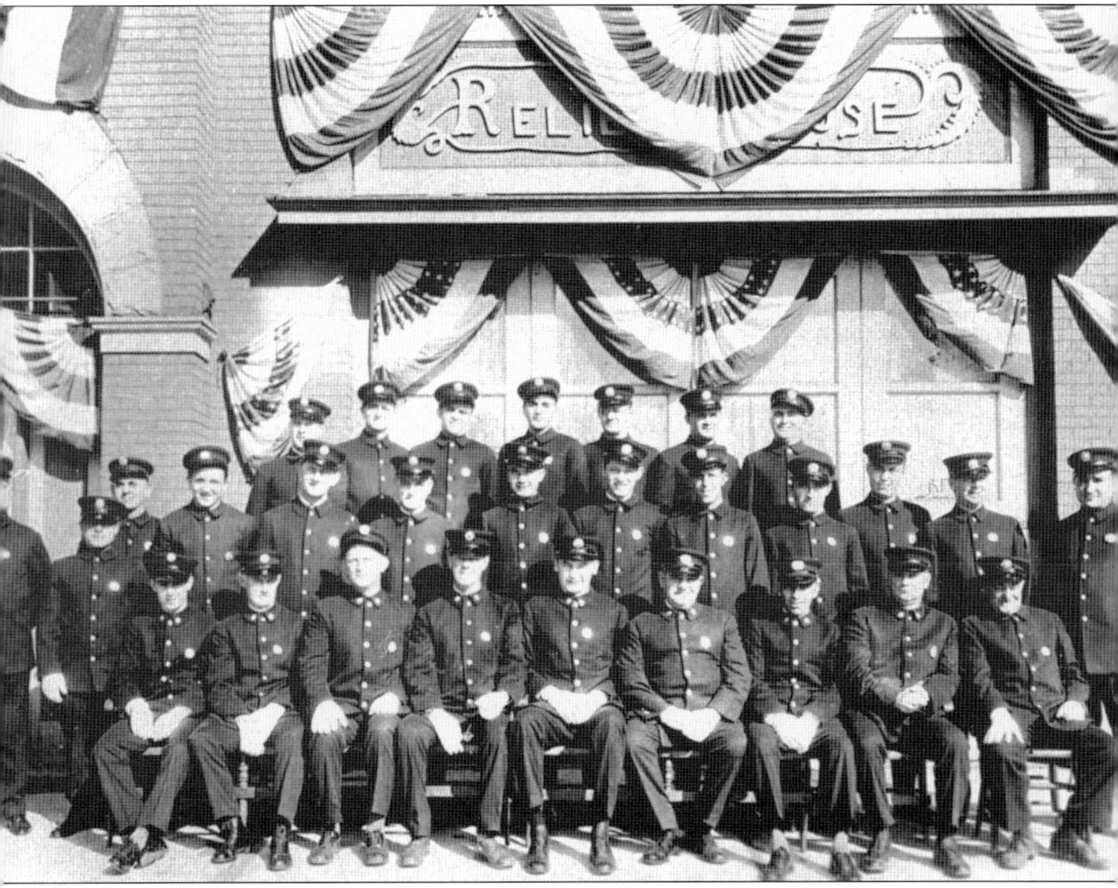

This 1927 photograph shows an ever-growing fire department posing in front of the engine house on Anderson Street.

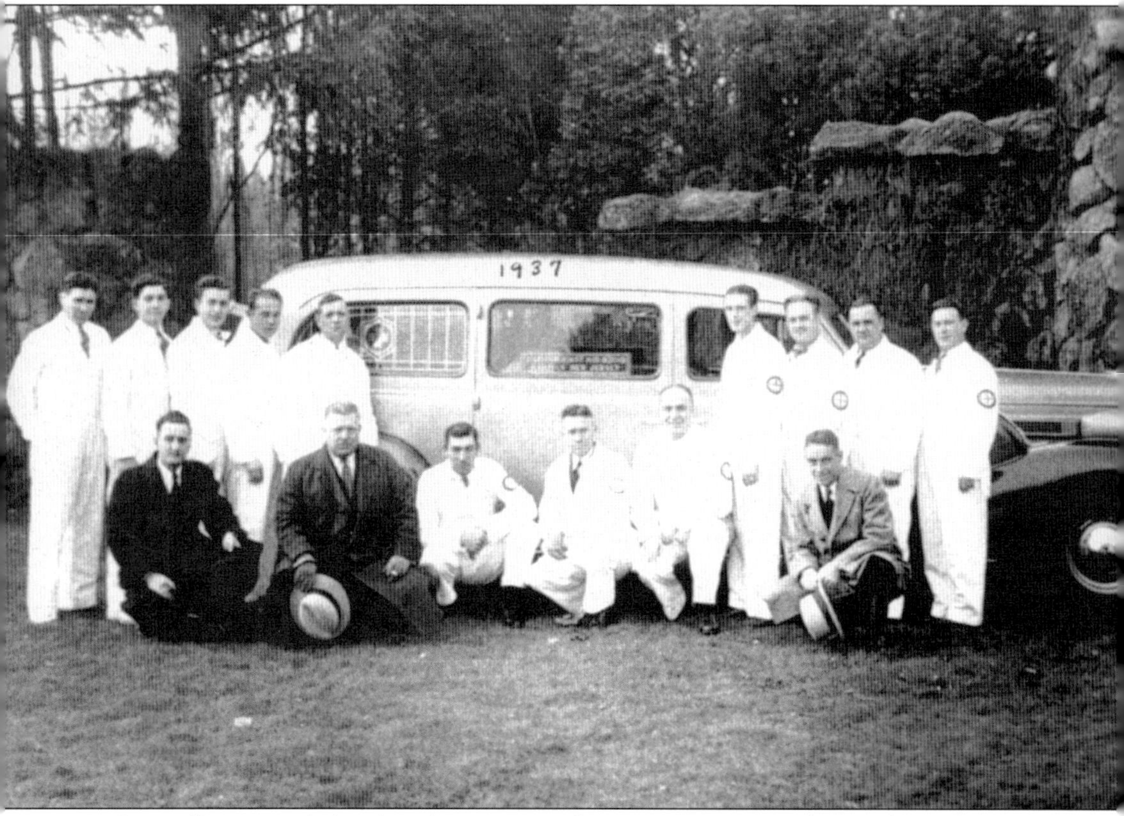

Originally part of the fire department, the Raritan First Aid Squad purchased a new state-of-the-art ambulance in 1937. From left to right are the following: (kneeling) J. Navatto Jr., E. Adams, F. Noble, G. Dixon, G. Mezzenotte, and J. Kelly; (standing) J. Sylvia, A. Navatto, T. Sancini, A. Valeri, R. Young, H. Young, F. Burns, J. Hudak, and J. Liptak.

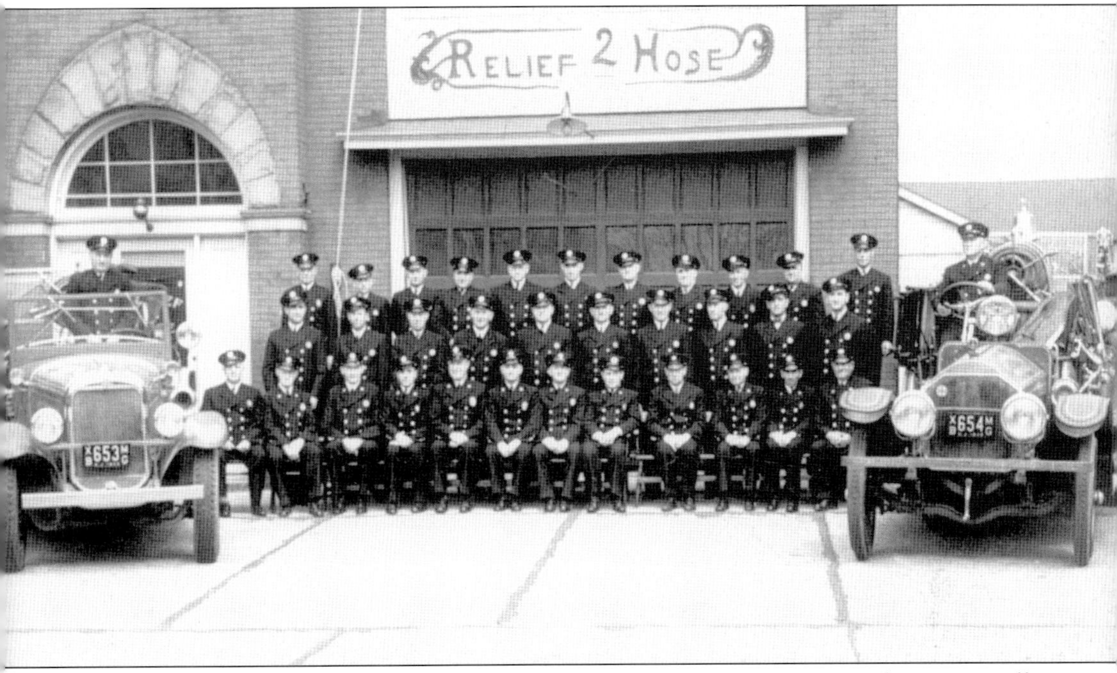

After World War II ended and soldiers returned home, the Relief Hose Company began to swell in ranks. The company is pictured here in front of the engine house.

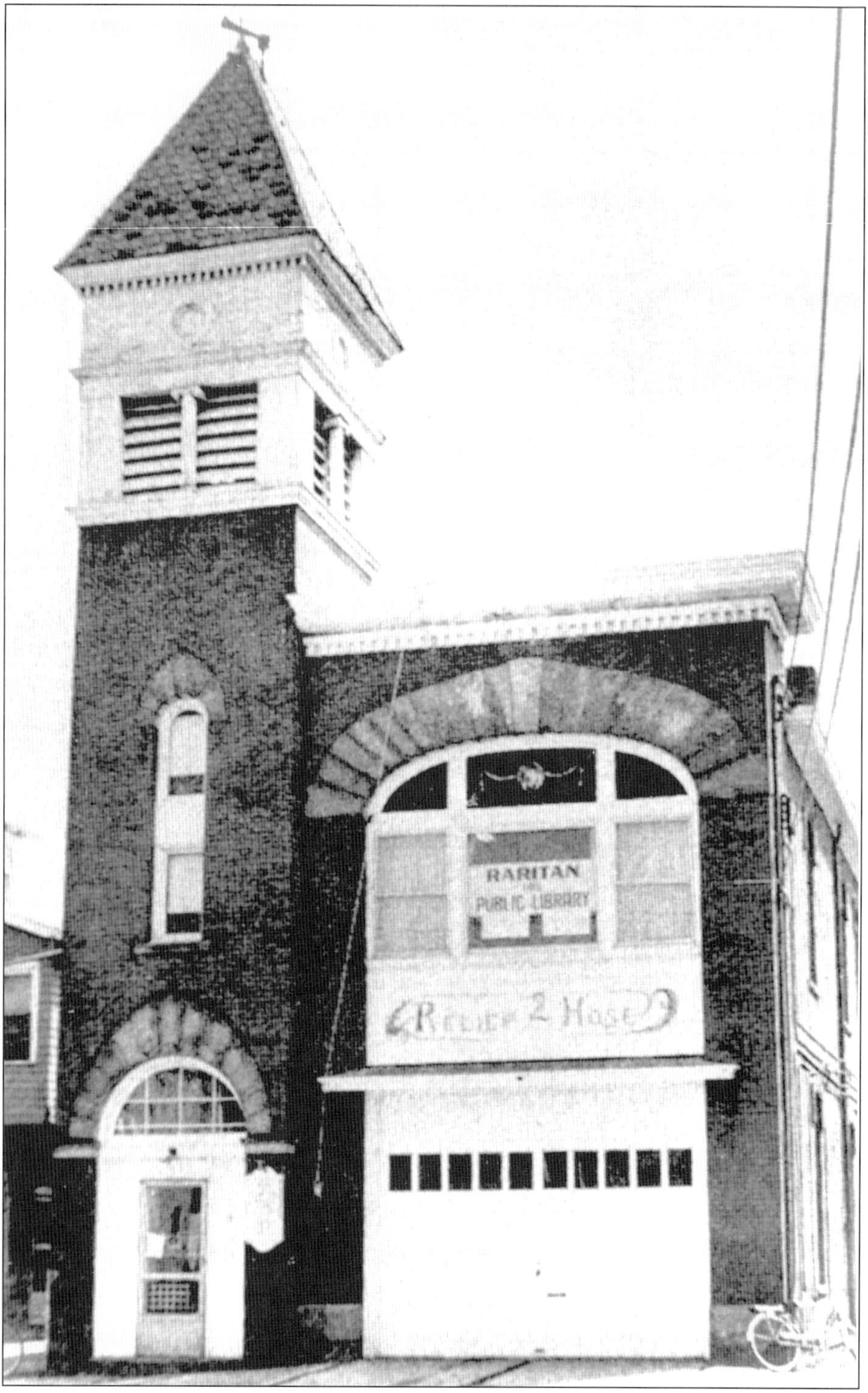

In 1892, the town purchased a lot for $475 from Mrs. A.H. Brokaw with the intention of building a firehouse. J. Van Derbeck was the architect. The building has been in continuous use as a firehouse, municipal court, council chambers, clerk's office, meetinghouse, and library.

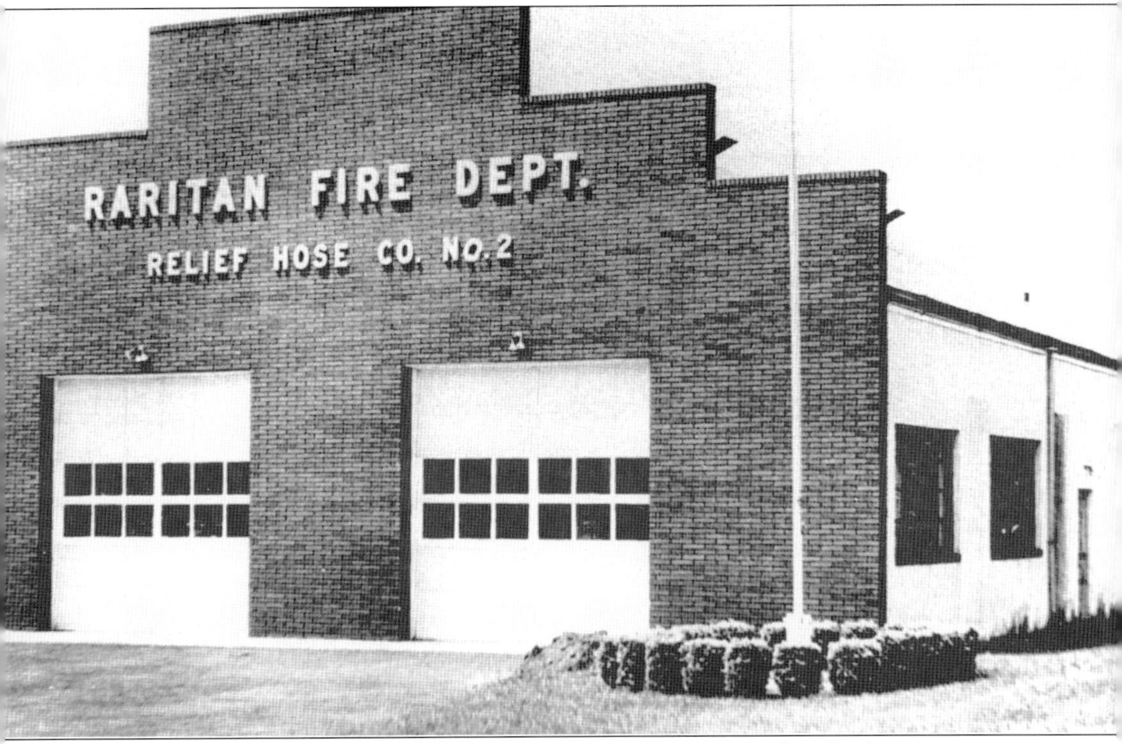

The North Thompson Street Firehouse was built in 1956 to accommodate the larger apparatus and provide firefighting coverage to an expanding part of town.

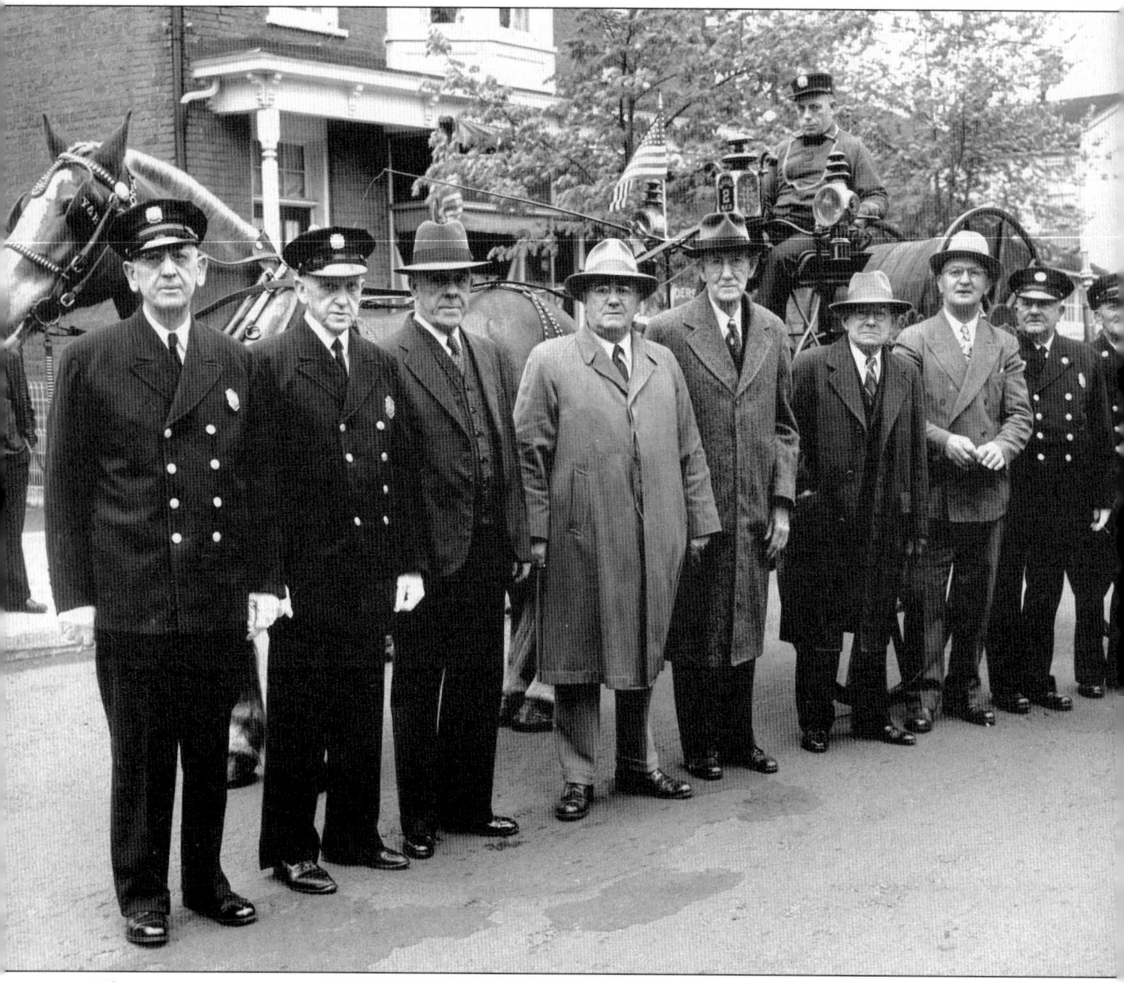

These men are part of the Exempt Firemen's Association. Standing, from left to right, are Charlie Becker, Michael Enright, Martin Kelly Sr., Nicholas DiPaolo, Thomas Brown, Matthew Purcell, Michael Petras, George Leibold, and Arthur Amey. Seated on the truck is Howard Young.

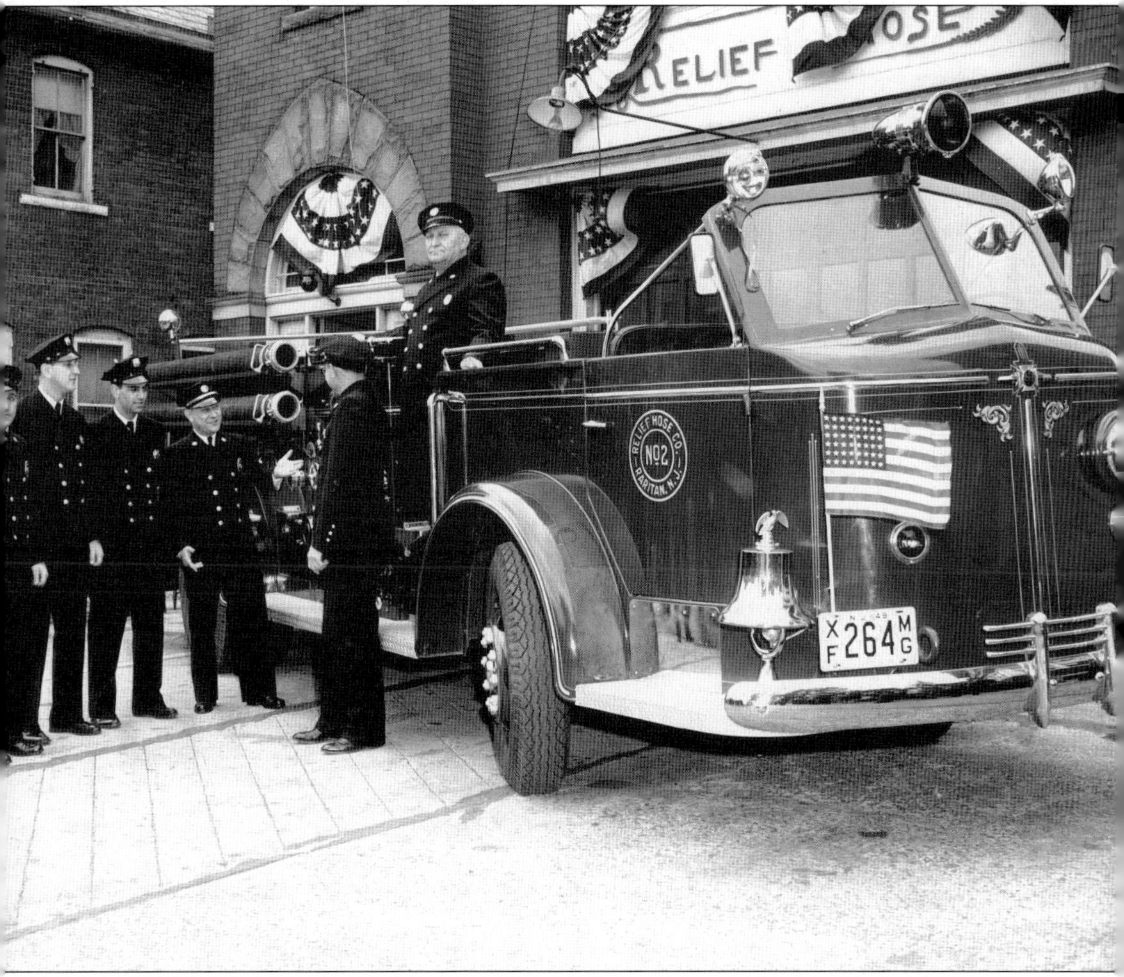

The men admire their new 1948 American LaFrance pumper. From left to right are Pat Esposito, Rocco Miele, Edward Minetti, Joseph Liptak, Henry Condo, and Edward Diesbusky.

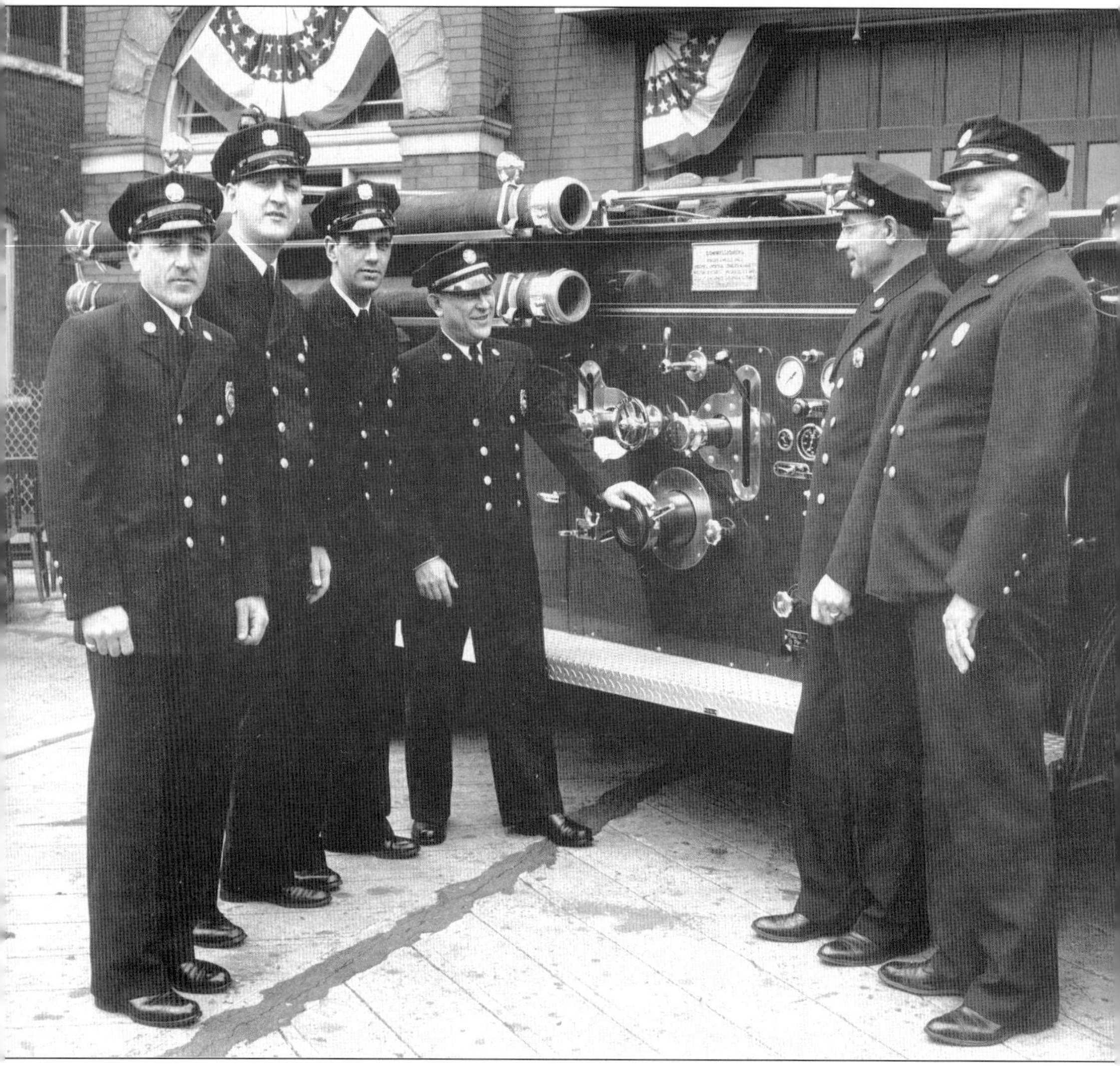

Chief Joseph Liptak (center) explains the pumping capacity of the new engine to fellow firefighters. They are, from left to right, Pat Esposito, Rocky Miele, Ed Minetti, Henry Condo, and Edward Diesbusky.

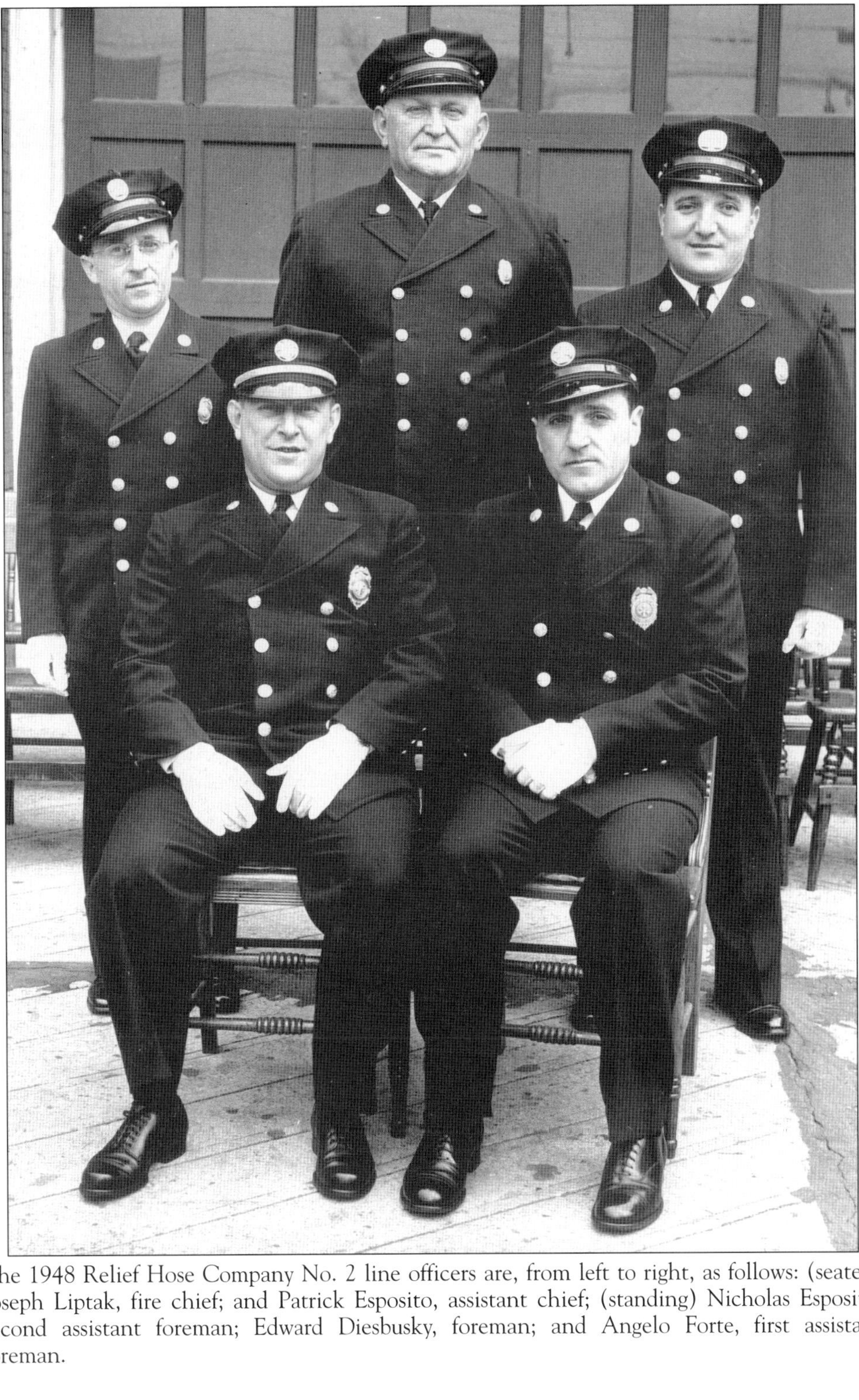

The 1948 Relief Hose Company No. 2 line officers are, from left to right, as follows: (seated) Joseph Liptak, fire chief; and Patrick Esposito, assistant chief; (standing) Nicholas Esposito, second assistant foreman; Edward Diesbusky, foreman; and Angelo Forte, first assistant foreman.

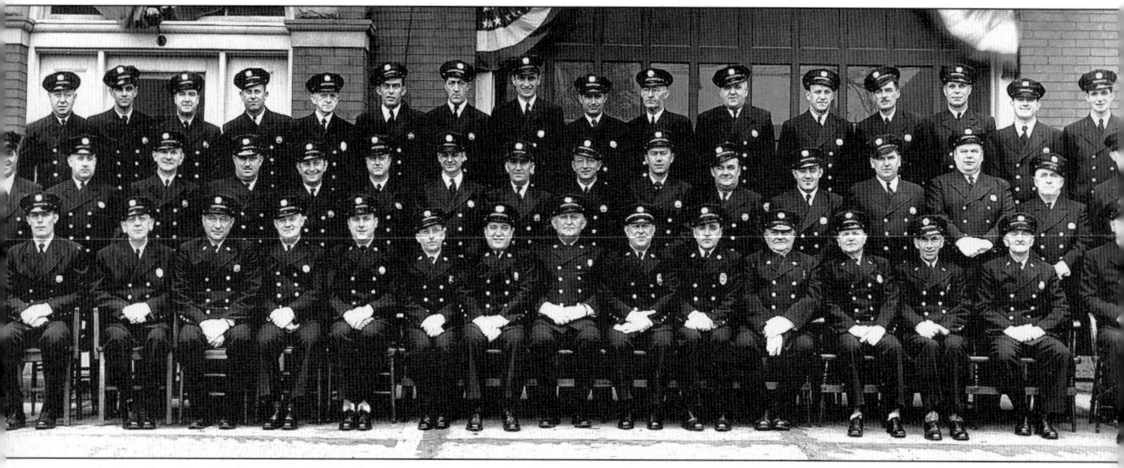

Members of the 1947 Relief Hose No. 2 pose for a group picture. They are, from left to right, as follows: (front row) George Gara, Charles Becker Sr., Henry Condo, Frank Burns, Joseph Amorosa, Nicholas Esposito, Angelo Forte, Edward Diesbusky, Joseph Liptak, Pat Esposito, George Liebold, Cyrenas Slack, Clarence Barclay, Arthur Amey, and Rocco Miele; (middle row) Henry Schiavi, Arthur Bencer, John Perantoni, John Poliesili, James Del Monte, Peter Carlino, Anthony DeCicco, Angelo Morano, Arthur Soriano, Maurice Bernabe, John Hudak, Pat DiPaolo, Andrew Ruzbarsky, William Haley, and Alfred Petras; (back row) Fred Corona, Edward Minetti, Angelo DeLorenzo, Michael Galaida, Michael Enright, Edward Swickle, Frank LaMonica, Vince Gara, John Comandini, Edward Kelly, Edward Lesko, Joseph Krachun, Herman Hannon, Louis Trepiccione, Albert Navatto, and Joseph Lovetri.

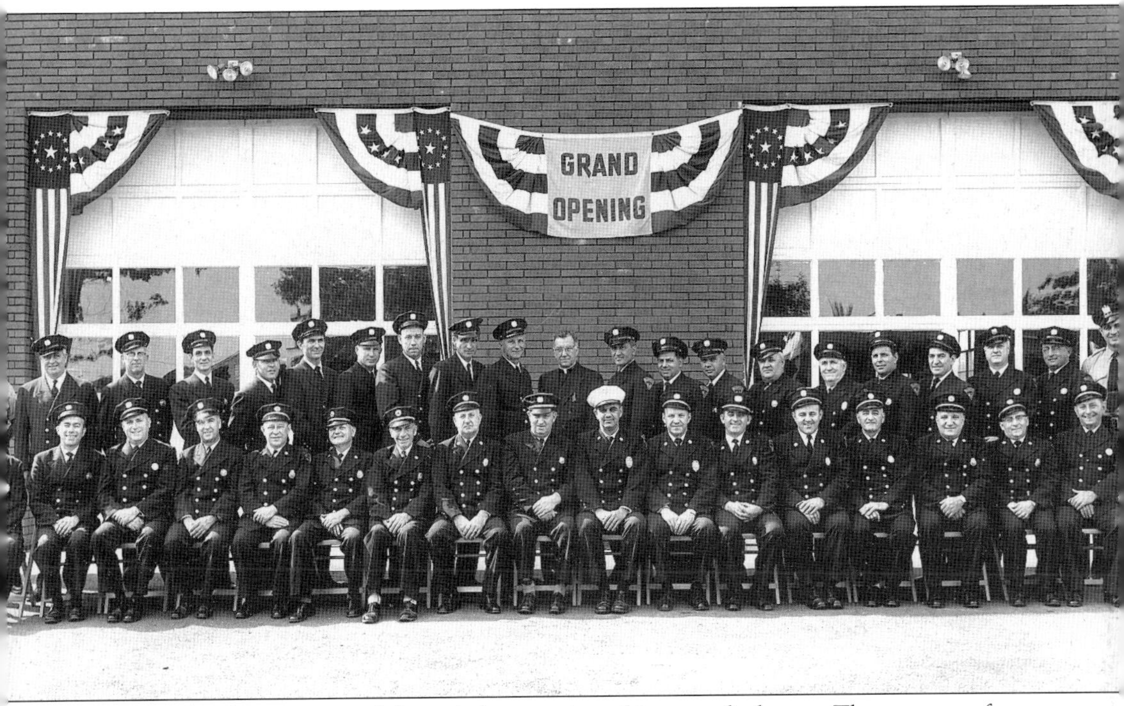

In 1957, the fire department celebrated the opening of its new firehouse. The men are, from left to right, as follows: (seated) M. Enright, M. Bernabe, J. Amorosa, A. DeLorenzo, J. Liptak, C. Slack, C. Barclay, A. Bencer, J. Poliselli, E. Minetti, J. Krachun, A. Navatto, P. DiPaolo, J. Navatto, A. Forte, N. Esposito, and J. Del Monte; (standing) J. Soriano, L. Schiavi, M. Galaida, J. Lovetri, D. Somlock, J. Bernabe, J. Azud, D. Seminara, V. Garo, J. Melitsky, Rev. J. Olsovsky (fire department chaplain), A. Caruso, L. Gandolfo, A. Kovac, J. Hudak, W. Haley, A. DeMaio, A. Morano, P. Carlino, A. Soriano, and C. Aversa.

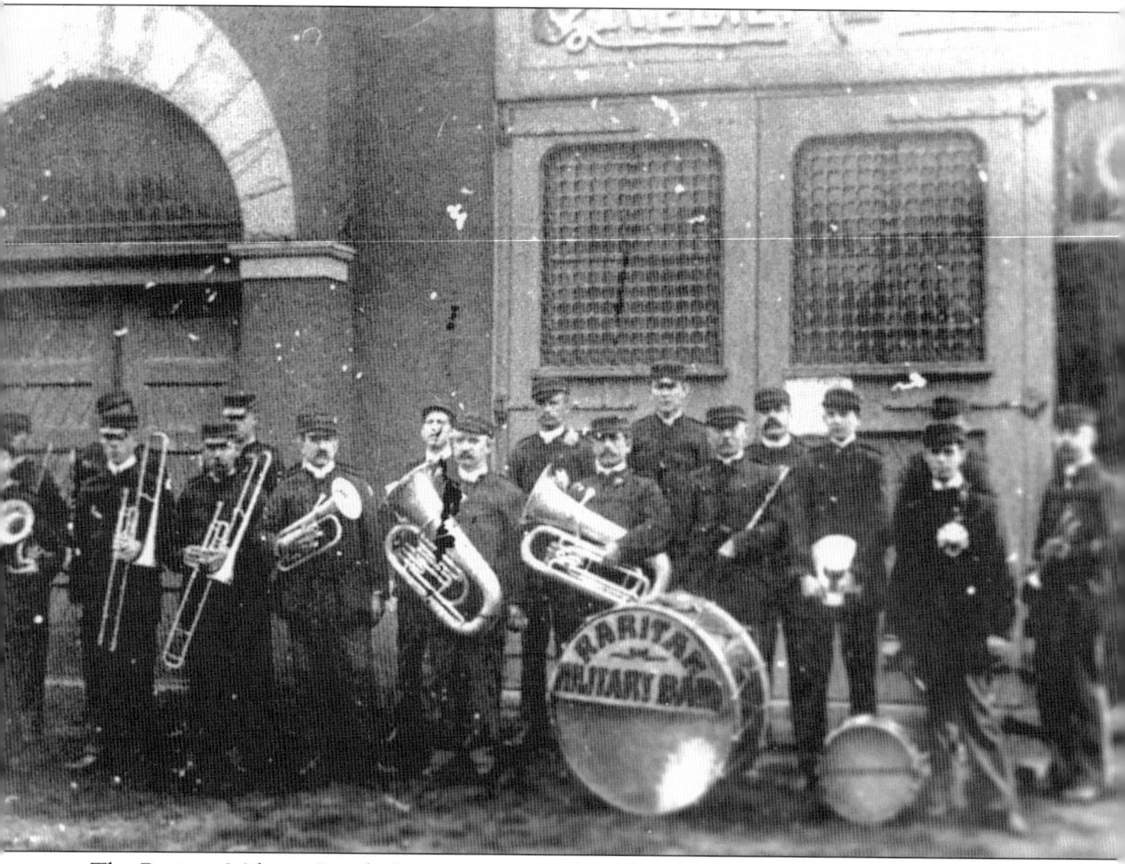

The Raritan Military Band often accompanied the fire department in parades.

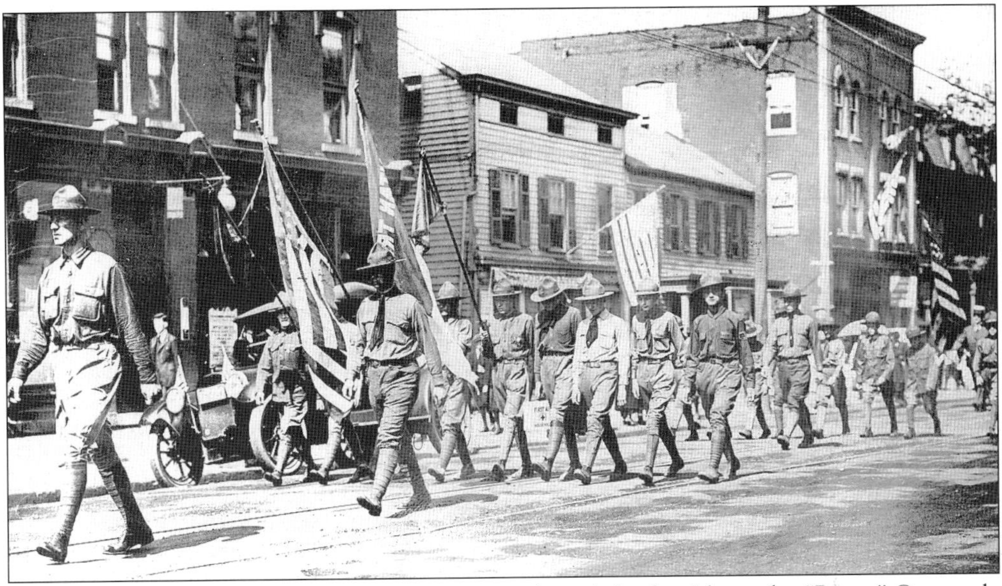

Raritan Boy Scout Troop No. 1 marches in a parade with leader Alexander "Pappy" Carnevale (left). (Courtesy of Barbara Navatto.)

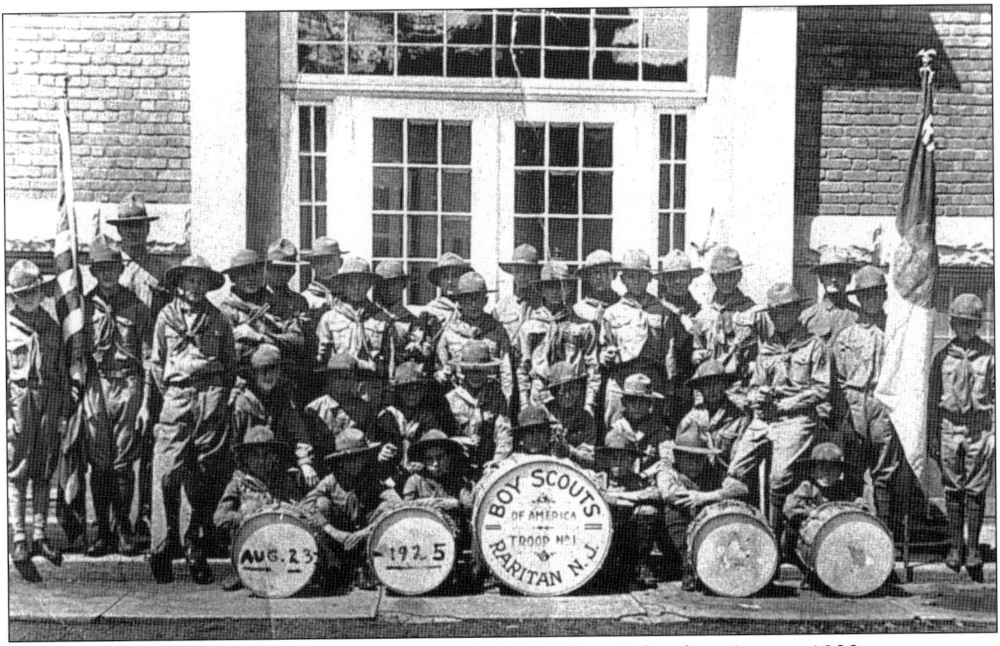

Boy Scouts assemble in front of the Raritan Intermediate School in August 1923.

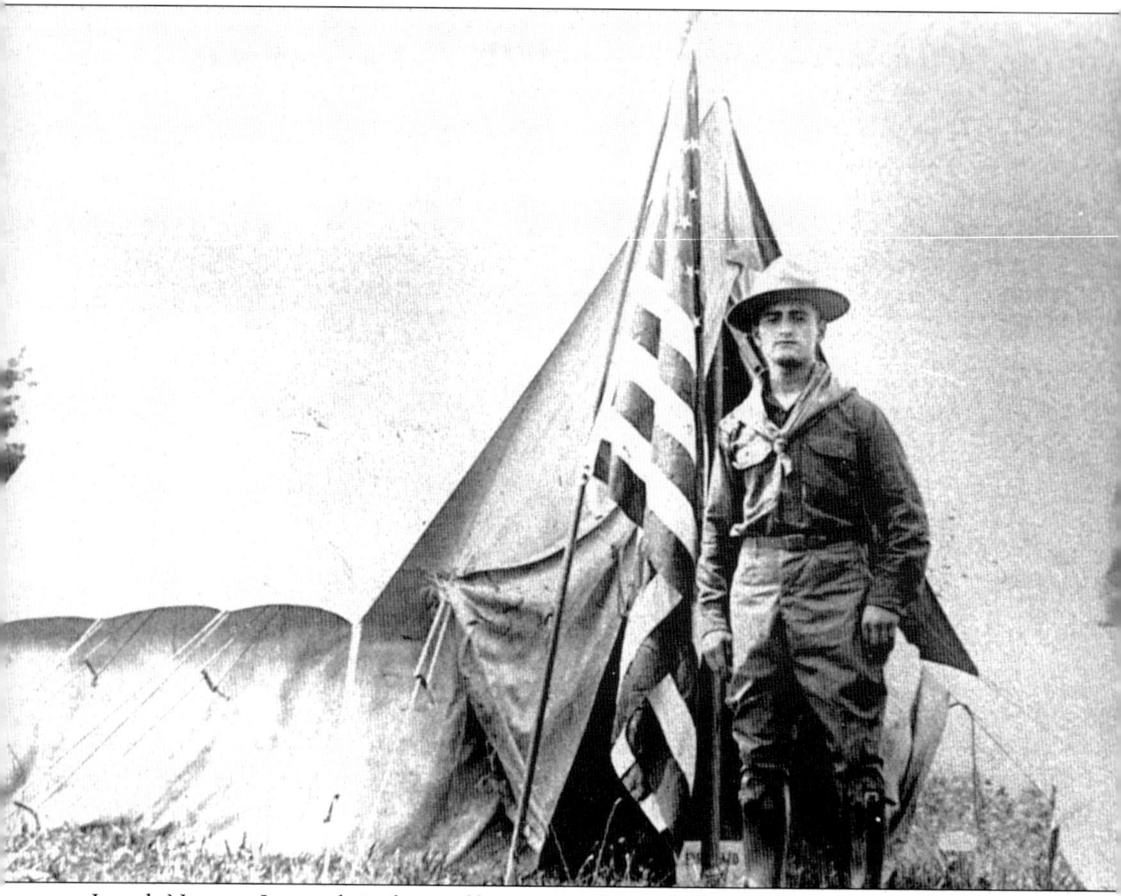

Joseph Navatto Jr. stands in front of his tent at Camp Gilbert, a local Boy Scout camp, in the summer of 1917. Camp Gilbert, on Milltown Road in Bridgewater, was located in an orchard owned by Joseph Gilbert.

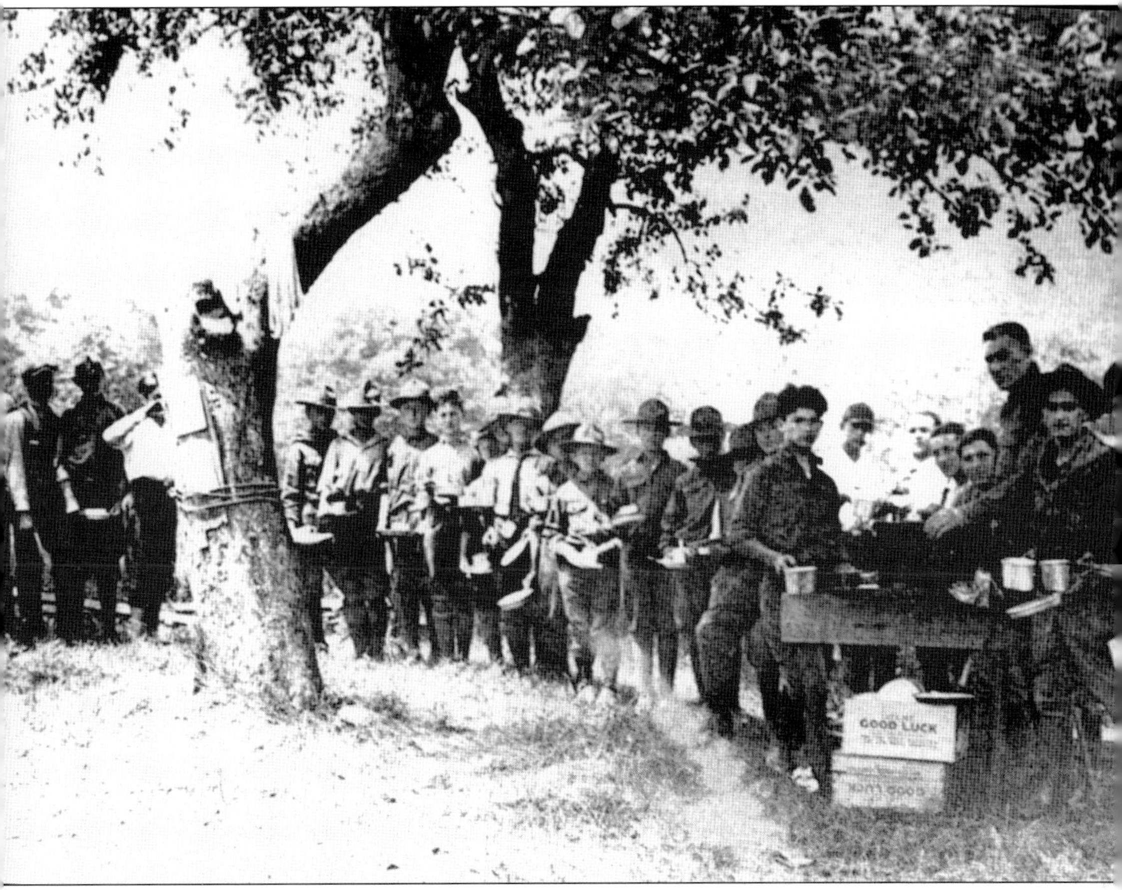

After a day of activities, the hungry Boy Scouts queue up for chow at Camp Gilbert.

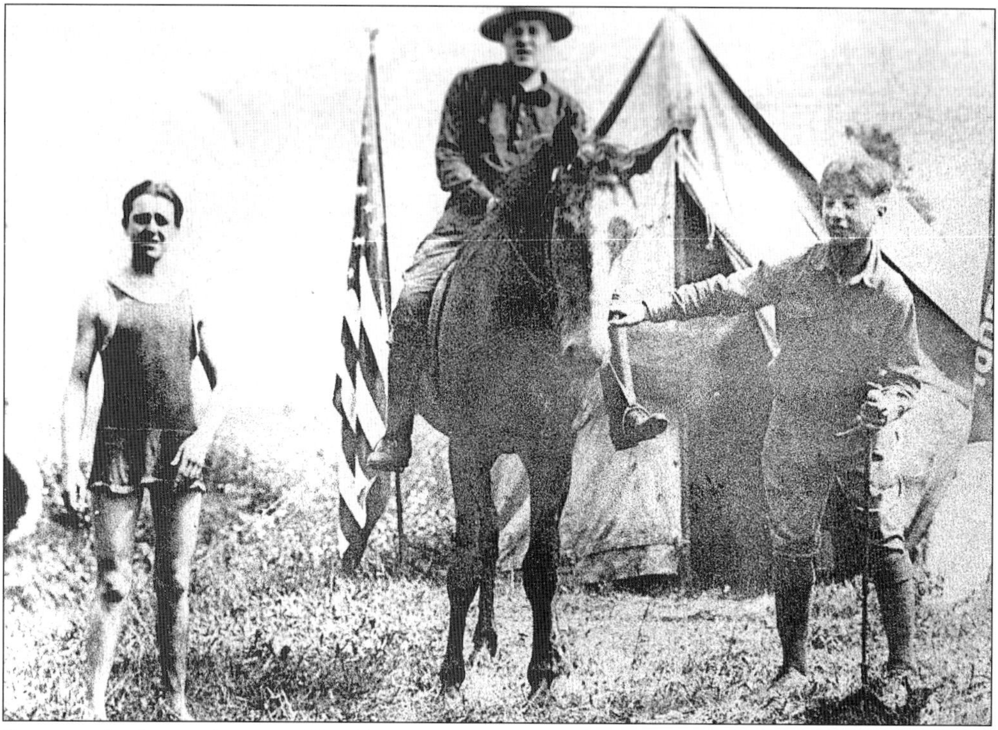

Everyone had a good time at Boy Scout camp.

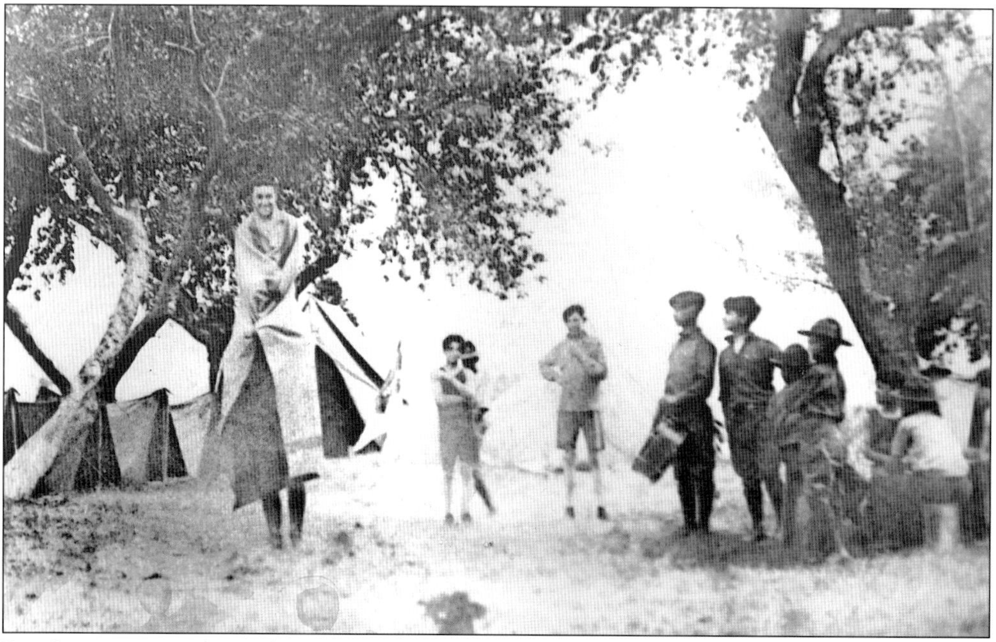

Boy Scouts amuse themselves with a little horseplay in the summer of 1917.

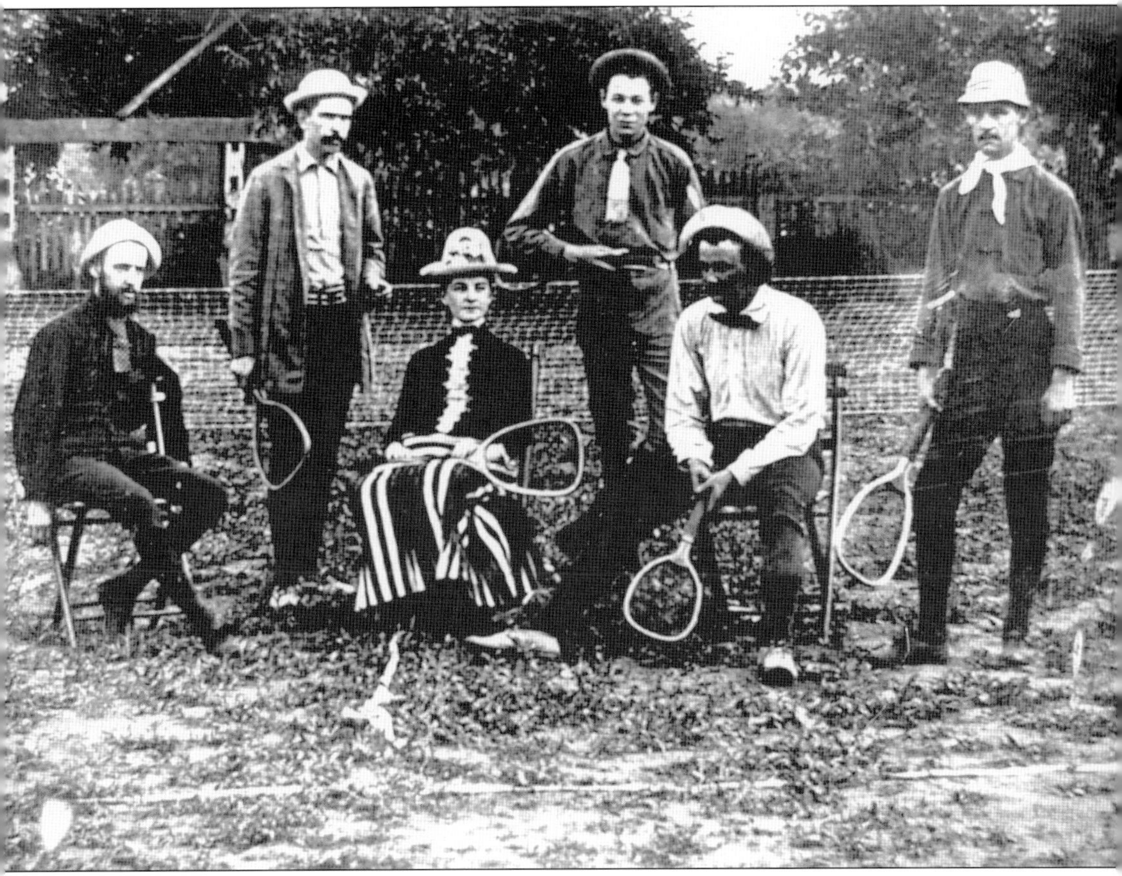
Pictured here is a group of early lawn tennis players—all wearing hats.

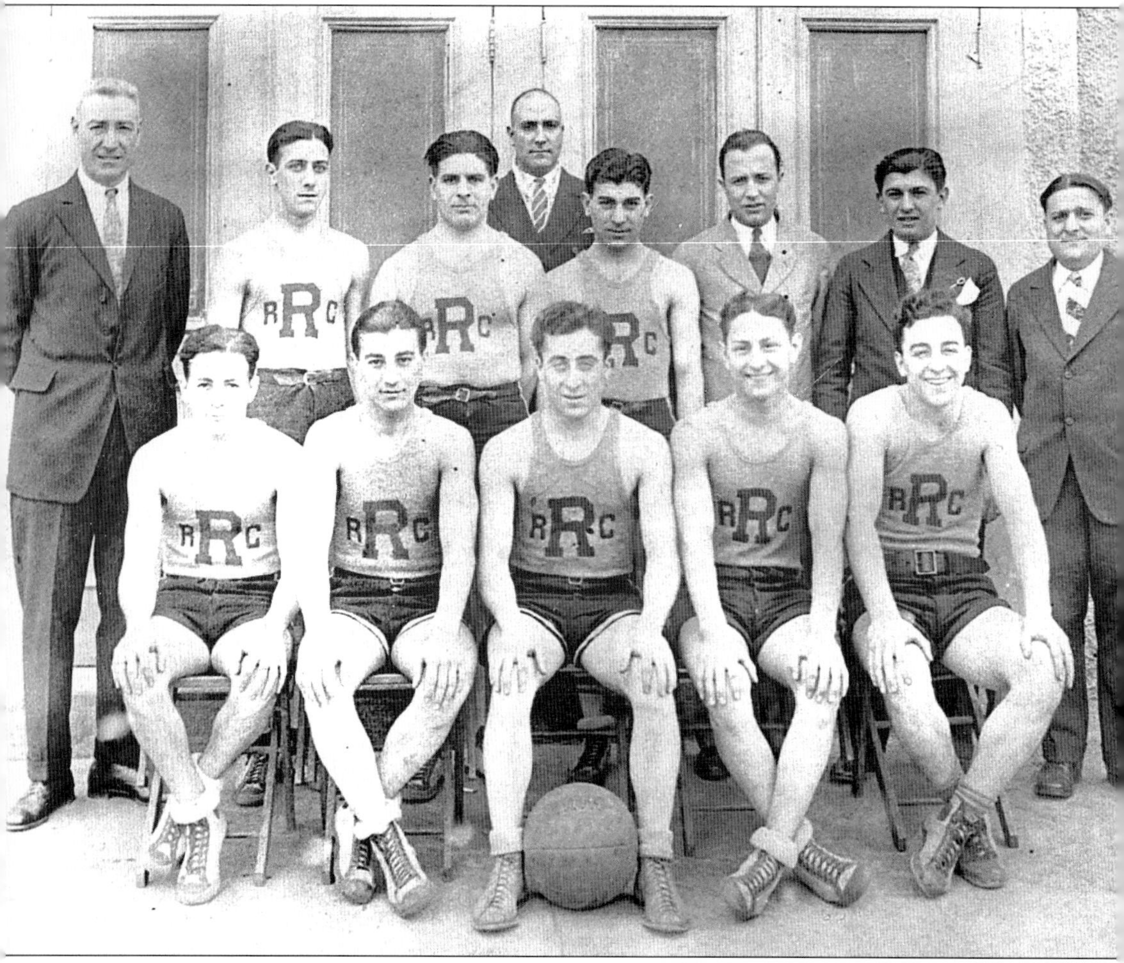

This *c.* 1929 Raritan Recreation Club basketball team photograph was taken in front of the Star of Italy Hall on Anderson Street. The team members are, from left to right, as follows: (front row) unidentified, Danny Soriano, Dr. Stabile, Jim DelMonte, and Patrick Navatto; (middle row) Alexander "Pappy" Carnevale, Al Soriano, Vince Minetti, Ray Soriano, Dominic Amorosa, Matty D'Ambola, and George Soriano Sr.; (back row) Dominick Natale.

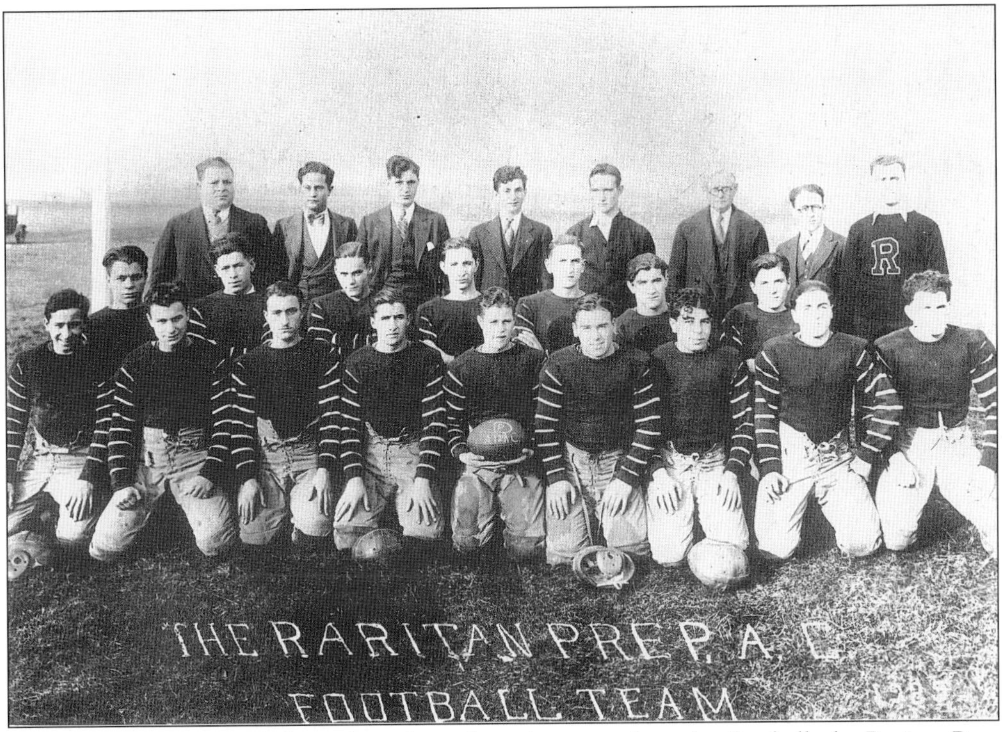

Founded in 1925 for eighth- and ninth-graders who wanted to play football, the Raritan Prep Athletic Club boasted 25 members. Later, the club expanded to include baseball and basketball. This photograph shows the 1929 football team.

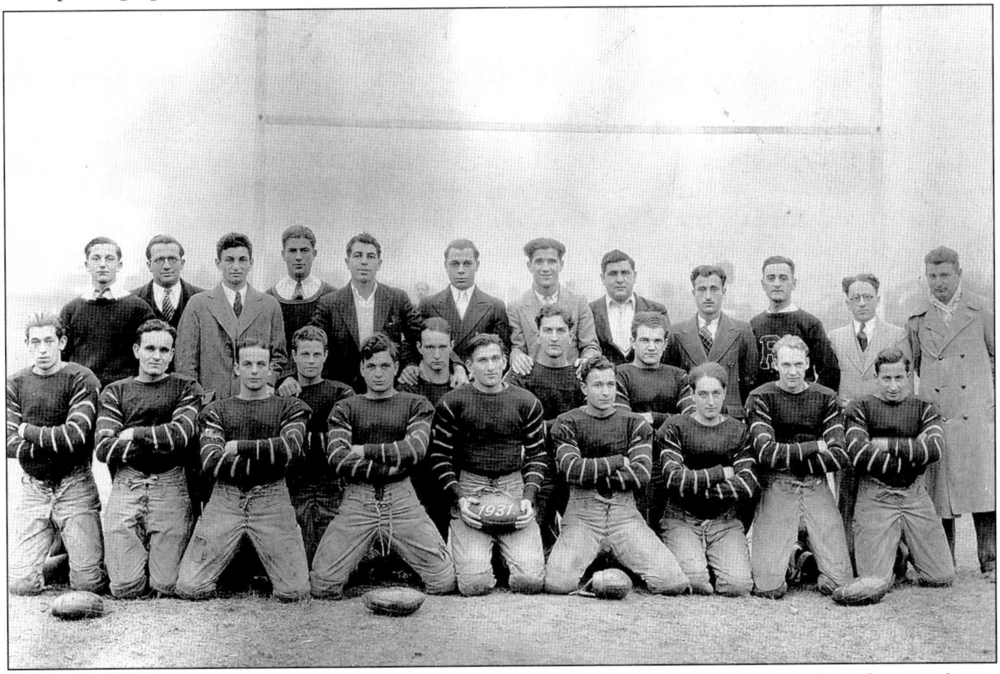

The 1931 Raritan Prep team was undefeated and untied. Pride shows in the players' faces. (Courtesy of Lilyan Navatto.)

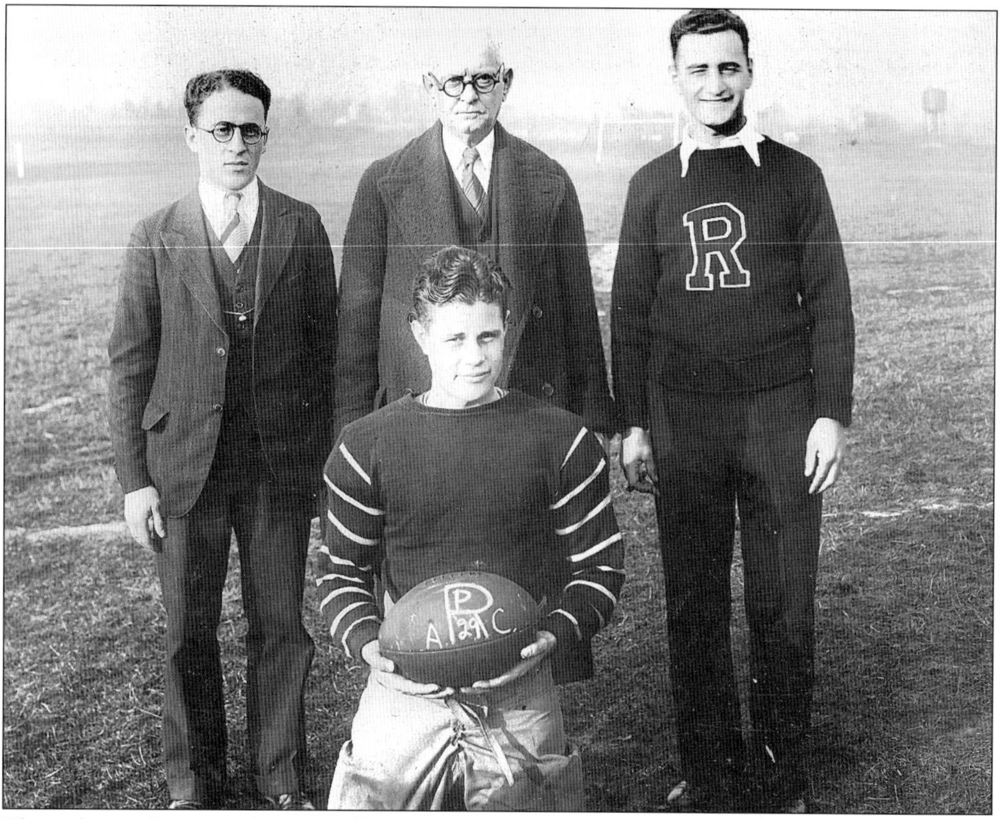

Through supplying uniforms, William Greene (standing, center) was a driving force in the organization of the Raritan Preps. He felt the team needed an identity, and uniforms helped the boys feel they were a team. Shown with him after the 1929 season are the coaches and organizer of team, from left to right, Anthony Esposito, unidentified, Joseph Navatto Jr. (Courtesy of Lilyan Navatto.)

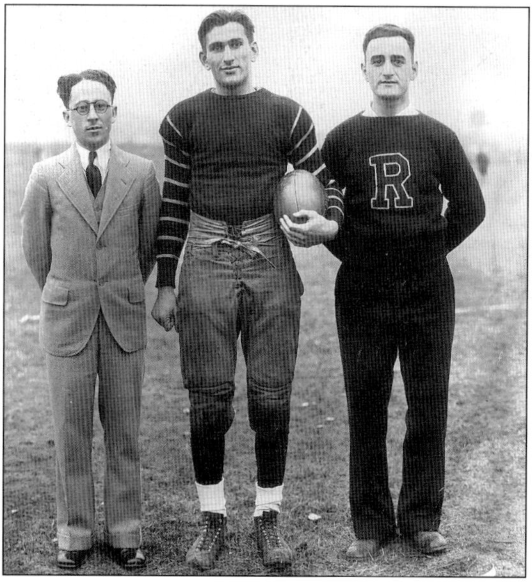

Coaches Anthony Esposito (left) and Joseph Navatto Jr. (right) pose with one of the players who helped the Raritan Preps achieve an undefeated 1931 season. (Courtesy of Lilyan Navatto.)

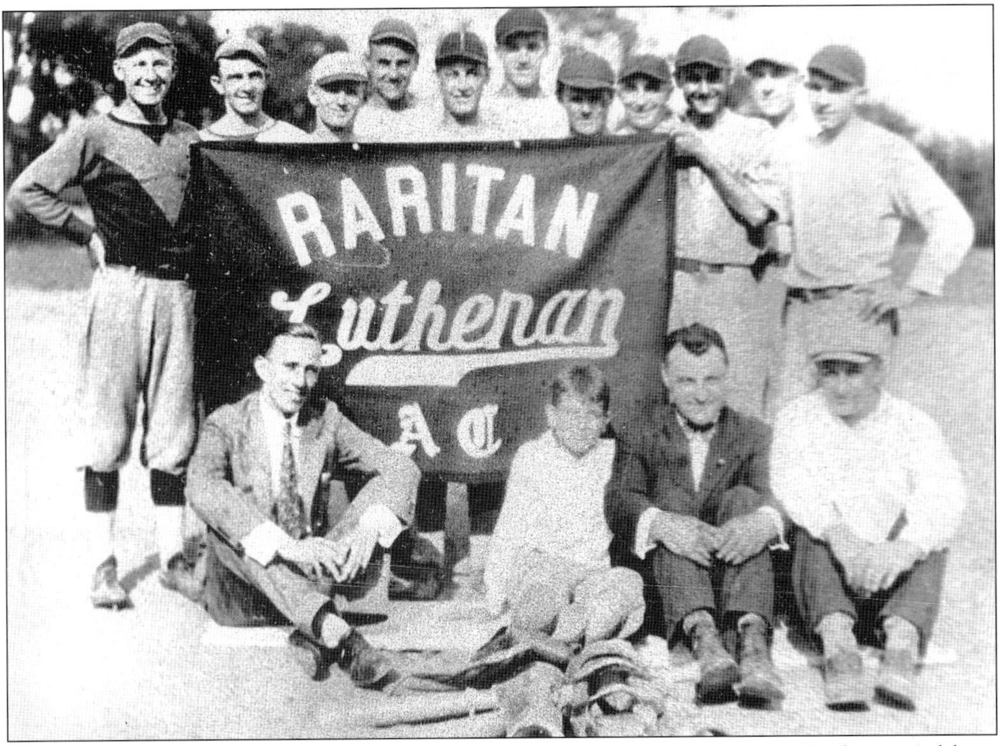

Many churches also sponsored athletic teams. Pictured here is the Raritan Lutheran Athletic Club baseball team in the 1920s.

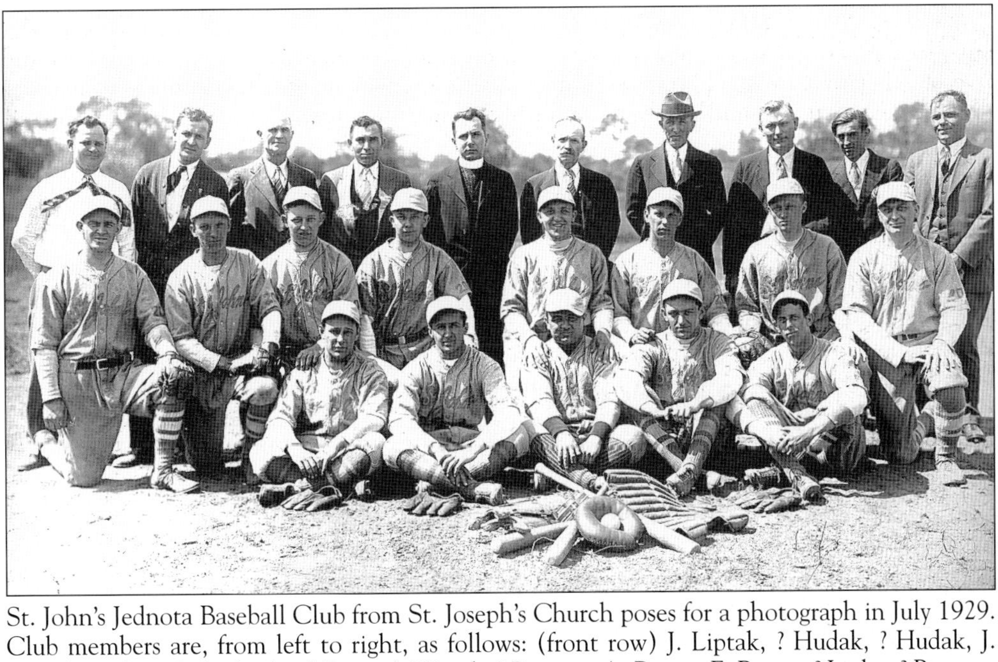

St. John's Jednota Baseball Club from St. Joseph's Church poses for a photograph in July 1929. Club members are, from left to right, as follows: (front row) J. Liptak, ? Hudak, ? Hudak, J. Yenick, and M. Galaida; (middle row) ? Yurek, ? Papcun, A. Petras, E. Petras, ? Lesko, ? Papcun, and J. Verba; (back row) two unidentified men, J. Suski, ? Kovac, Father Batcho, unidentified, ? Lesko, ? Liska, and J. Valko.

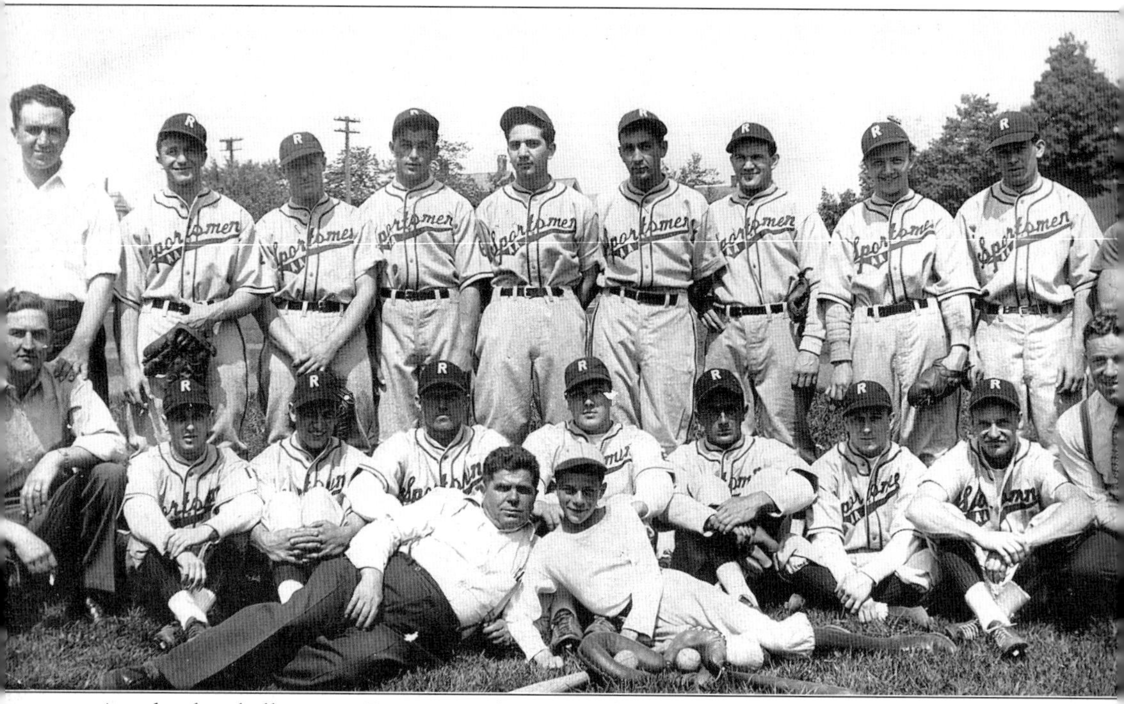

Another baseball team in Raritan was known as the Raritan Sportsmen. Team members in this 1935 photograph are, from left to right, as follows: (front row) Nick Micharone and ? Orlando; (middle row) Rocky Miele, Natie Kerr, Pete Pryzwozny, George Pfister, Carl Mehlenback, Joe Musz, Bernie Navatto, James Shug, and William Poliselli; (back row) Nick Russo, Armando Gabinelli, Lou Poliselli, Mike Musz, Tony Russo, Angelo Crisci, Joe Mattel, Andy Mattoe, Lou Schiavi, and Art Amey. (Courtesy of Bernard Navatto Sr.)

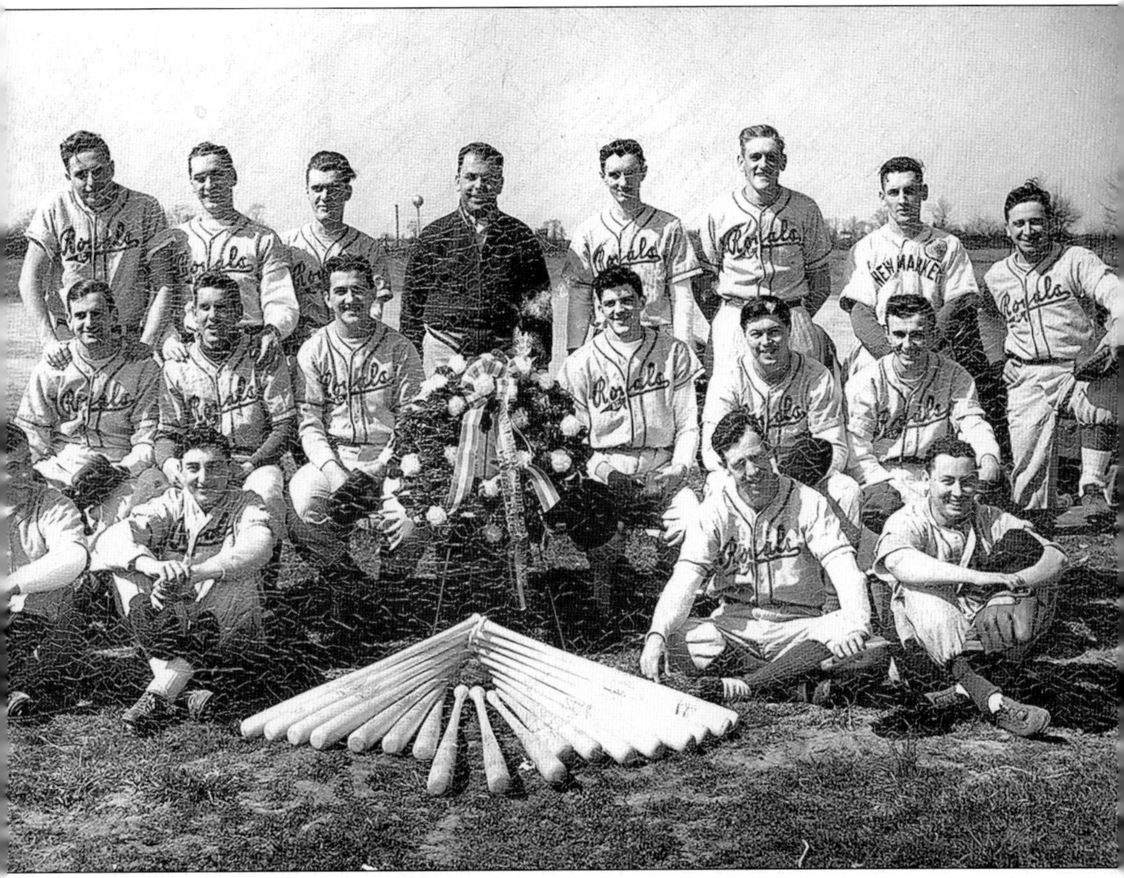

The 1950 Raritan Royals baseball team poses with coach Tom Esposito (back, center). (Courtesy of the Raritan Public Library.)

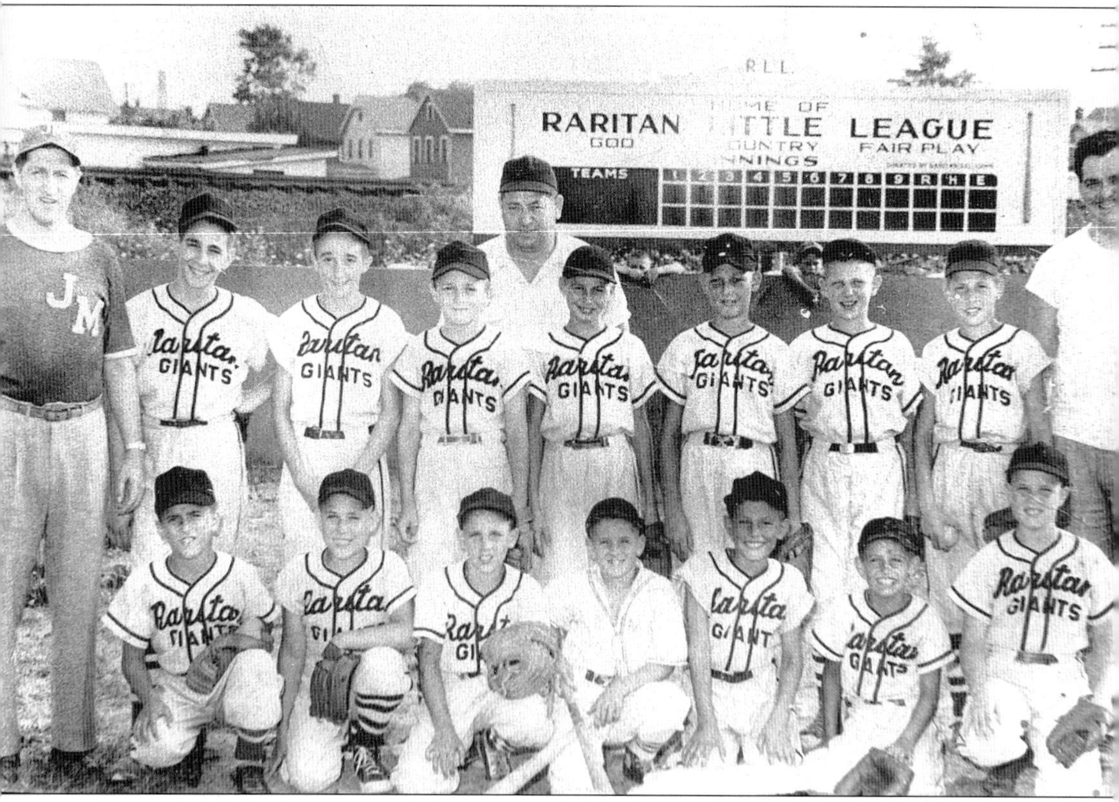

The style of the uniforms and the names of the players may change, but the Raritan Little League Giants still love baseball. This 1950s team poses with its coaches at the Frelinghuysen Park Field.

Three

Government

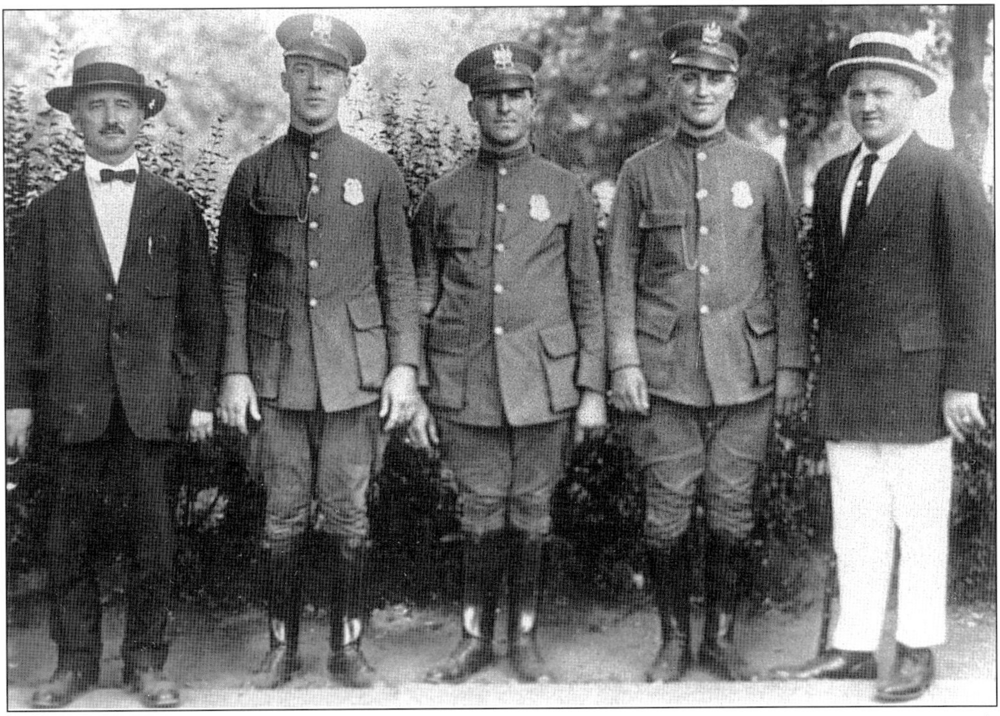

The Raritan Police Department is pictured here in the early 1920s. From left to right are Joseph Navatto Sr., chief of police and commissioner; James Mansfield, Joseph Malang, and Lorenzo Rossi—all patrolman; and Charles Mattoe, police commissioner.

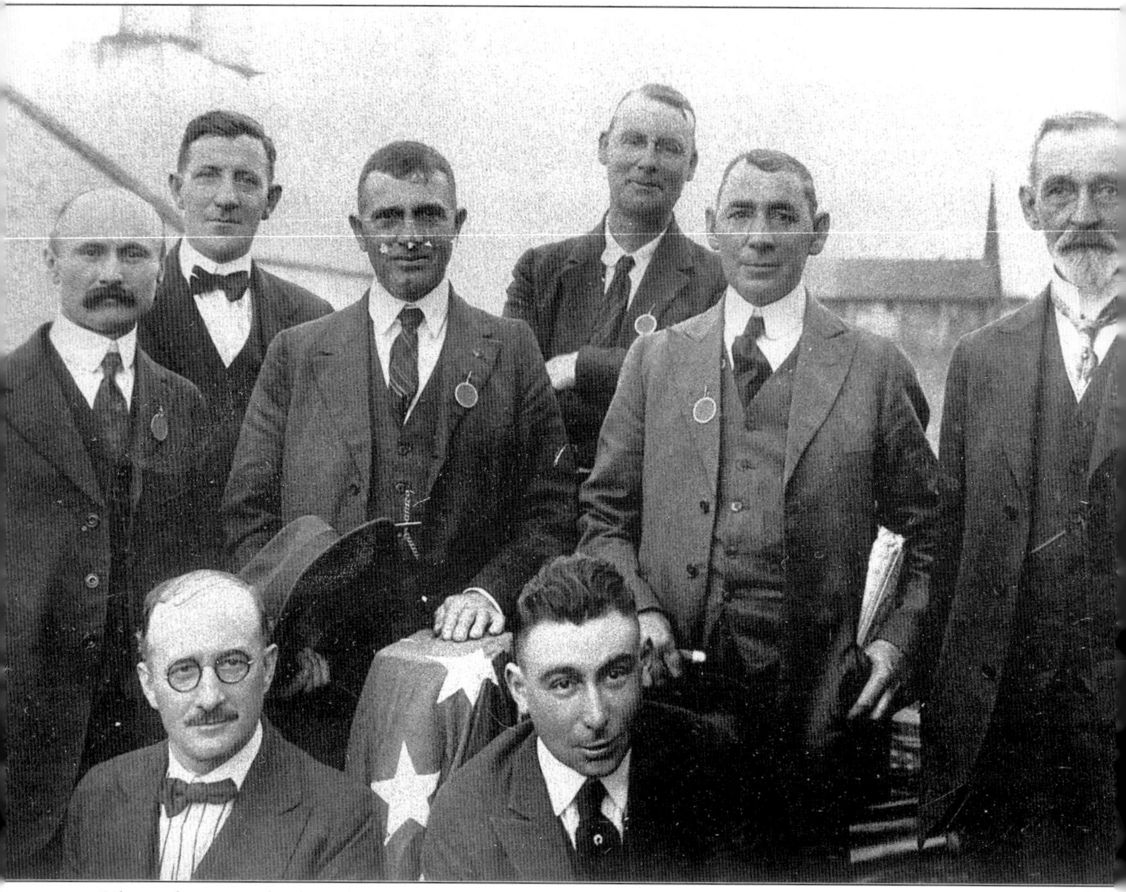

These distinguished-looking gentlemen made up the Raritan Board of Commissioners and were elected to run the town government. They are, from left to right, as follows: (front row) Joseph Navatto Sr. and James Soriano, town clerk; (middle row) Andrew Sabol, George Leibold, Sam Glaser, and George West; (back row) P. Findley Wyckoff and Dick Dahoney.

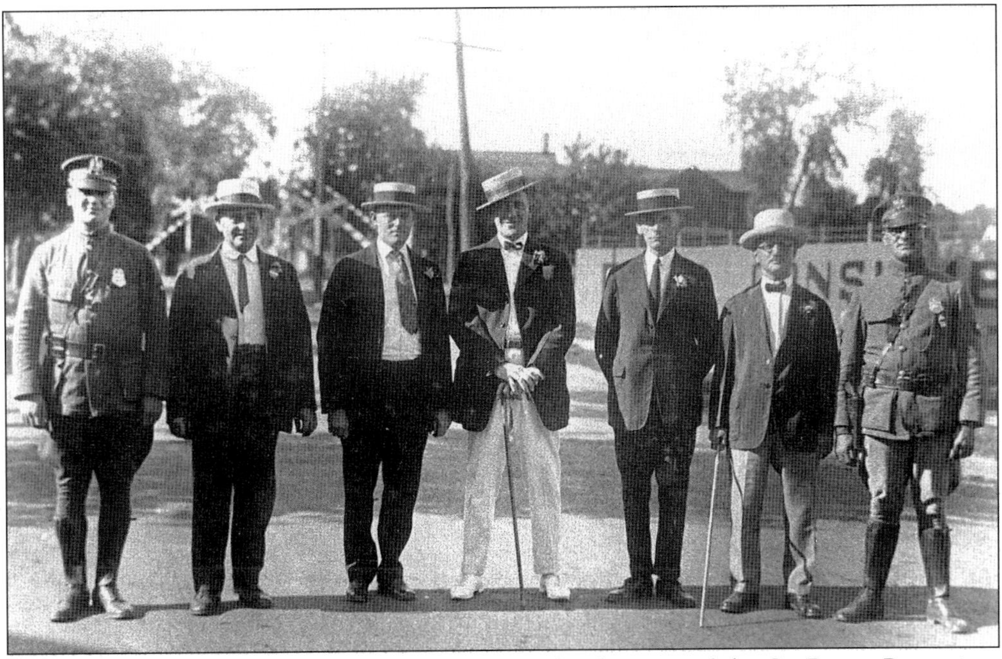

Raritan dignitaries queue up on Anderson Street for the start of the St. Rocco Procession. From left to right are Lorenzo Rossi (patrolman), George Leibold, ? Griffin, P. Findley Wyckoff, Albert Van Tine, Joseph Navatto Sr., and Joseph Malang (patrolman).

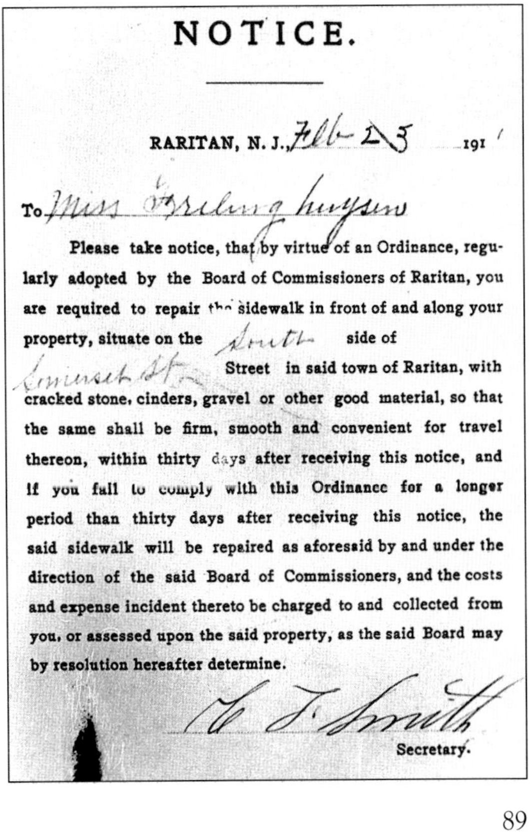

NOTICE.

RARITAN, N. J., Feb 23 1911

To Miss Frelinghuysen

Please take notice, that by virtue of an Ordinance, regularly adopted by the Board of Commissioners of Raritan, you are required to repair the sidewalk in front of and along your property, situate on the South side of Somerset St Street in said town of Raritan, with cracked stone, cinders, gravel or other good material, so that the same shall be firm, smooth and convenient for travel thereon, within thirty days after receiving this notice, and if you fail to comply with this Ordinance for a longer period than thirty days after receiving this notice, the said sidewalk will be repaired as aforesaid by and under the direction of the said Board of Commissioners, and the costs and expense incident thereto be charged to and collected from you, or assessed upon the said property, as the said Board may by resolution hereafter determine.

C. T. Smith

Secretary.

This Notice to Fix Property was issued to Miss Frelinghuysen on February 23, 1911. Her property is now the home of the Raritan Public Library.

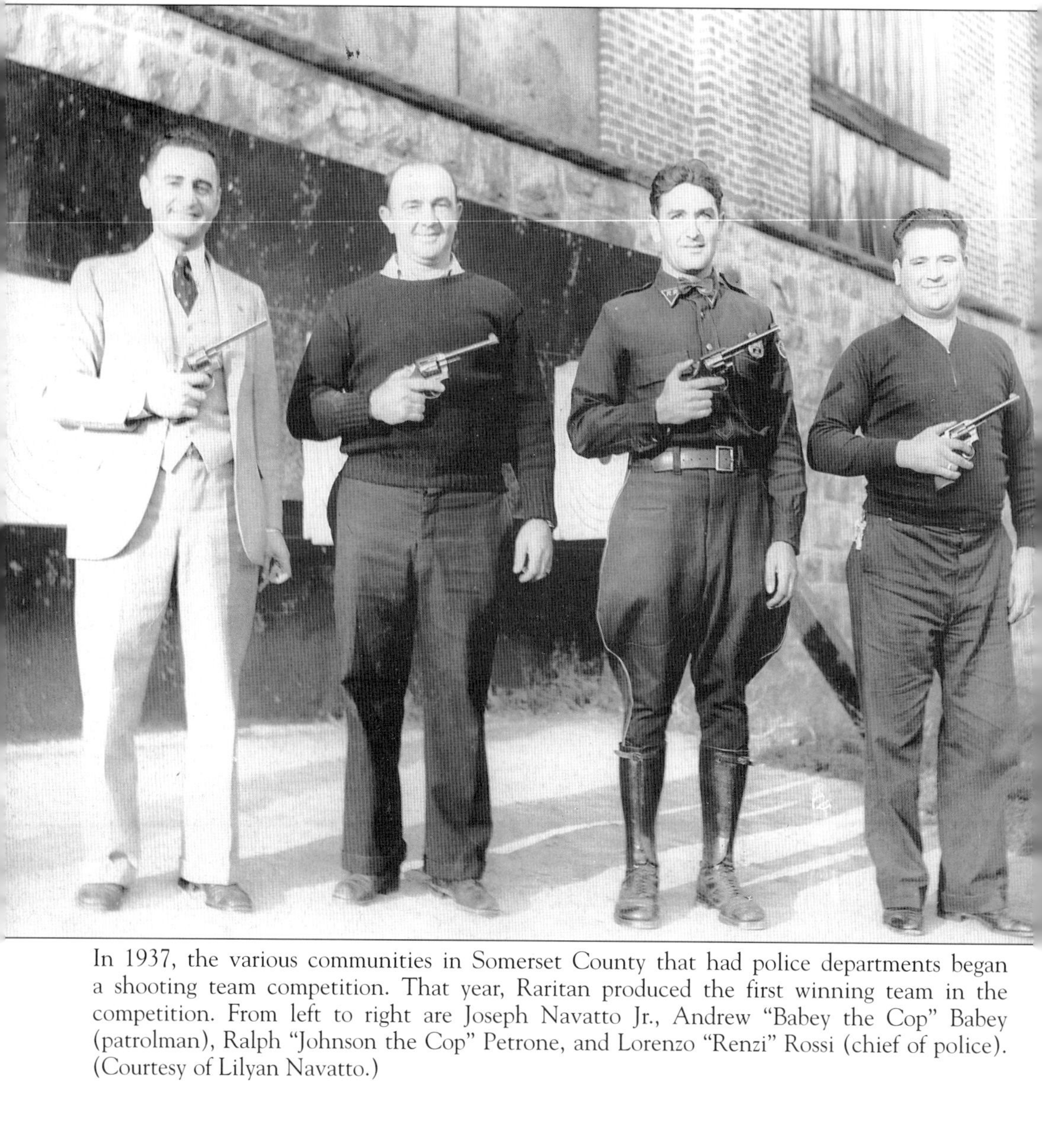

In 1937, the various communities in Somerset County that had police departments began a shooting team competition. That year, Raritan produced the first winning team in the competition. From left to right are Joseph Navatto Jr., Andrew "Babey the Cop" Babey (patrolman), Ralph "Johnson the Cop" Petrone, and Lorenzo "Renzi" Rossi (chief of police). (Courtesy of Lilyan Navatto.)

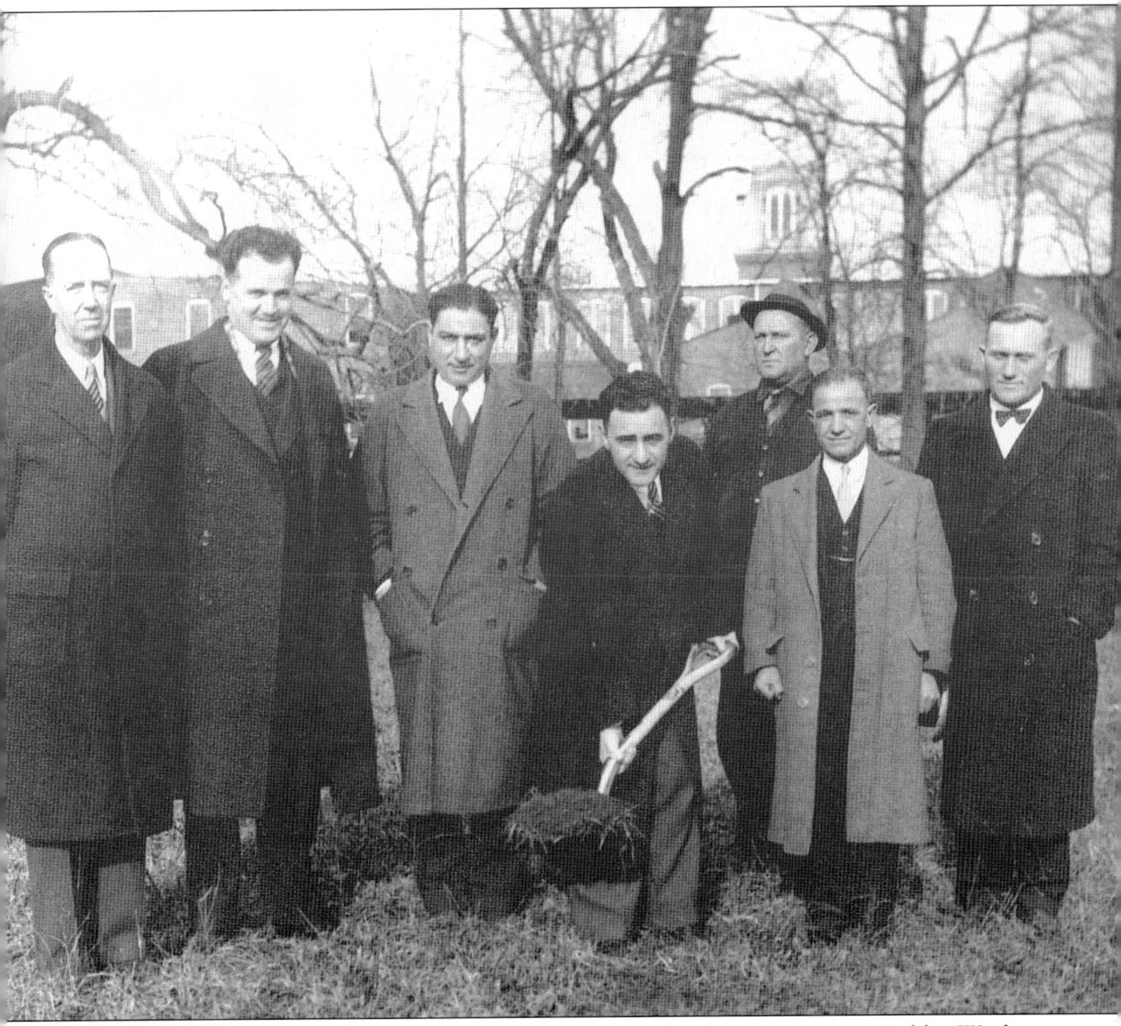

Mayor Joseph Navatto Jr. removes the first shovel of dirt for the new Raritan Public Works garage in 1937. Other members of the board of commissioners are pictured with him. They are, from left to right, unidentified, John Macko, Henry Condo, Edward Diesbusky (public works director), Terry Minetti, and unidentified. (Courtesy of Lilyan Navatto.)

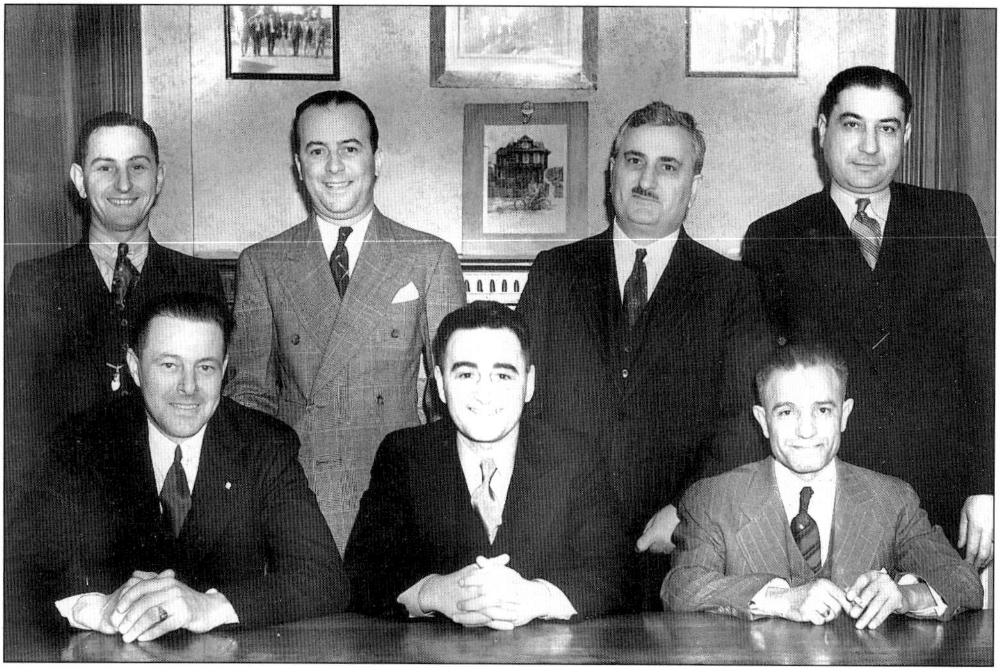

The 1939 board of commissioners poses for a photograph. From left to right are the following: (front row) unidentified, Mayor Joseph Navatto Jr., and Terry Minetti; (back row) James Del Monte, Angelo Soriano, Peter Mencaroni, and Henry Condo. (Courtesy of Lilyan Navatto.)

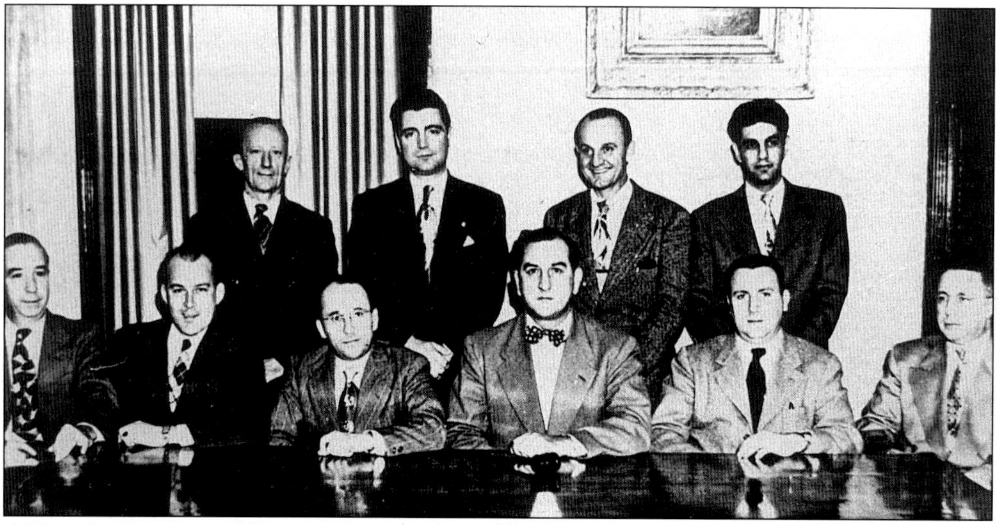

Although the town of Raritan dates back to 1868, the borough was officially incorporated on May 12, 1948, after a long battle for independence from Bridgewater Township. Pictured is the first mayor and council elected in the borough of Raritan. They are, from left to right, as follows: (seated) William Cunningham Sr., borough engineer; Milton Kovac, councilman; Nicholas Esposito, borough clerk; Rocco J. Miele, mayor; Joseph Amorosa, council president; and George W. Allgair, borough attorney; (standing) Michael Tkacik, Anthony J. Santora, Steve Timko, and Edward Minetti—all councilmen.

Four

Around Town

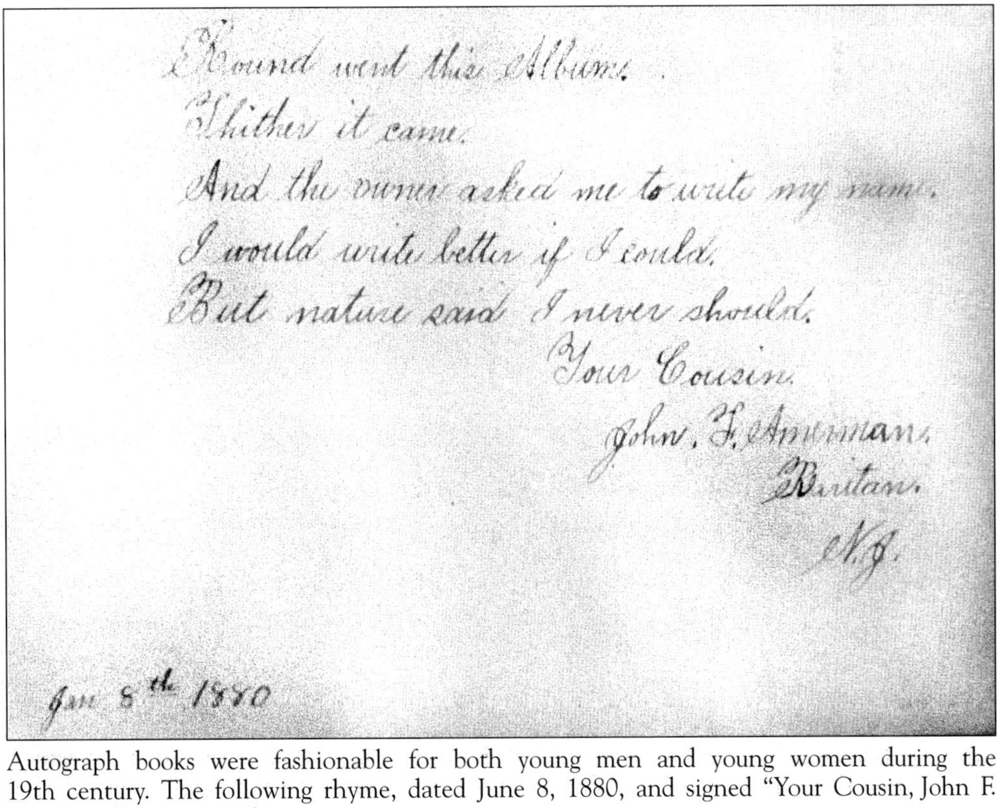

Autograph books were fashionable for both young men and young women during the 19th century. The following rhyme, dated June 8, 1880, and signed "Your Cousin, John F. Amerman," was a popular one:

> Round went this Album
> Hither it came
> And the owner asked me to write my name.
> I would write better if I could,
> But nature said I never should.

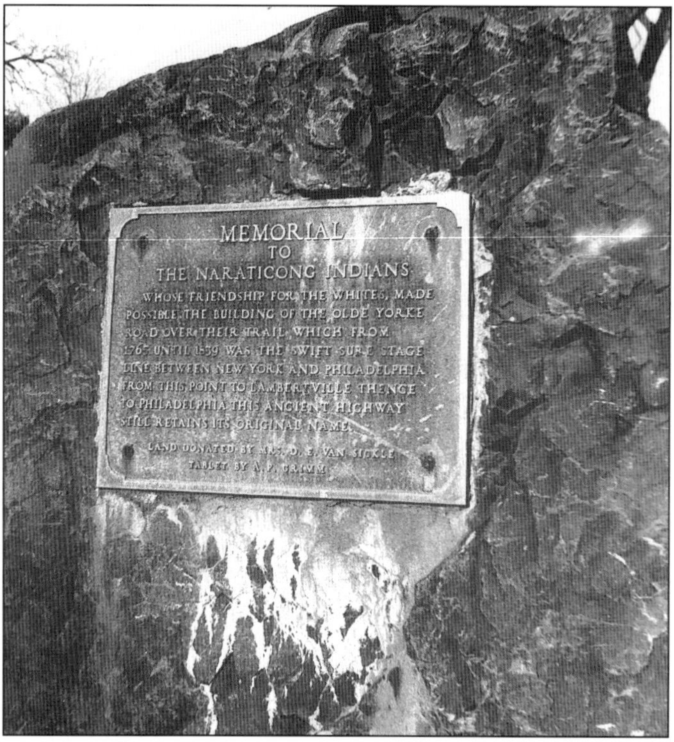

The Naraticong tribe of the Lenape was very helpful to the Europeans who came to this wilderness. This memorial to the Naraticong Indians is on Old York Road and reads: "Whose friendship for the whites, made possible the building of the Olde Yorke Road over their trail which from 1765 until 1859 was the Swift Sure Stage Line between New York and Philadelphia from this point to Lambertville thence to Philadelphia. This ancient highway still retains its original name."

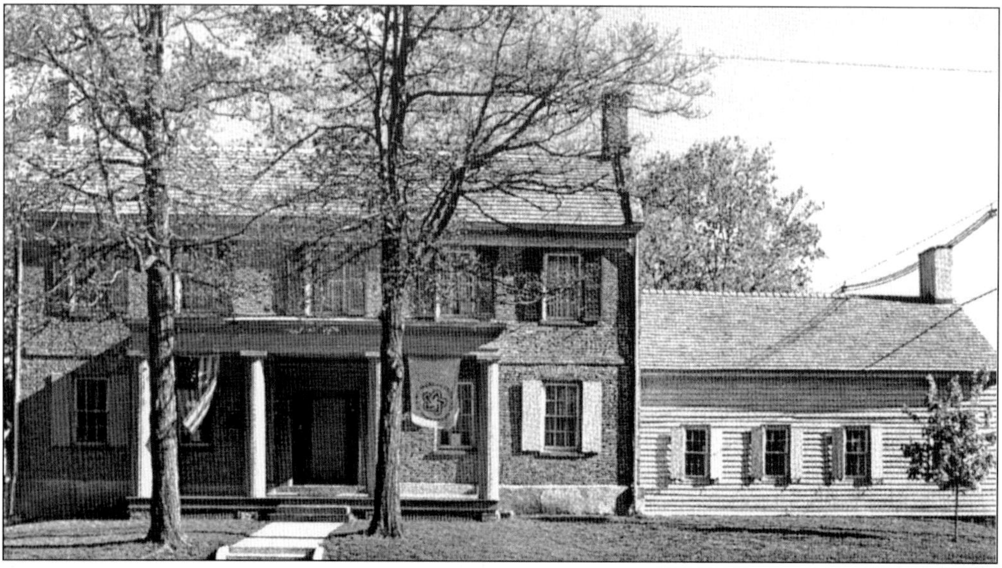

The General John Frelinghuysen House is listed on the National Register of Historic Places. Frederick Frelinghuysen purchased the property from Cornelius Middaugh. Each change in the building's structure represents a different period in U.S. history. The first floor, built sometime between 1740 and 1780, has glazed headers, a type of brick. These were popular during the time of the Boston Tea Party, the Declaration of Independence, and the early years of the Revolutionary War. The lower wooden wing is the oldest section of the house. In 1859, the Frelinghuysens added a new porch of Neoclassical architecture. Today, the General John Frelinghuysen House is the home of the Raritan Public Library. (Courtesy of Barbara Navatto.)

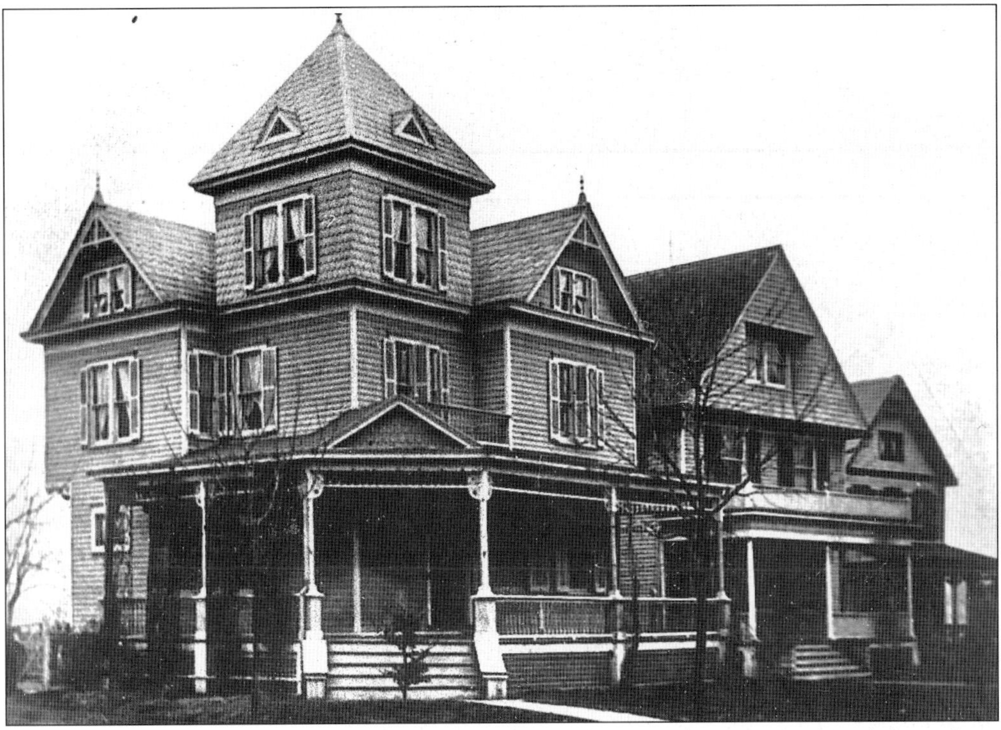

Many homes were built along Somerset Street east of the main business district. A large front porch assured a buffer from the busy streets filled with horses, buggies, trolley cars, and the newest invention—the horseless carriage.

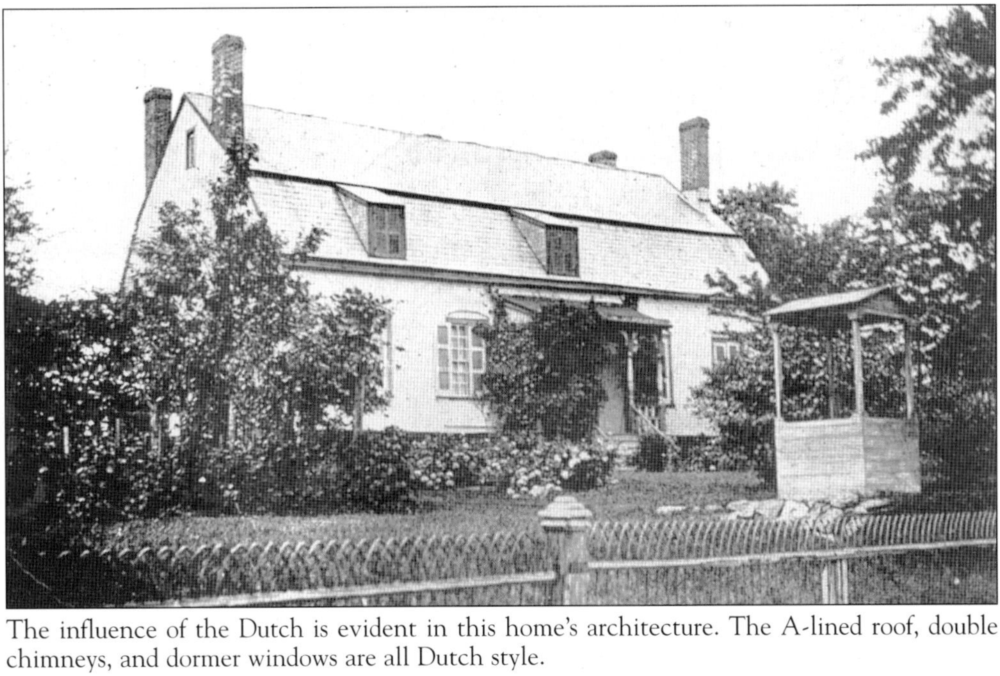

The influence of the Dutch is evident in this home's architecture. The A-lined roof, double chimneys, and dormer windows are all Dutch style.

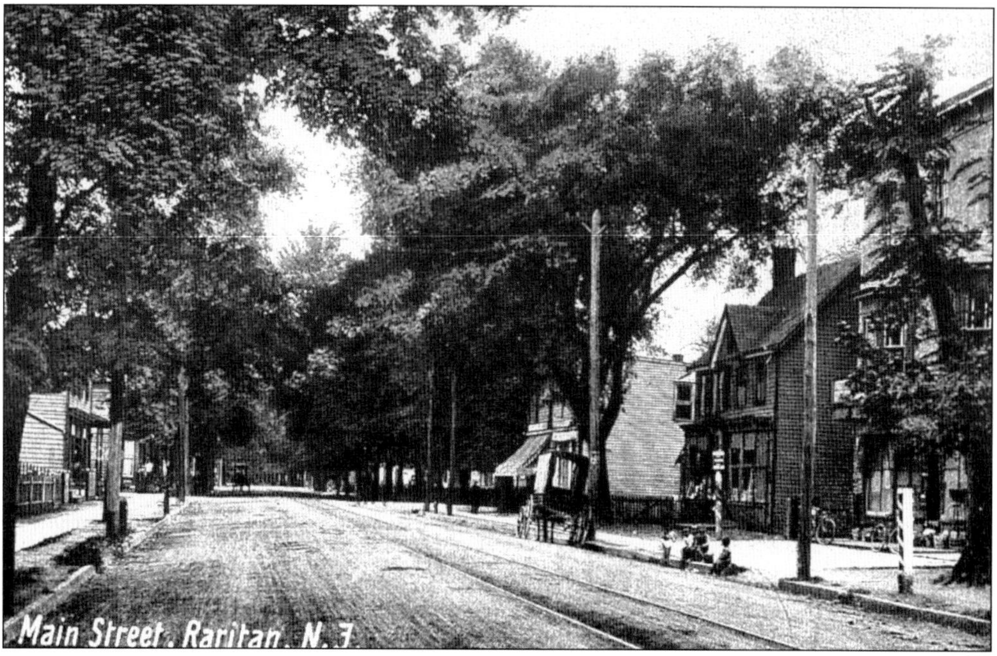

Horses, buggies, and bicycles were the popular modes of transportation when this 1907 photograph was taken. (Courtesy of Frank Tropiano.)

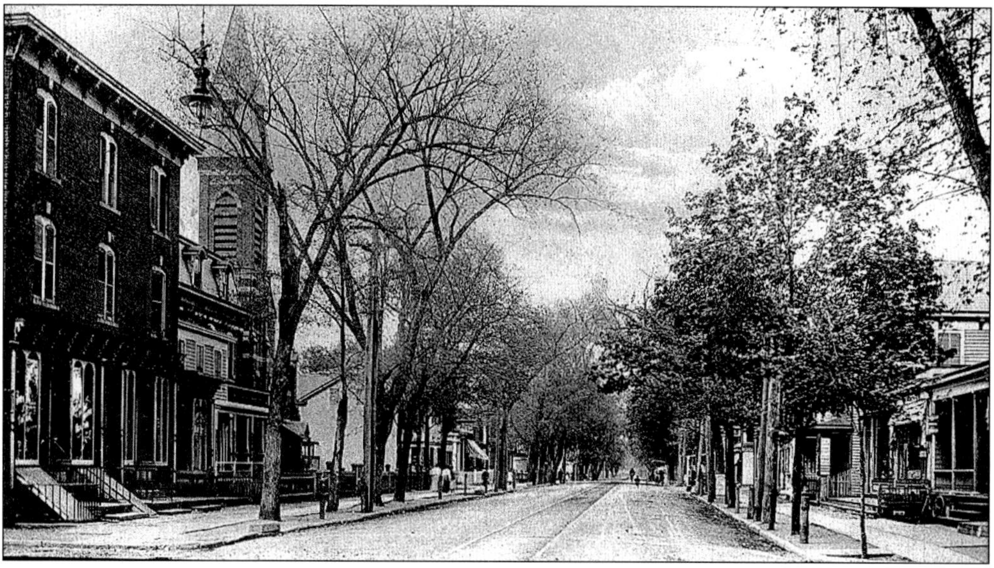

This view, taken from Wall Street looking east down Somerset Street, shows the trolley tracks and the imposing steeple of St. Bernard's Church. (Courtesy of Barbara Navatto.)

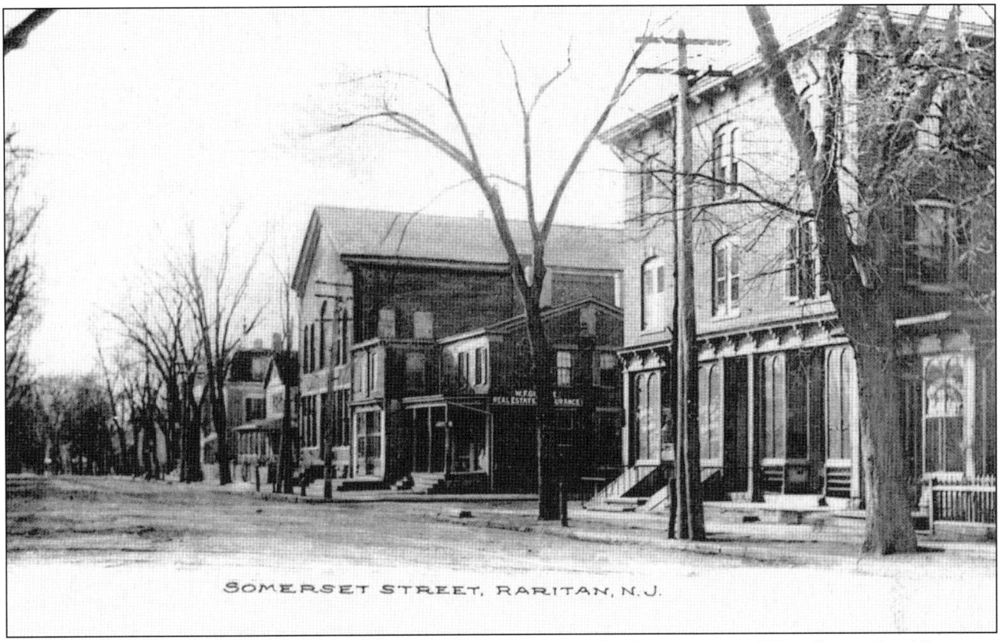

This *c.* 1910 scene was taken from Somerset Street looking west. The large building in the middle with the pitched roof is St. Bernard's Parochial School. (Courtesy of Barbara Navatto.)

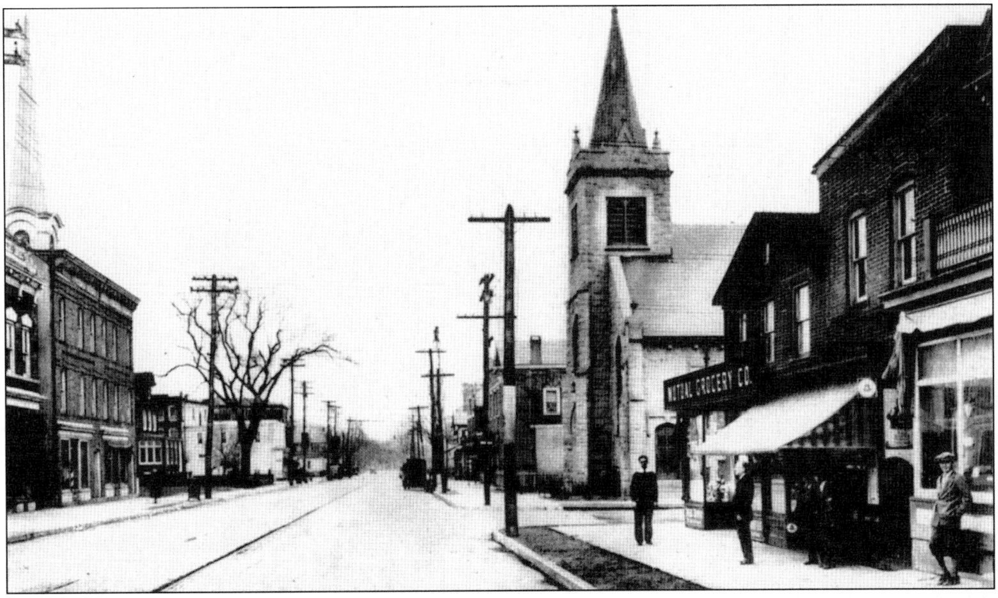

The main business section of Somerset Street can be seen in this photograph. St. Paul's Church (right) and the Third Reformed Dutch Church (left) date this scene to the 1920s. The Third Reformed Church's steeple was replaced in 1931 with a smaller rounded steeple after it was toppled by a windstorm. (Courtesy of Barbara Navatto.)

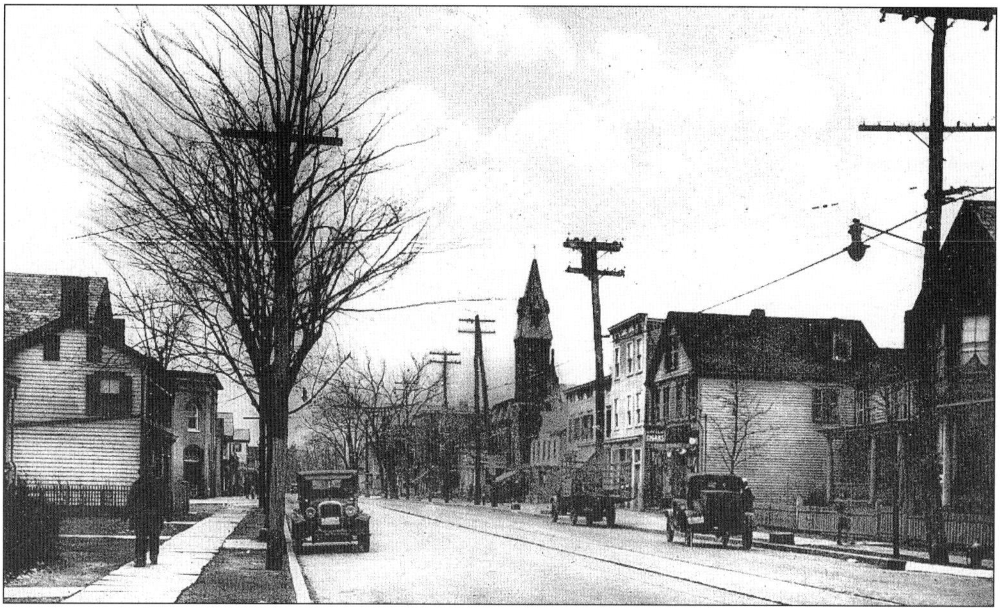

The trolley tracks are still visible in this picture of West Somerset Street in the 1930s. The spire of St. Bernard's Church can also be seen. (Courtesy of Barbara Navatto.)

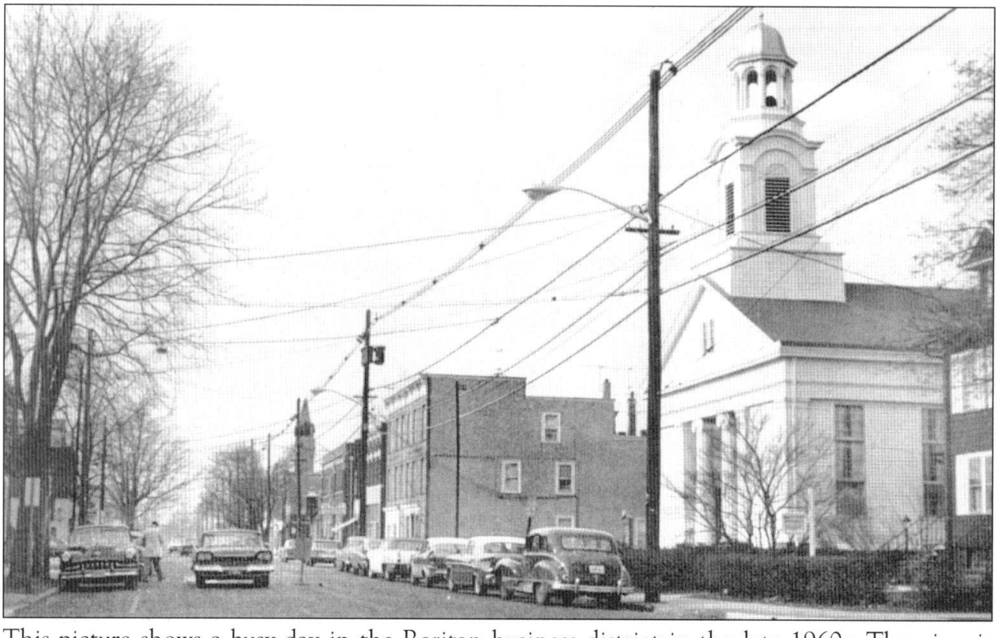

This picture shows a busy day in the Raritan business district in the late 1960s. The view is looking west from Thompson Street. (Courtesy of Barbara Navatto.)

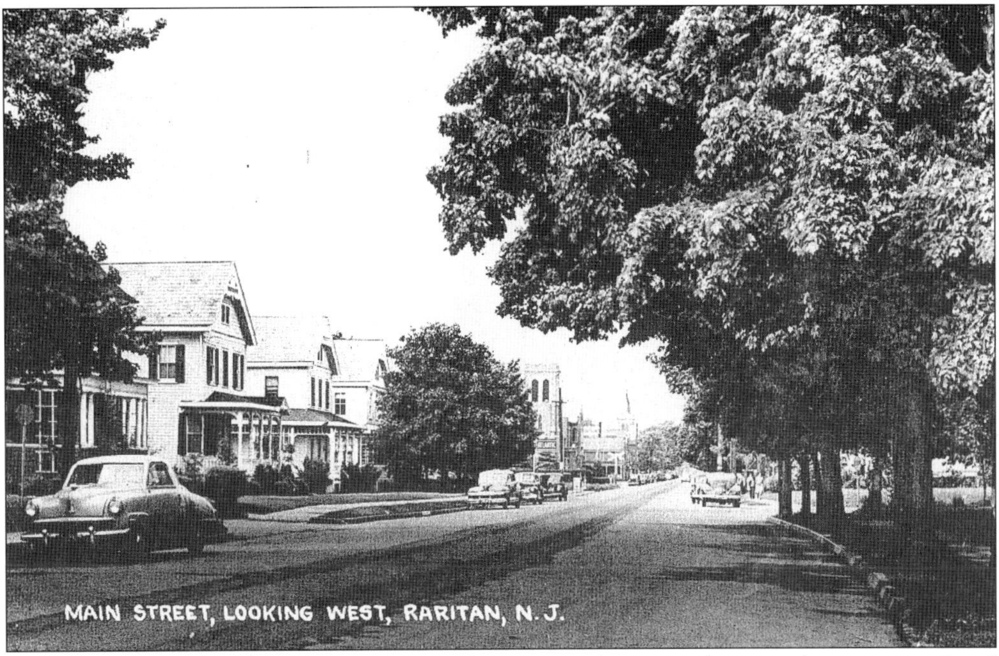

This pleasant scene, looking west toward Raritan's business district, shows a tree-lined Somerset Street. The bell tower of St. Joseph's Church can be seen in the distance. (Courtesy of Barbara Navatto.)

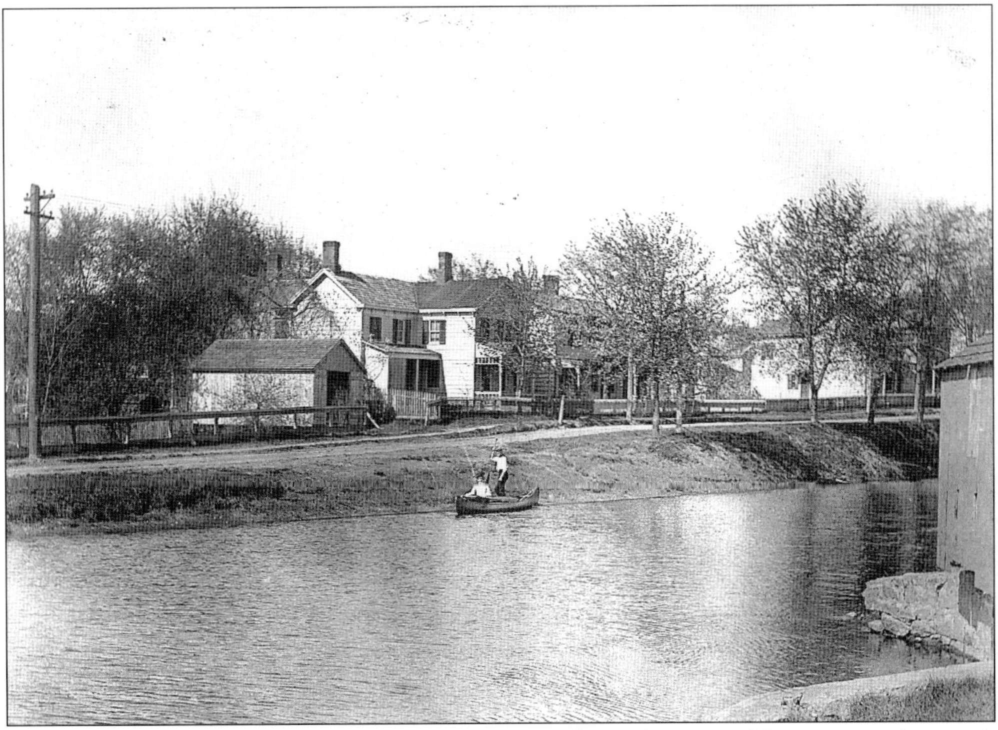

Early homes along Canal Street had boathouses, and people enjoyed boating on the canal. (Courtesy of Linda Barth.)

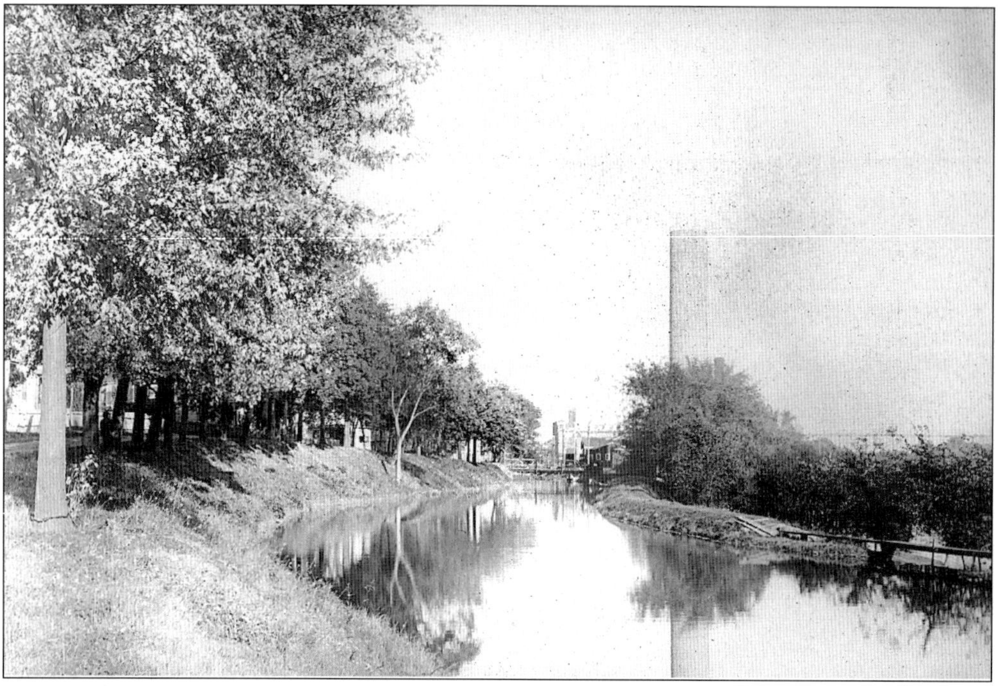

The Raritan Waterpower Canal flows between the Raritan River and Canal Street. Note that the canal is so still that it reflects the standpipe. (Courtesy of Linda Barth.)

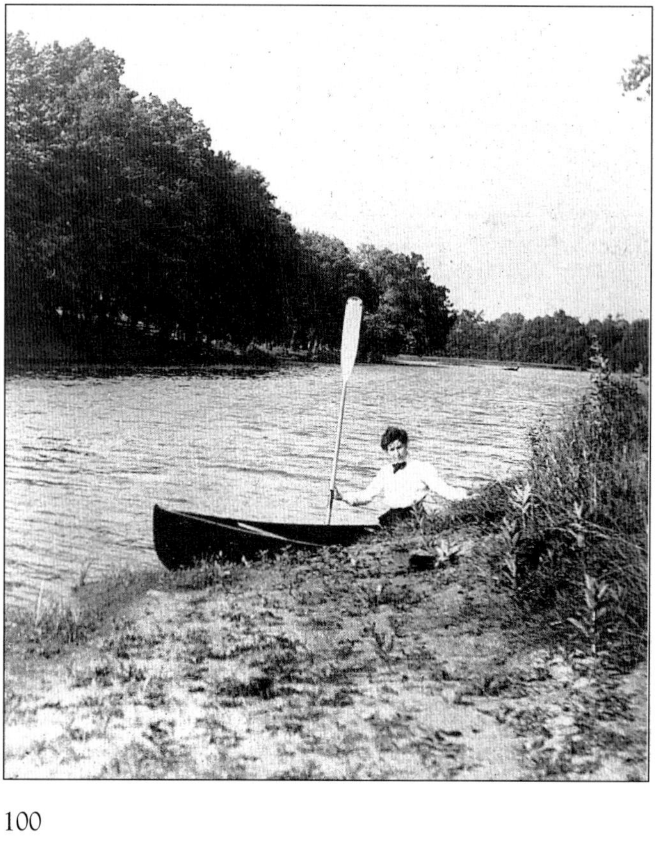

A daring young woman brings her canoe to shore along the Raritan River. (Courtesy of Linda Barth.)

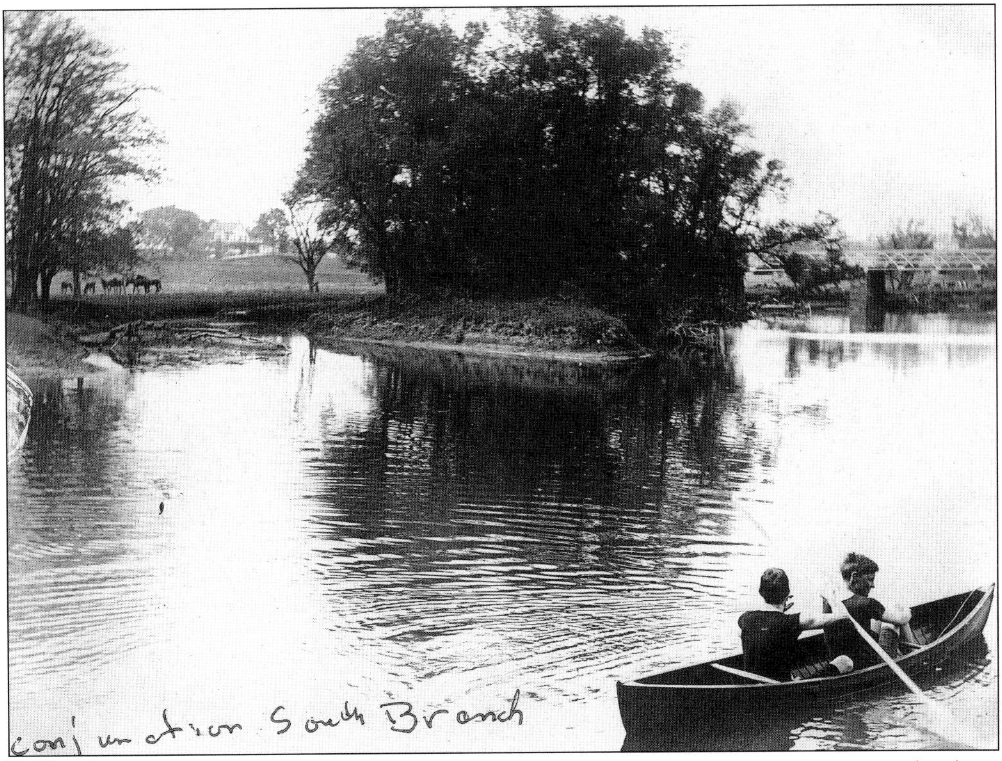

The confluence of the South Branch and the North Branch of the Raritan River provides these young men with an enjoyable afternoon. (Courtesy of Linda Barth.)

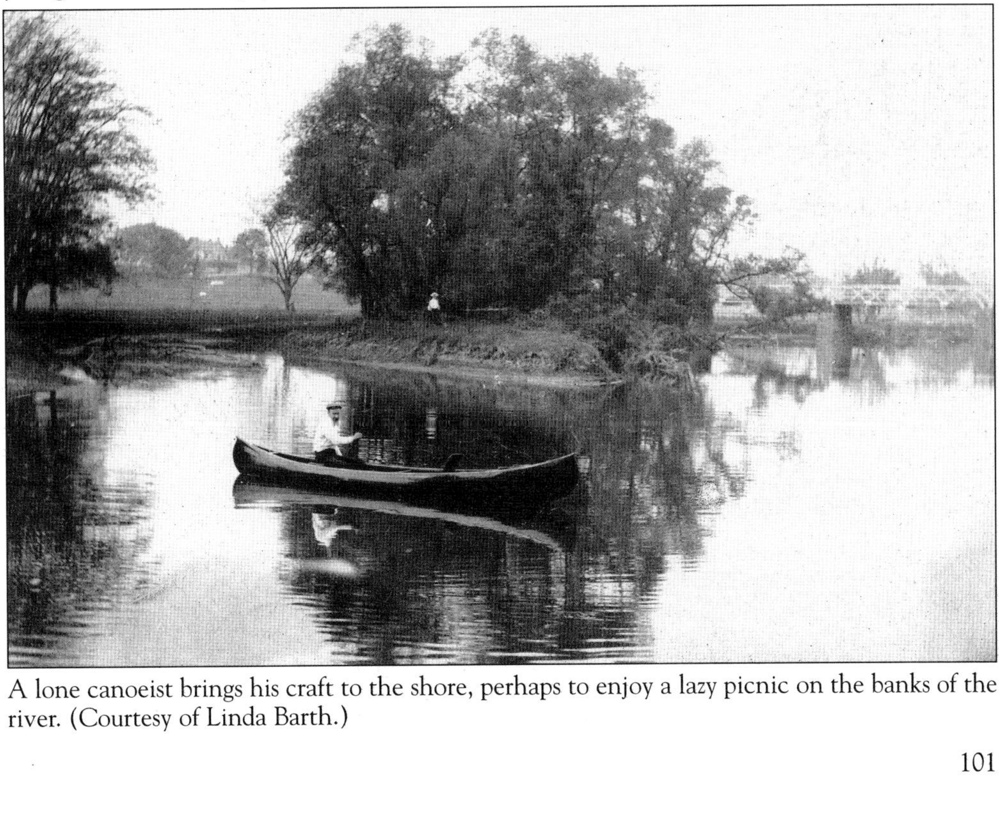

A lone canoeist brings his craft to the shore, perhaps to enjoy a lazy picnic on the banks of the river. (Courtesy of Linda Barth.)

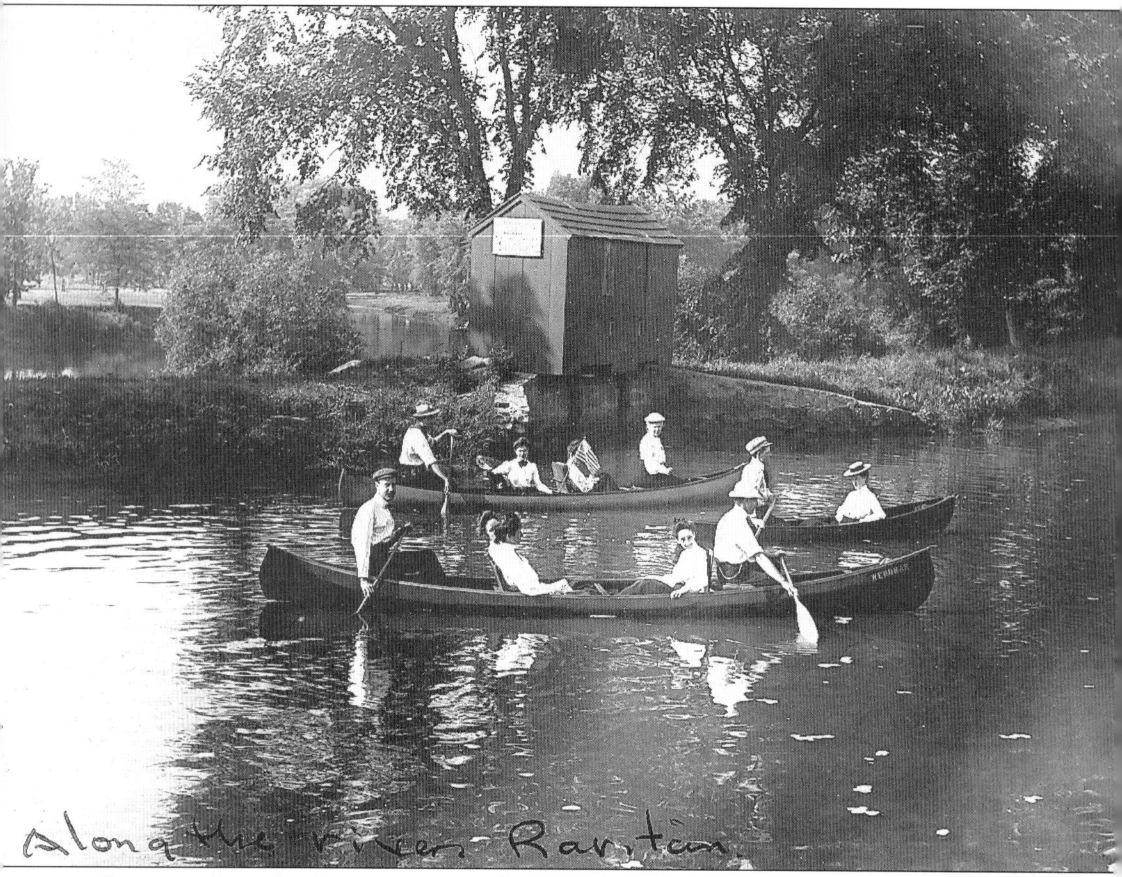

Canoeing along the slow-moving canal was a relaxing way to spend a summer afternoon with your best beau. (Courtesy of Linda Barth.)-

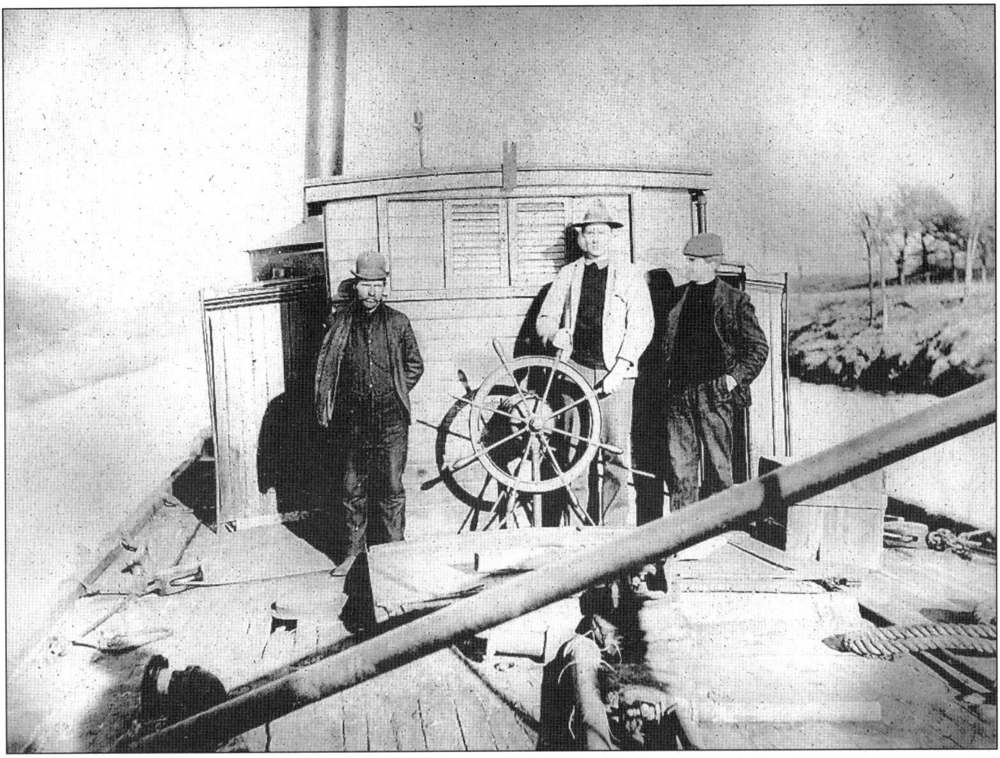

Boats larger than rowboats and canoes traveled on the Raritan Waterpower Canal. Pictured here is the crew of one of those vessels. (Courtesy of Linda Barth.)

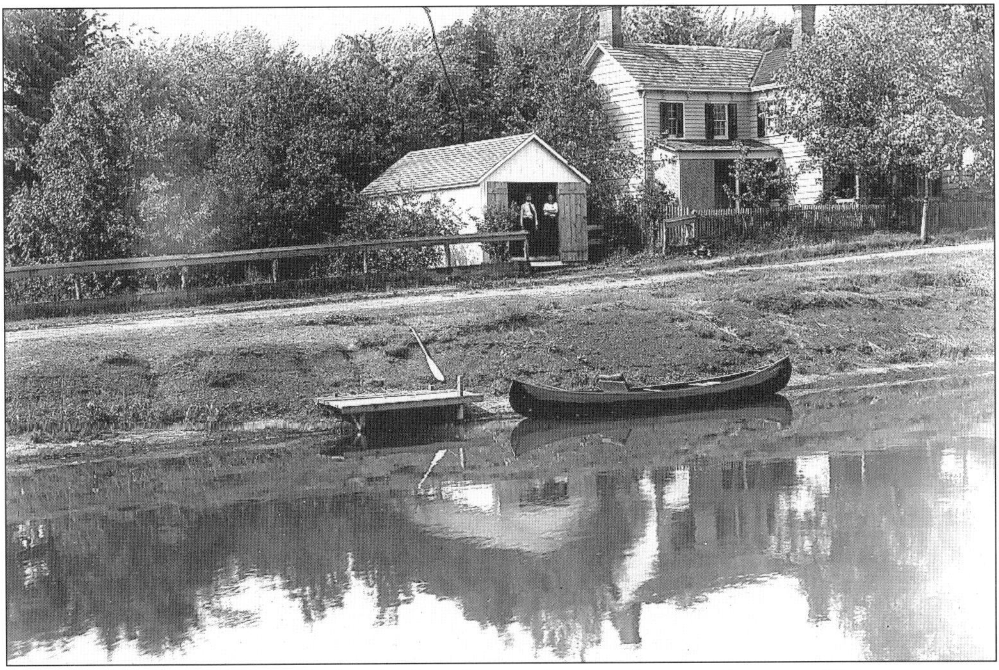

People living along the canal often had enclosures for their boats and canoes. This photograph shows one of the boathouses along Canal Street. (Courtesy of Linda Barth.)

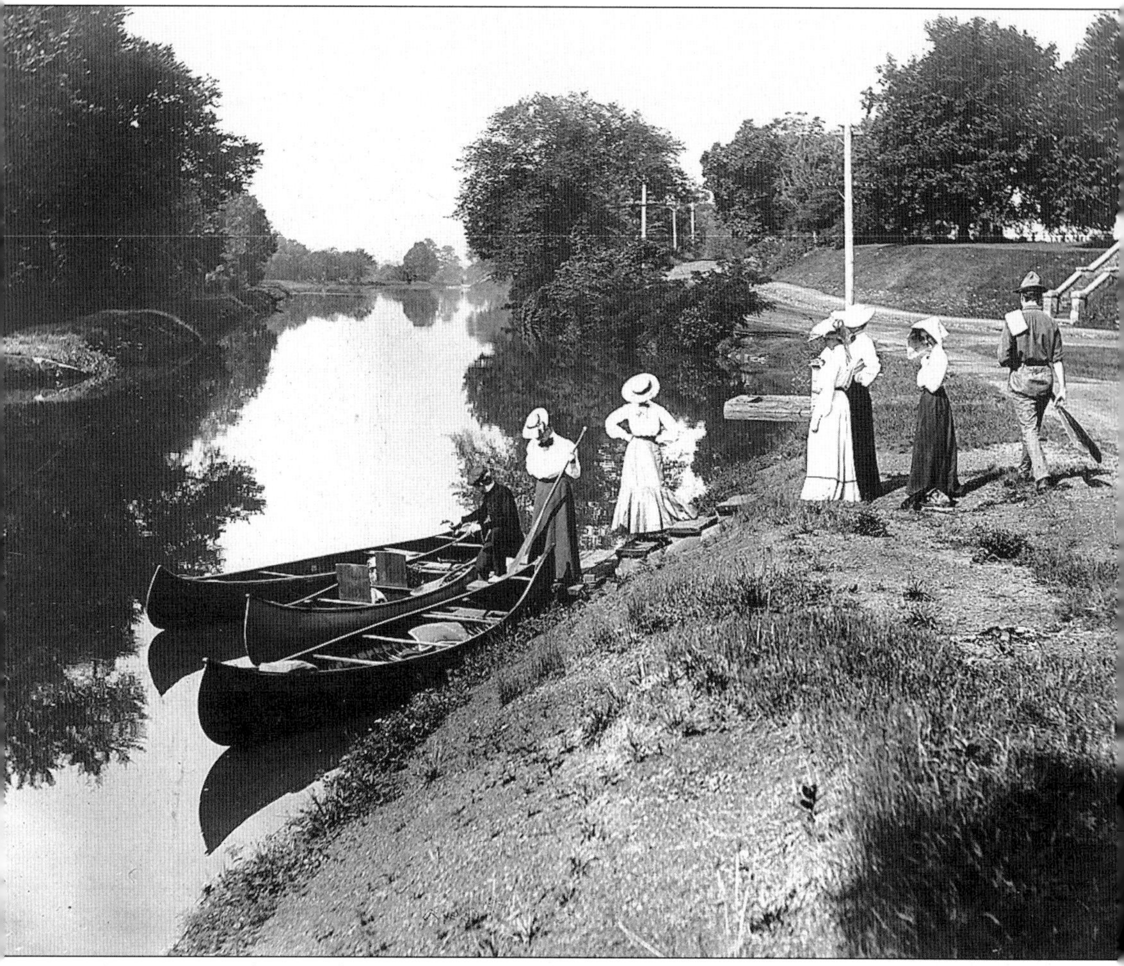

Canoeing on the canal was a popular Sunday afternoon activity. Young people also enjoyed taffy pulls and eggnog making. Eggnog was a clever way to mask the taste of milk that often had the flavor of the wild onions the cows ate during the spring. (Courtesy of Linda Barth.)

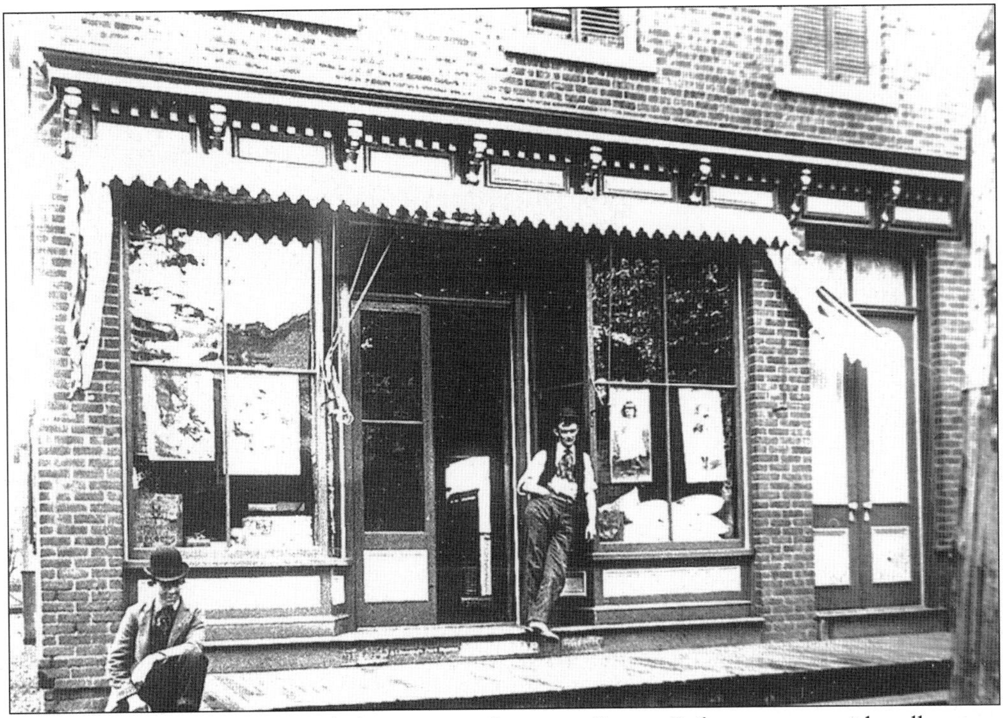

A local merchant stands outside his store on Somerset Street. Before concrete sidewalks came into use, stores like this one had boardwalks for pedestrians.

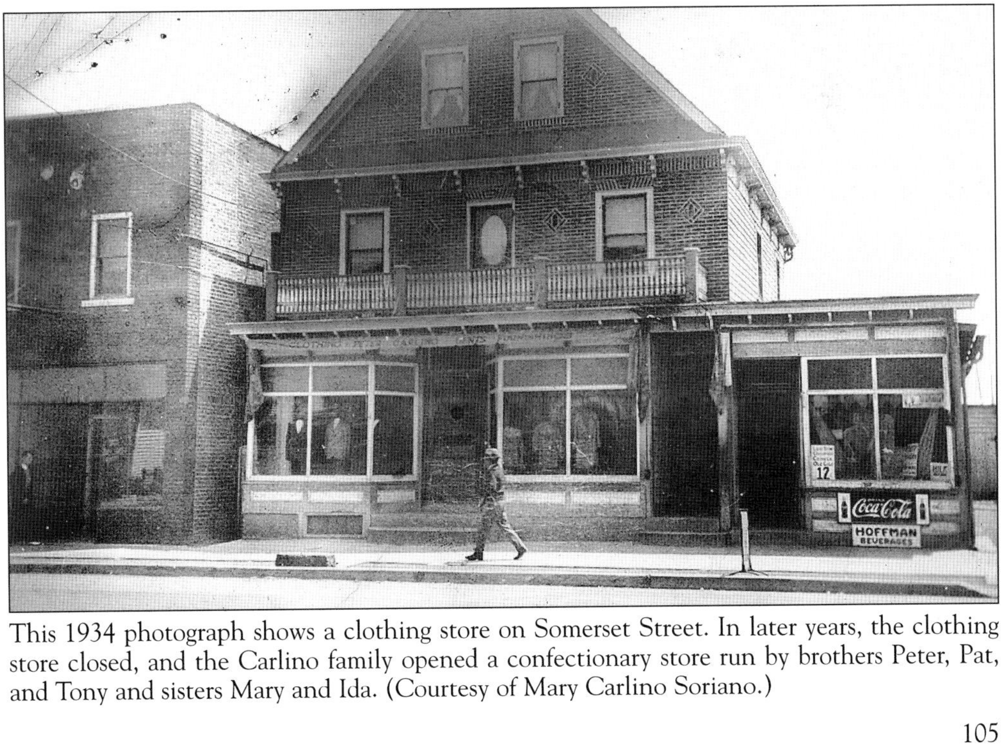

This 1934 photograph shows a clothing store on Somerset Street. In later years, the clothing store closed, and the Carlino family opened a confectionary store run by brothers Peter, Pat, and Tony and sisters Mary and Ida. (Courtesy of Mary Carlino Soriano.)

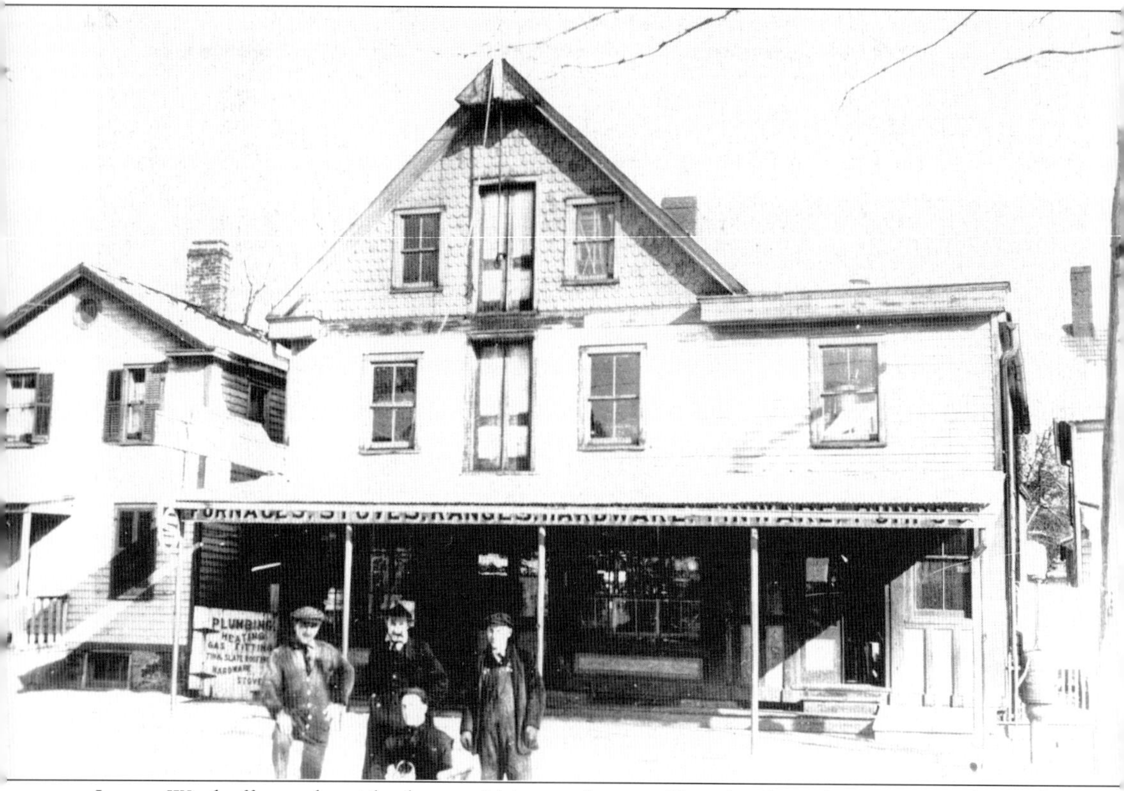

James Wyckoff stands with three of his employees. His plumbing business was located on Thompson Street. (Courtesy of Lilyan Navatto.)

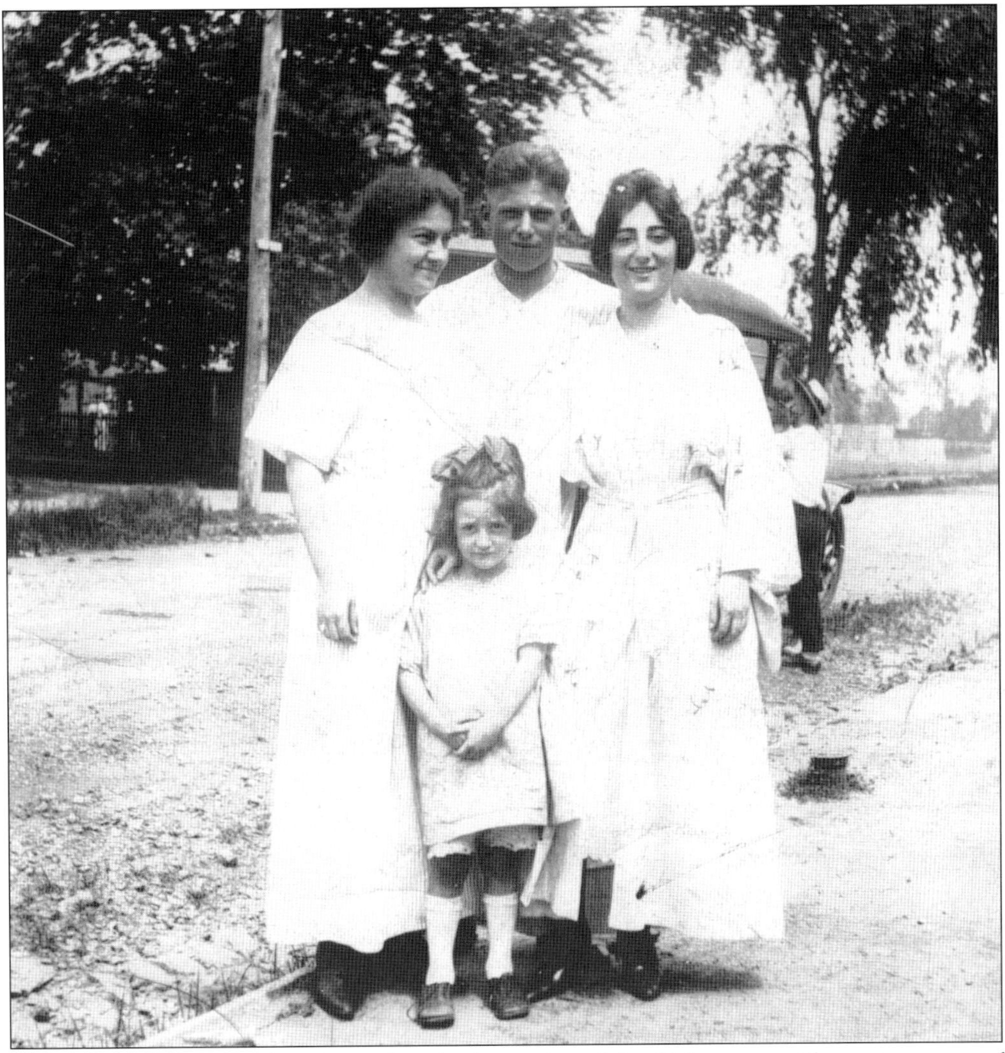

Not all roads were smooth and paved at the beginning of the 20th century. Shown is a group of four people standing on what is now First Avenue. (Courtesy of Lilyan Navatto.)

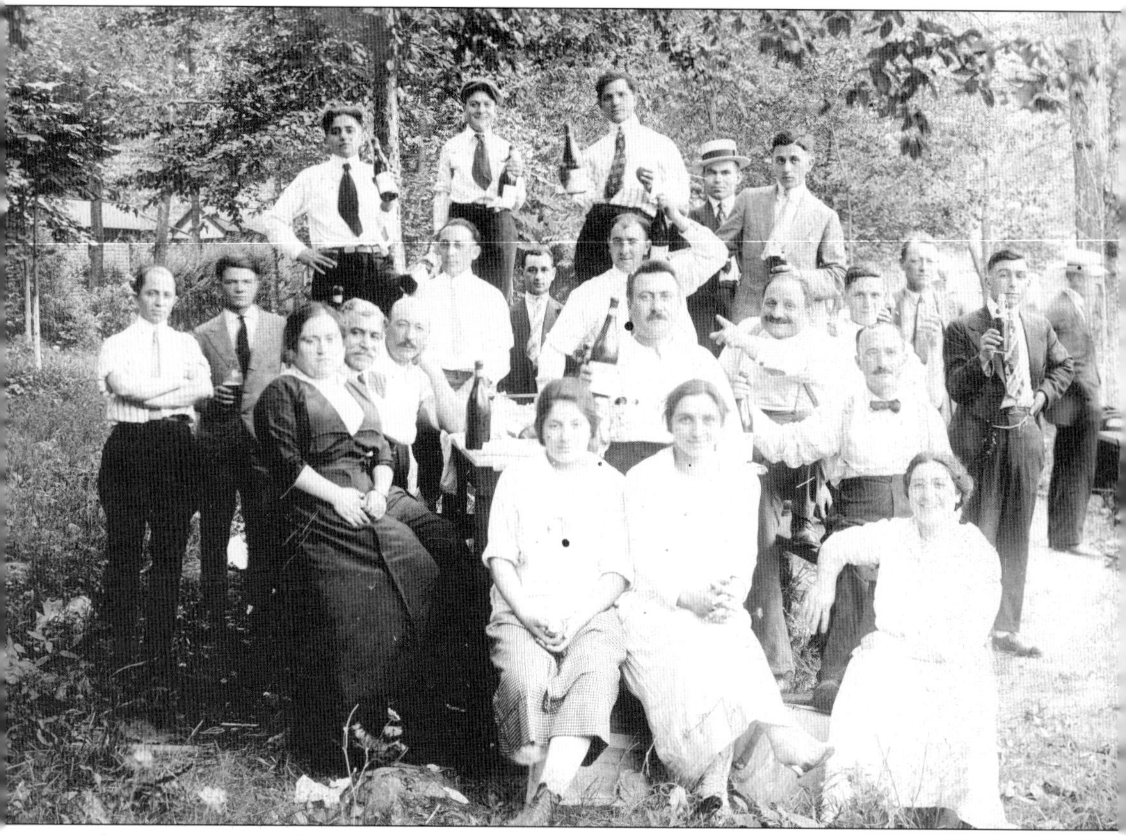

Quiet summer Sunday outings were popular among the Italian community in Raritan. Among those pictured in this photograph are Anna and Joseph Navatto, Minnie and Rocco Stabile, Marie and Terry Minetti, Michael Ruggieri, Lena Minetti Spinelli, Pat Soriano, Joseph Soriano, Alex Stabile, Nunnzio Longordo, Mr. Longordo Sr., Old "Zepp" Johnson, John Soriano, "Babe" Speri, Nicholas DiPaolo, and Louis Minetti.

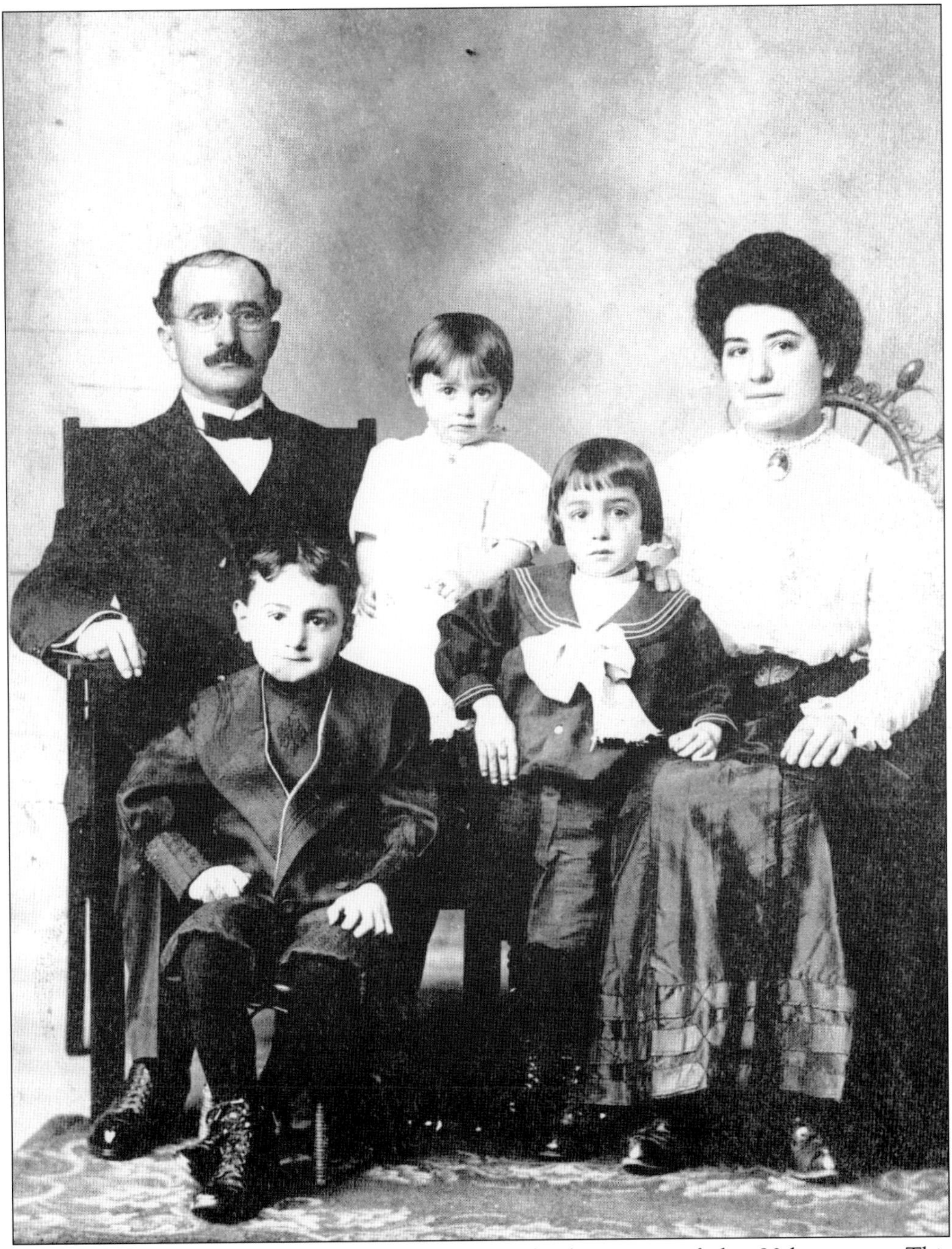

Family portraits were an important occasion at the beginning of the 20th century. This c. 1911 photograph shows the Navatto family. From left to right are the following: (front row) Joseph Jr. and Patrick; (back row) Joseph Sr., Stella, and Anna Carnevale Navatto.

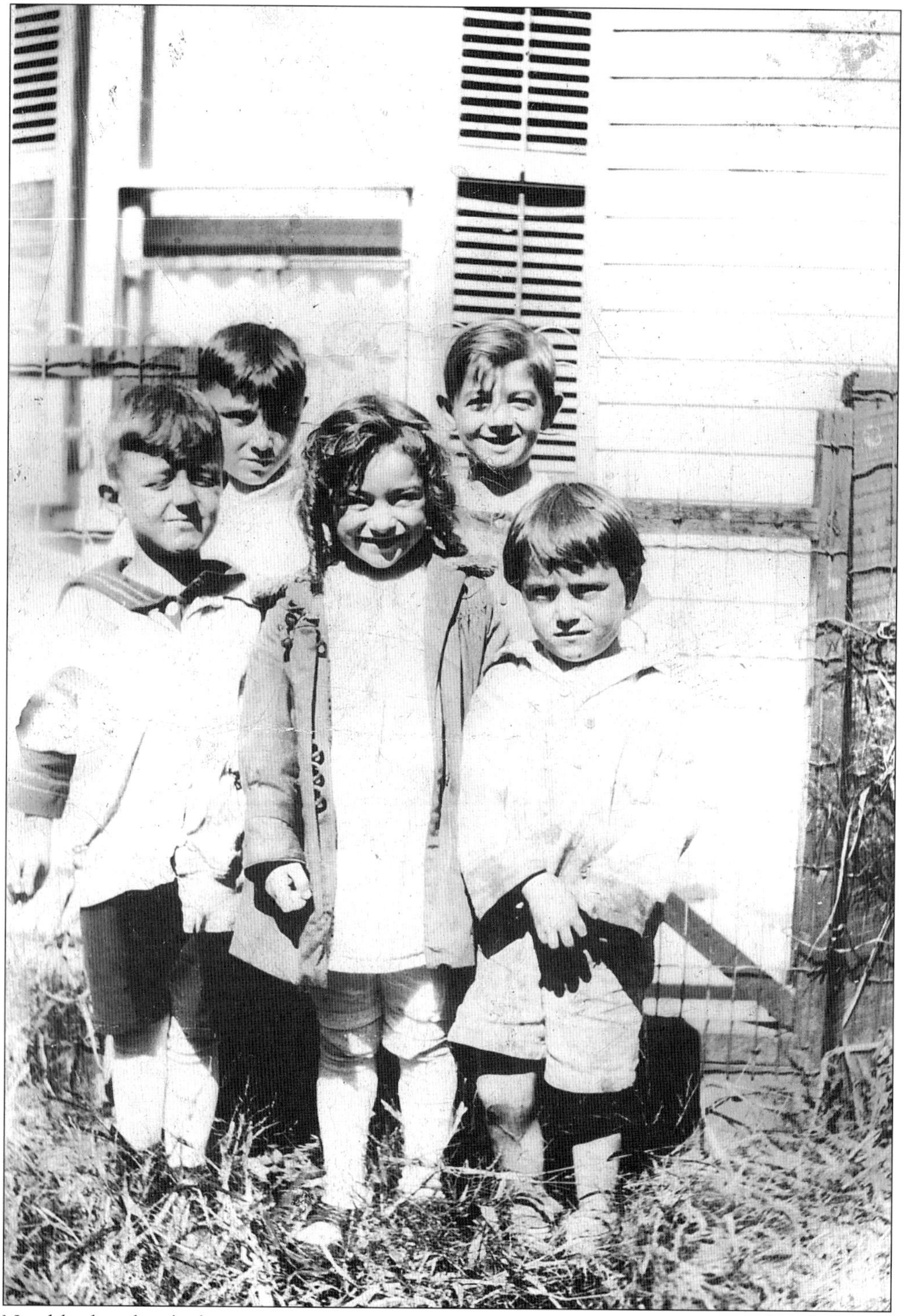

Neighborhood pals from 1929 remain good friends even today. From left to right are the following: (front row) James Menci, Anna Marie Navatto, and James Sorace; (back row) Frank Sacino and Dominick Menci. (Courtesy of Ann Navatto.)

Five

Notable Events

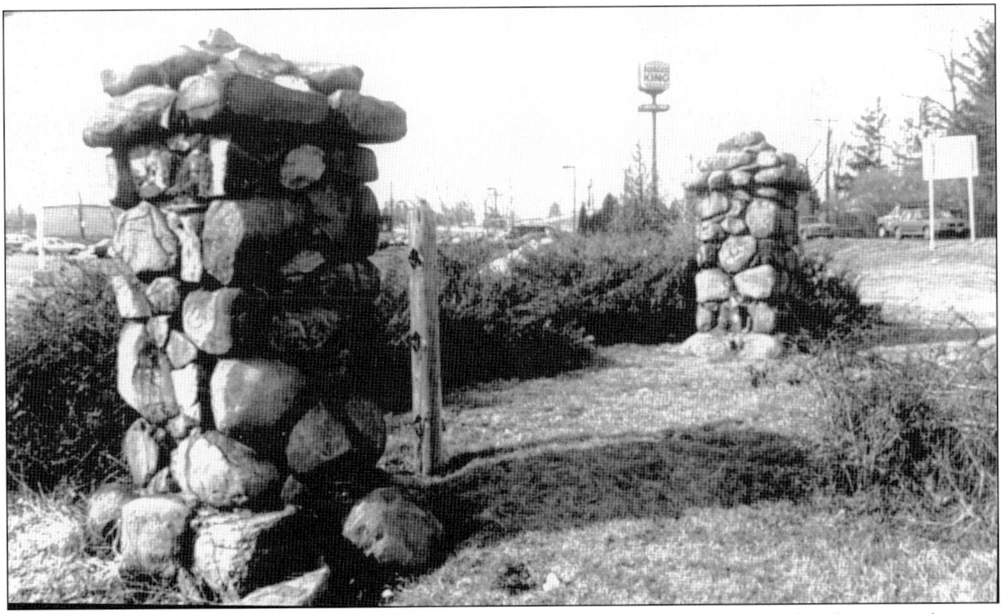

These stone pillars are the only remains of the estate of Sen. Joseph S. Frelinghuysen, the site of the signing of the Knox-Porter Resolution, the official end to World War I. A mysterious fire destroyed the house in 1957 while it was being dismantled for demolition.

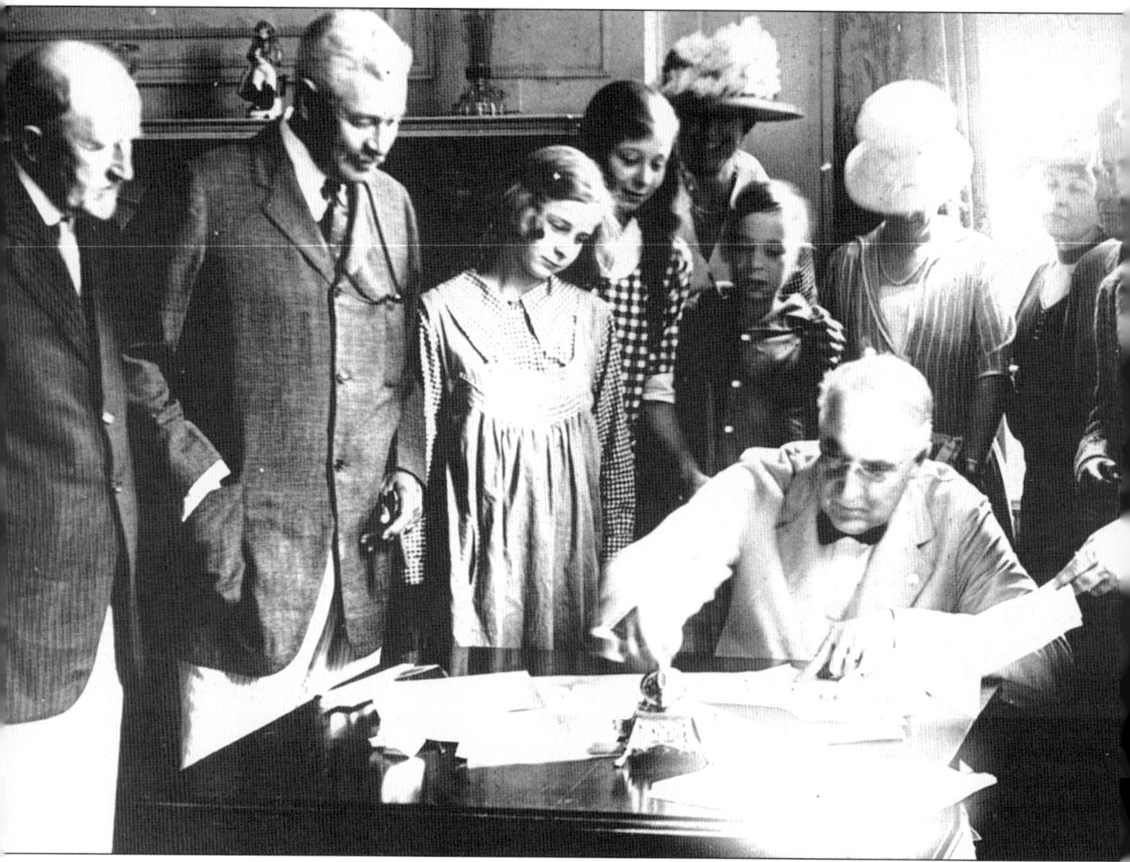

At the Frelinghuysen Estate on July 2, 1921, Pres. Warren G. Harding signs the Knox-Porter Resolution officially ending World War I. From left to right are Sen. Hale Kellogg, Sen. Joseph S. Frelinghuysen, Emily Frelinghuysen, Victoria Frelinghuysen, Mrs. Frelinghuysen, and Joseph S. Frelinghuysen Jr.

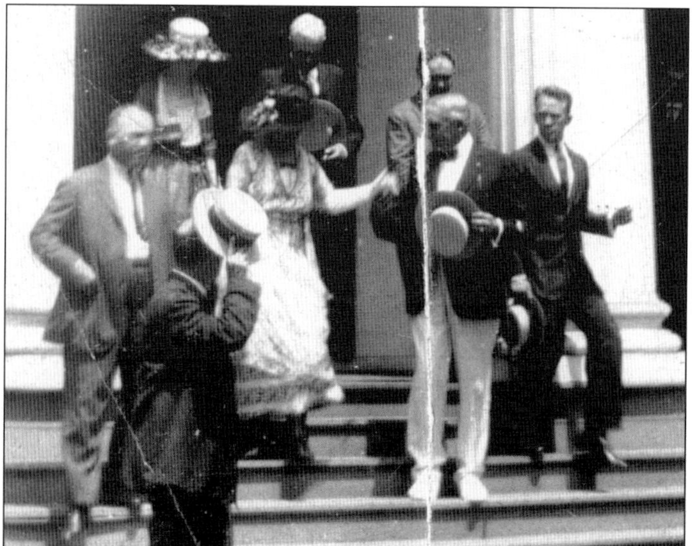

The Hardings emerge from the Third Reformed Dutch Church after Sunday service. The president and first lady often attended church here during their frequent visits with the Frelinghuysens.

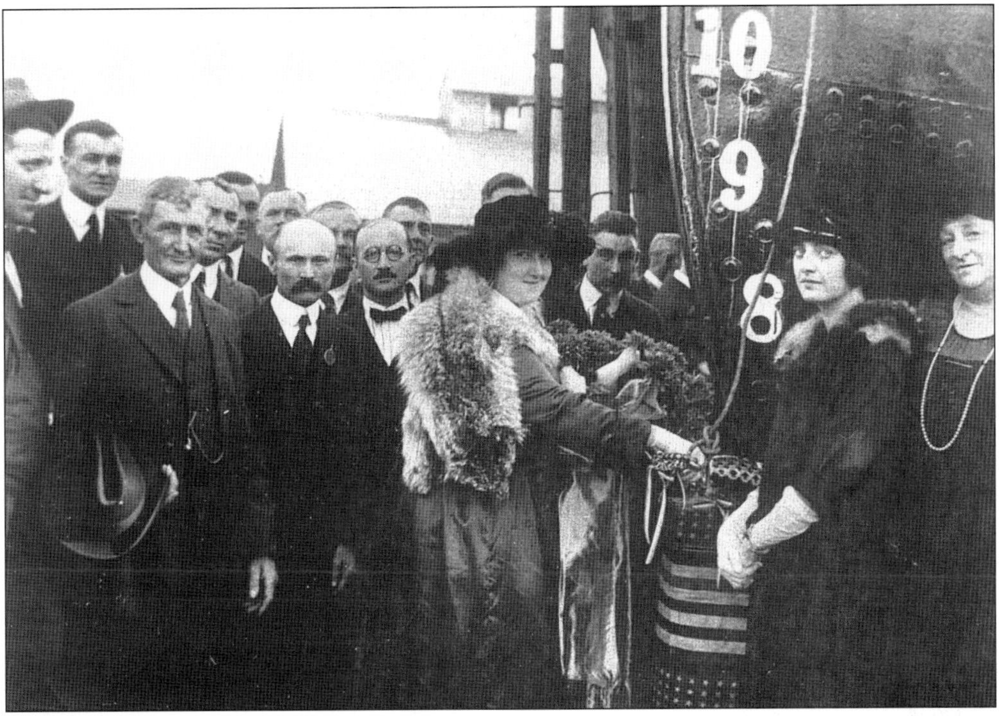

On October 16, 1920, a group of Raritan town officials traveled to Wilmington, Delaware, to christen the SS *Natirar.* This ship was named after the town (Raritan spelled backwards) in appreciation for the thousands of dollars in war bonds purchased by the citizens of Raritan during World War I. Pictured from left to right are P. Findley Wyckoff, W. Slattery, Samuel Glaser, Andrew Sabol, Joseph Navatto Sr., Katherine Slattery, James Soriano, and two unidentified women.

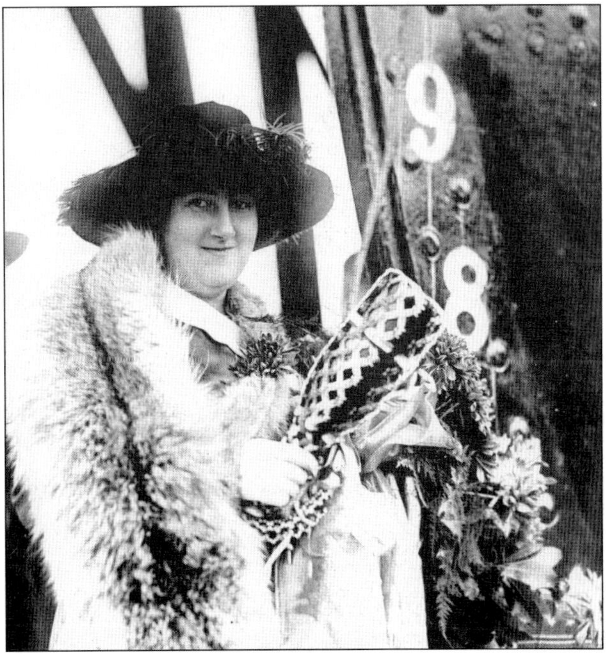

Katherine Slattery christens the SS *Natirar* on October 16, 1920 at Wilmington, Delaware. (Courtesy of the Raritan Public Library.)

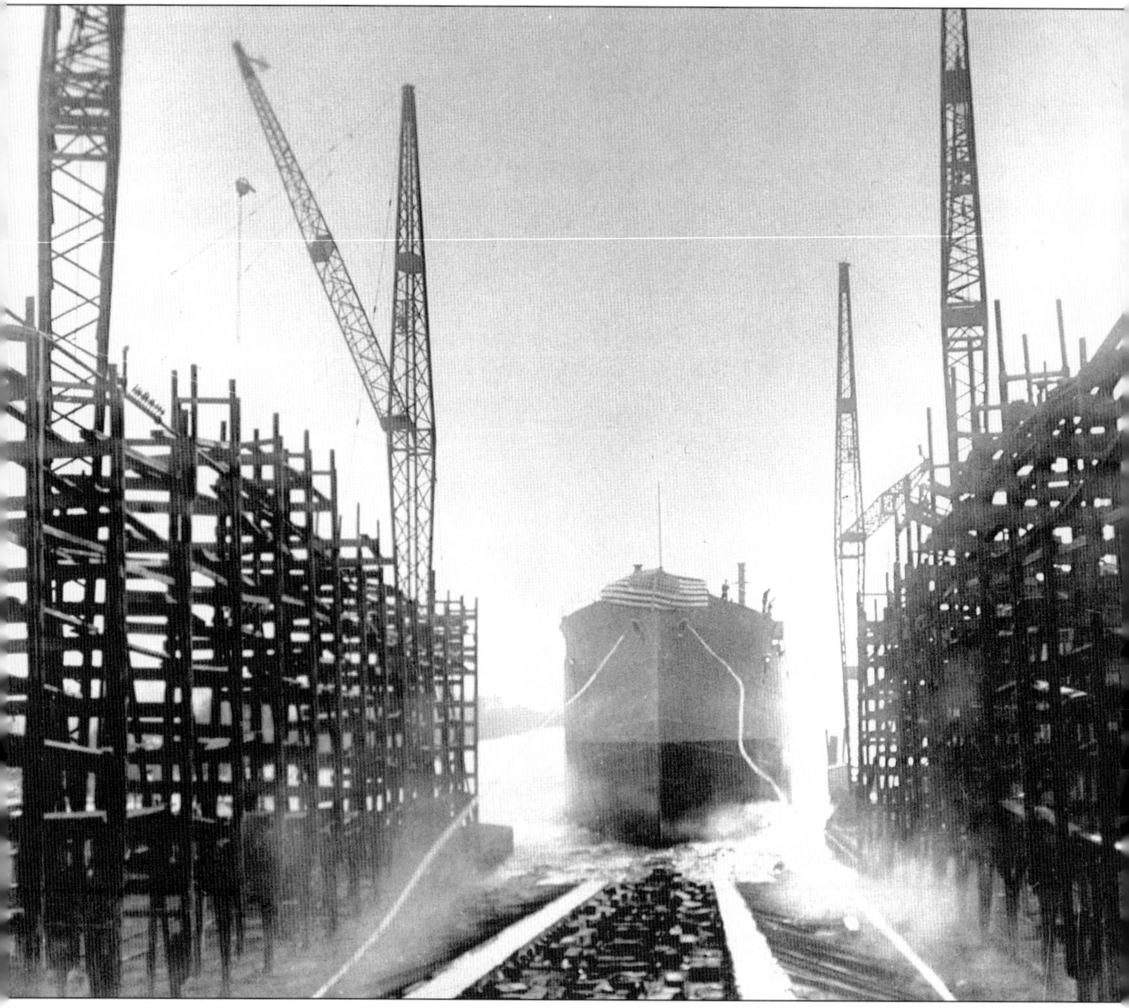

The SS *Natirar* slips from its berth at Wilmington, Delaware, after being christened by a group of Raritan dignitaries. Active for many years, the ship eventually became part of the Lend-Lease Agreement and was sent to the Soviet Union. (Courtesy of the Raritan Public Library.)

Six

"MANILA JOHN"

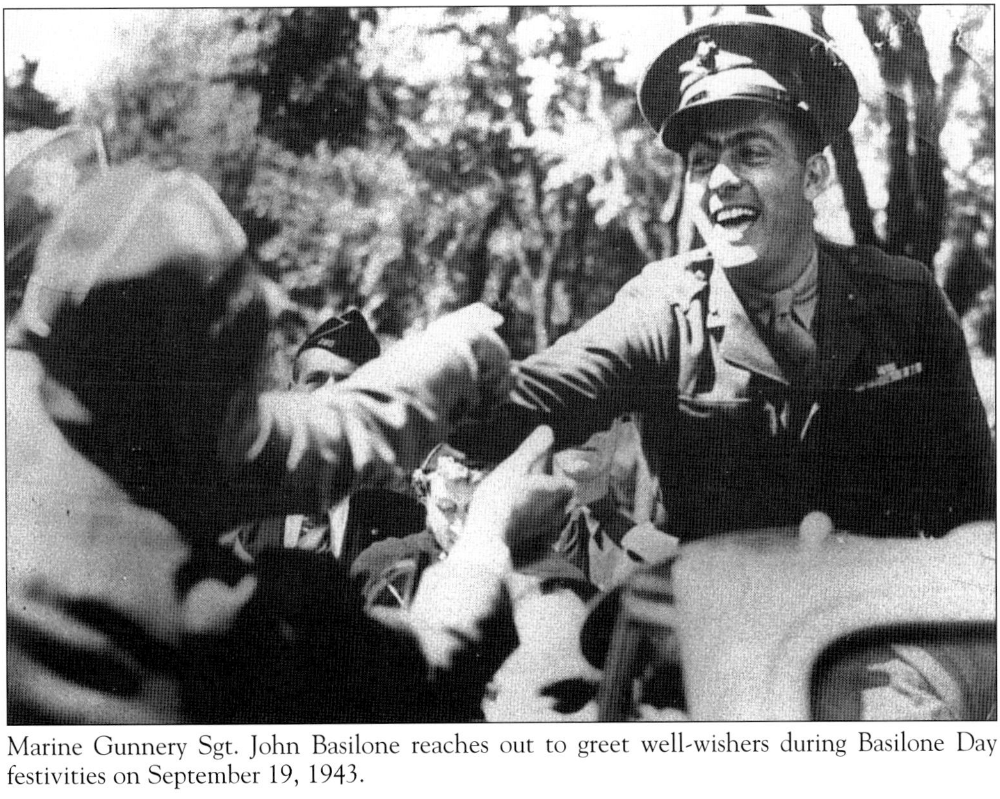

Marine Gunnery Sgt. John Basilone reaches out to greet well-wishers during Basilone Day festivities on September 19, 1943.

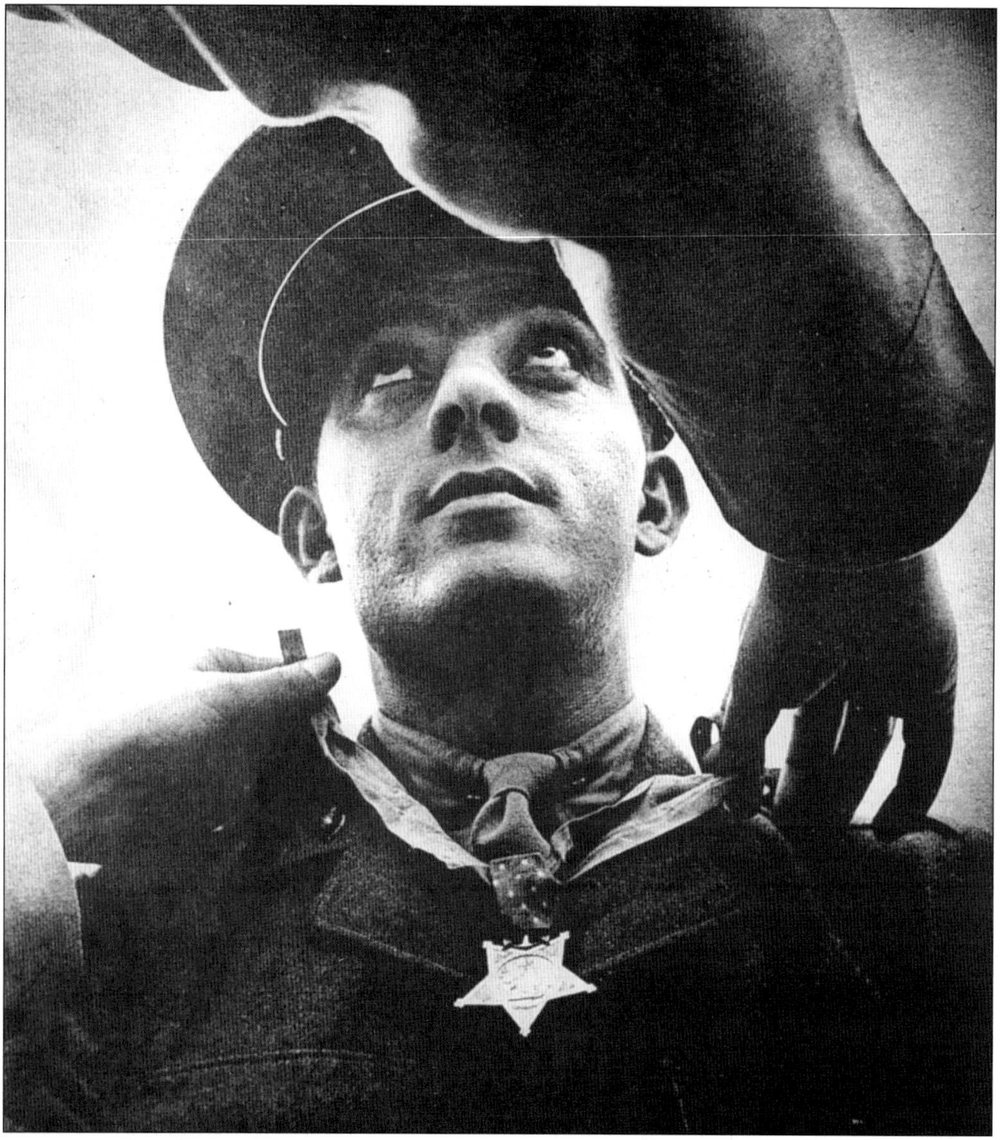

A serious Sgt. John Basilone receives the Congressional Medal of Honor for conspicuous gallantry in action above and beyond the call of duty. The citation that accompanied his medal says, in part, "In a fierce frontal attack with the Japanese blasting his guns with grenades and mortar fire, one of Sergeant Basilone's sections, with its gun crews, was put out of action, leaving only two men to carry on. Moving an extra gun into position, he placed it in action, then under continual fire repaired another and personally manned it. A little later, with ammunition critically low and the supply lines cut off, Basilone at great risk to his life and in the face of continued enemy attack, battled his way through hostile lines with urgently needed shells for his gunner." (Courtesy of the *Somerset Messenger Gazette*.)

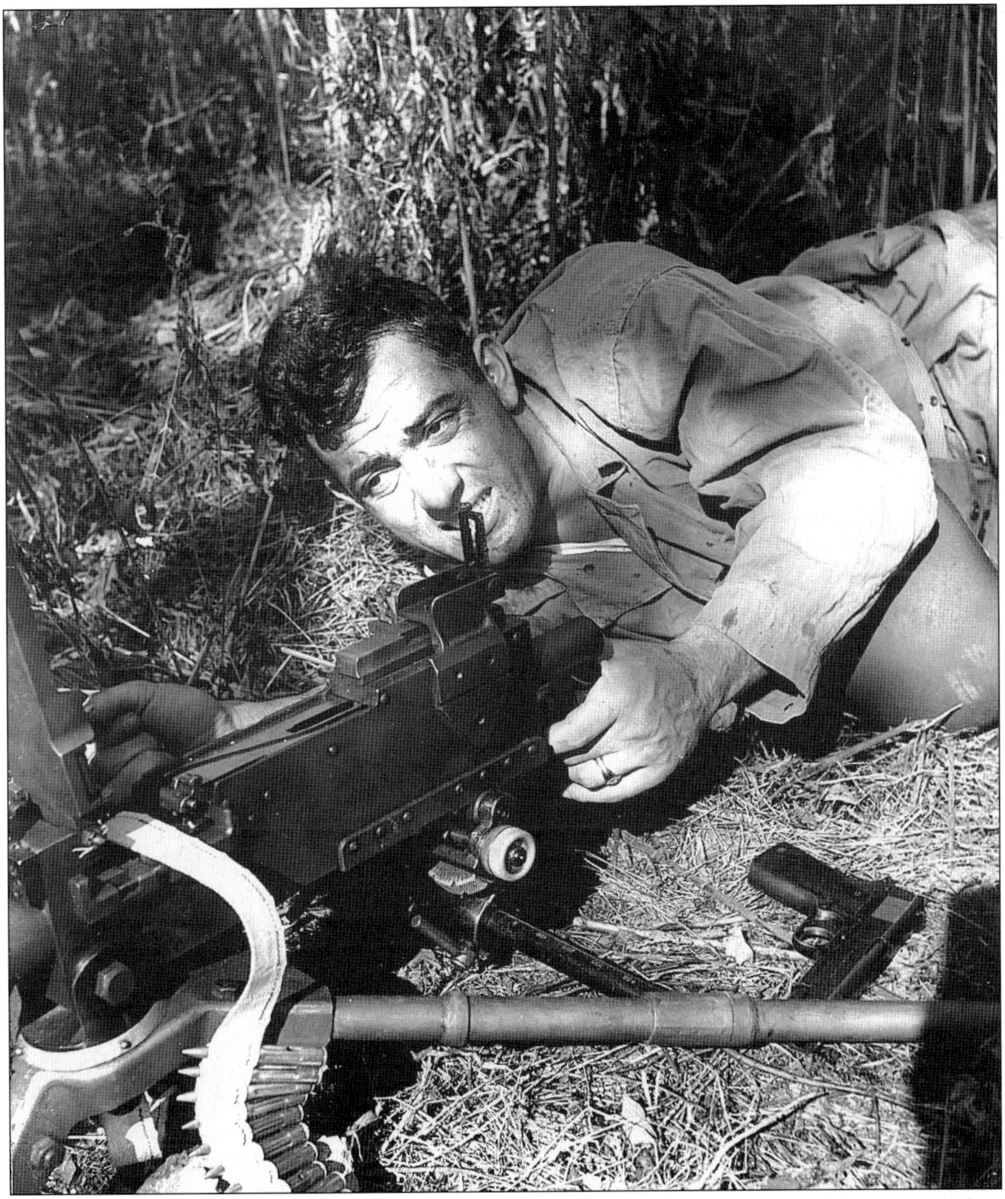

Sgt. John Basilone was ordered to duty stateside after his heroic action. He grew restless participating in war bond drives and requested to be returned to his fellow Marines. He was part of the first assault wave on Iwo Jima on February 19, 1945, and was killed in action. For his heroic actions on that day, he received a second Congressional Medal of Honor nomination. Since no one had ever earned two Congressional Medals of Honor, he was awarded the Navy Cross posthumously. He is buried at Arlington National Cemetery. (Courtesy of the Raritan Public Library.)

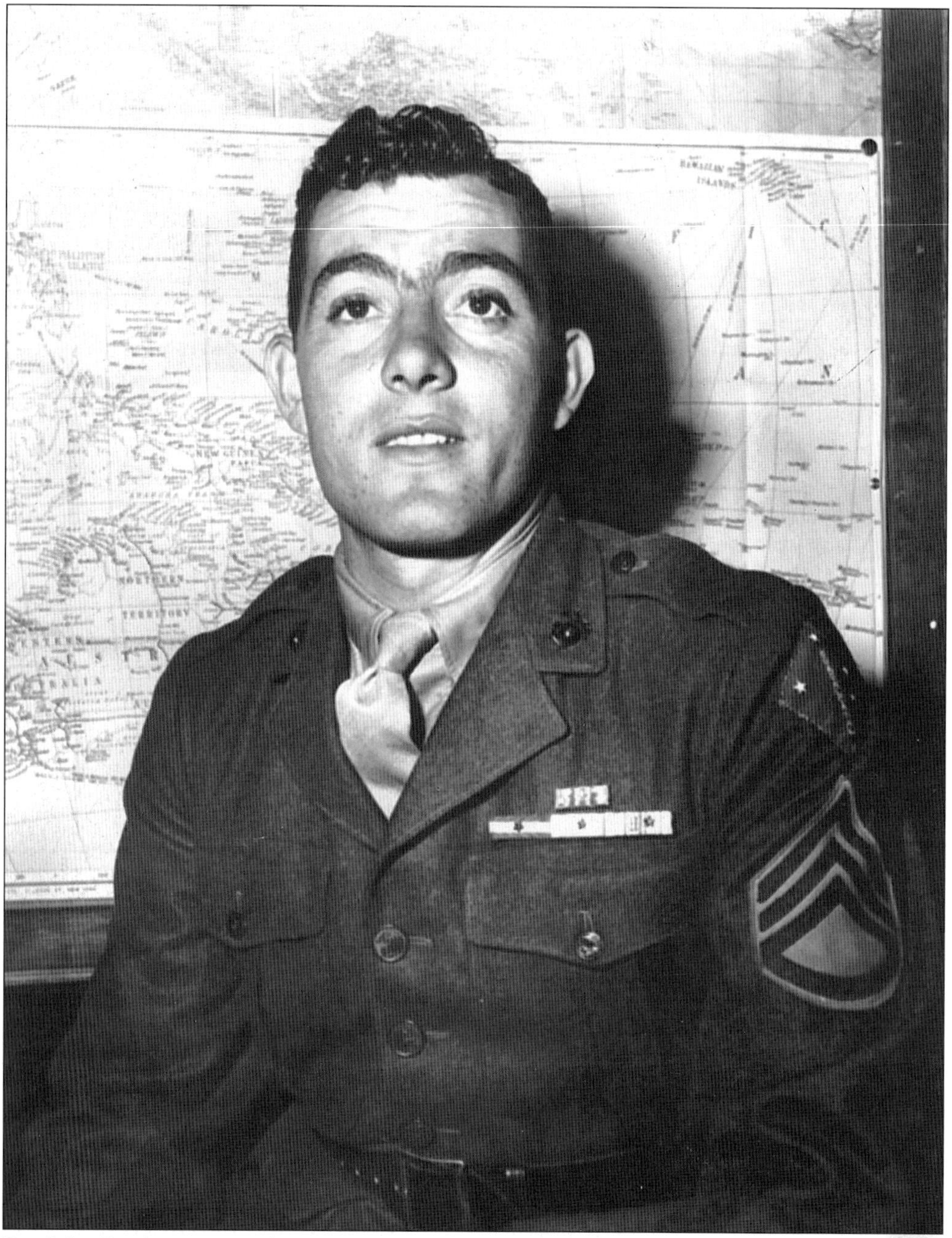

Sgt. John Basilone sits at the Marine Corps headquarters in Washington, D.C., waiting to be interviewed. (Courtesy of the *Somerset Messenger Gazette*.)

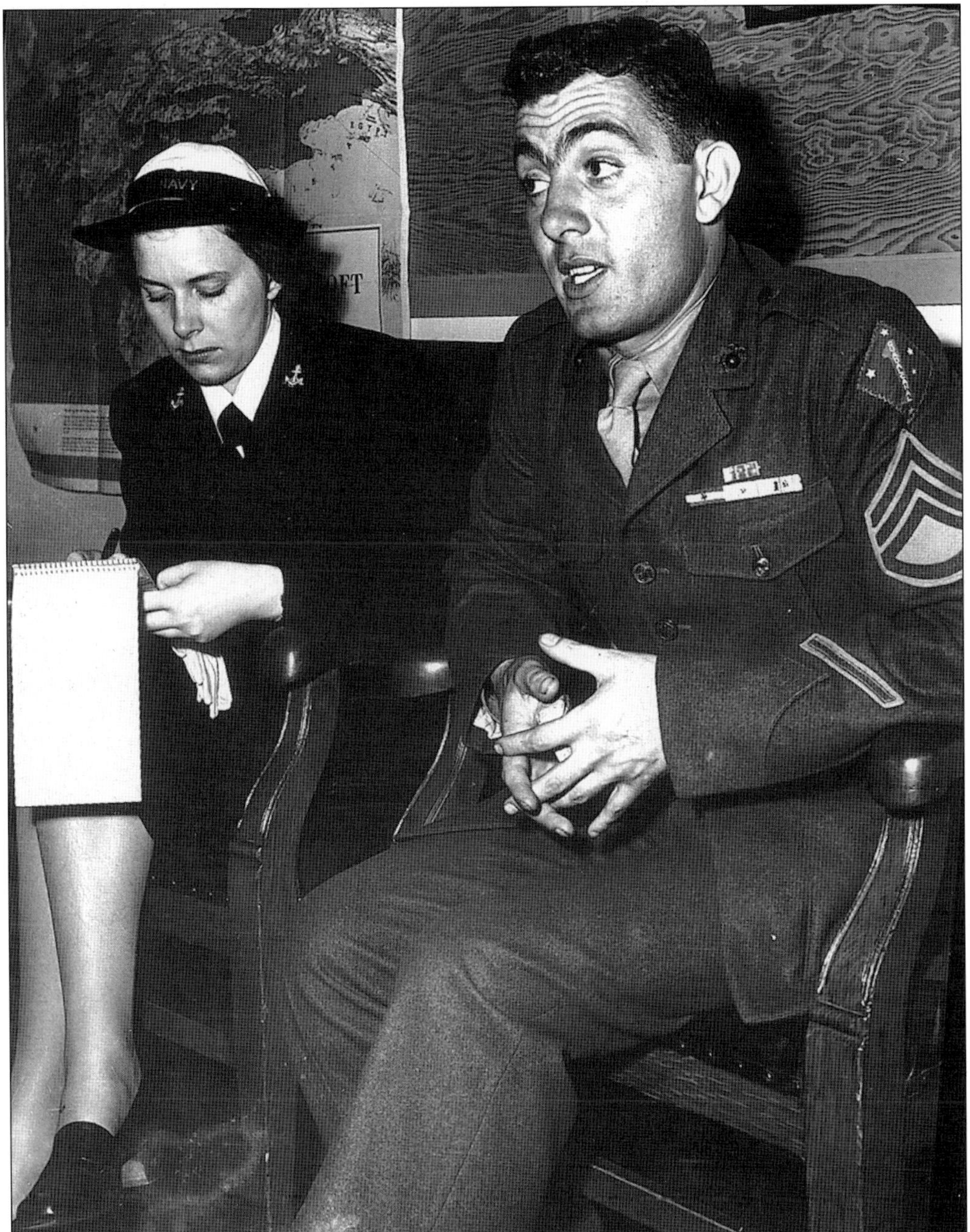

In September 1943, Sgt. John Basilone was interviewed at the Marine Corps headquarters in Washington, D.C., by WAVE 3/C Sigrid Shield. (Courtesy of the *Somerset Messenger Gazette*.)

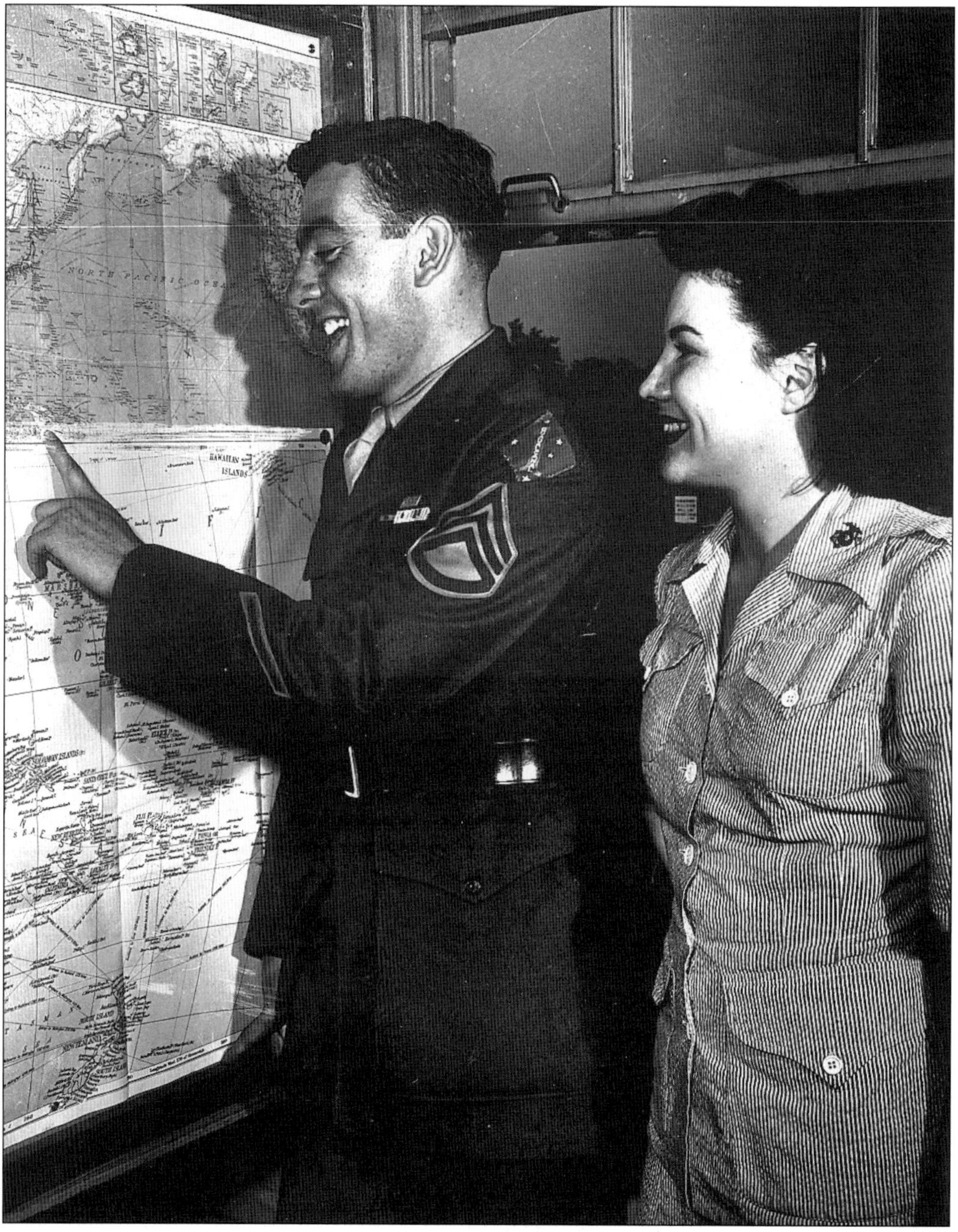

This photograph shows Sgt. John Basilone (left) meeting with Cpl. M. Beerworth in the public relations office at Marine headquarters. (Courtesy of the *Somerset Messenger Gazette*.)

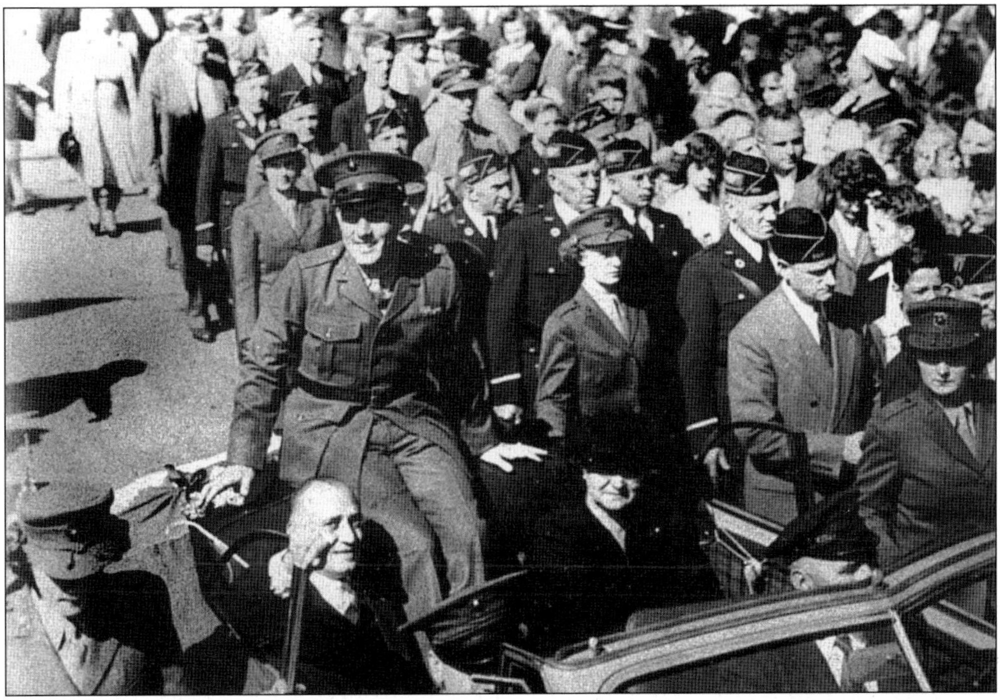

Salvatore and Theodora Basilone ride with their son during the massive celebration honoring him on his return to Raritan after receiving the Congressional Medal of Honor.

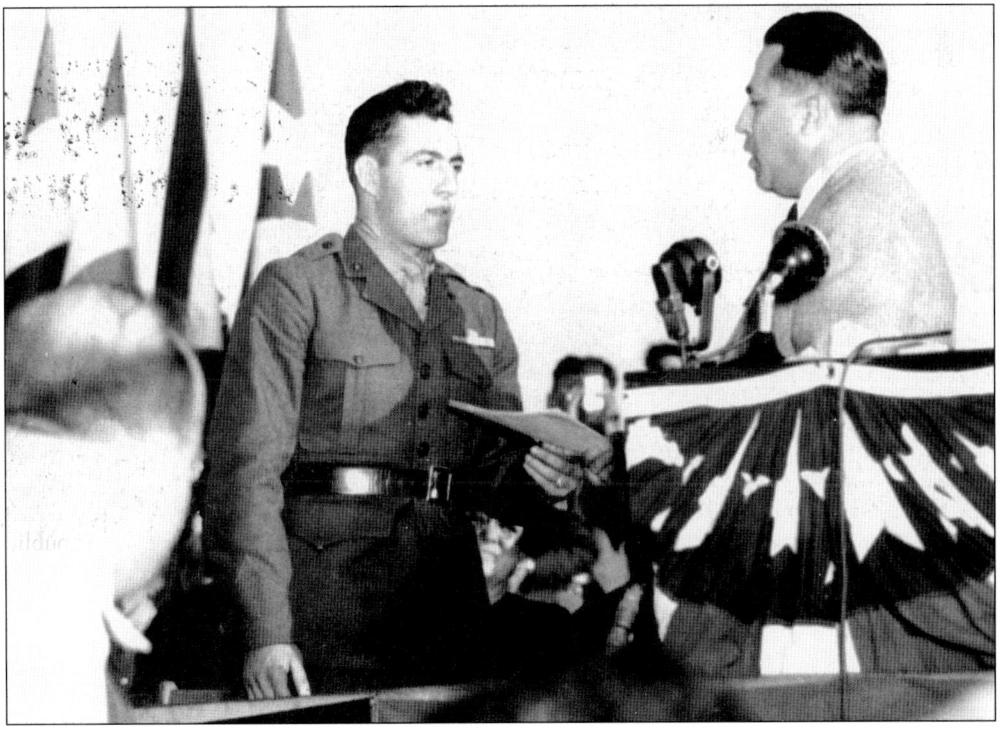

Sgt. John Basilone receives a citation from Judge George W. Allgair, chairman of the John Basilone Day Committee.

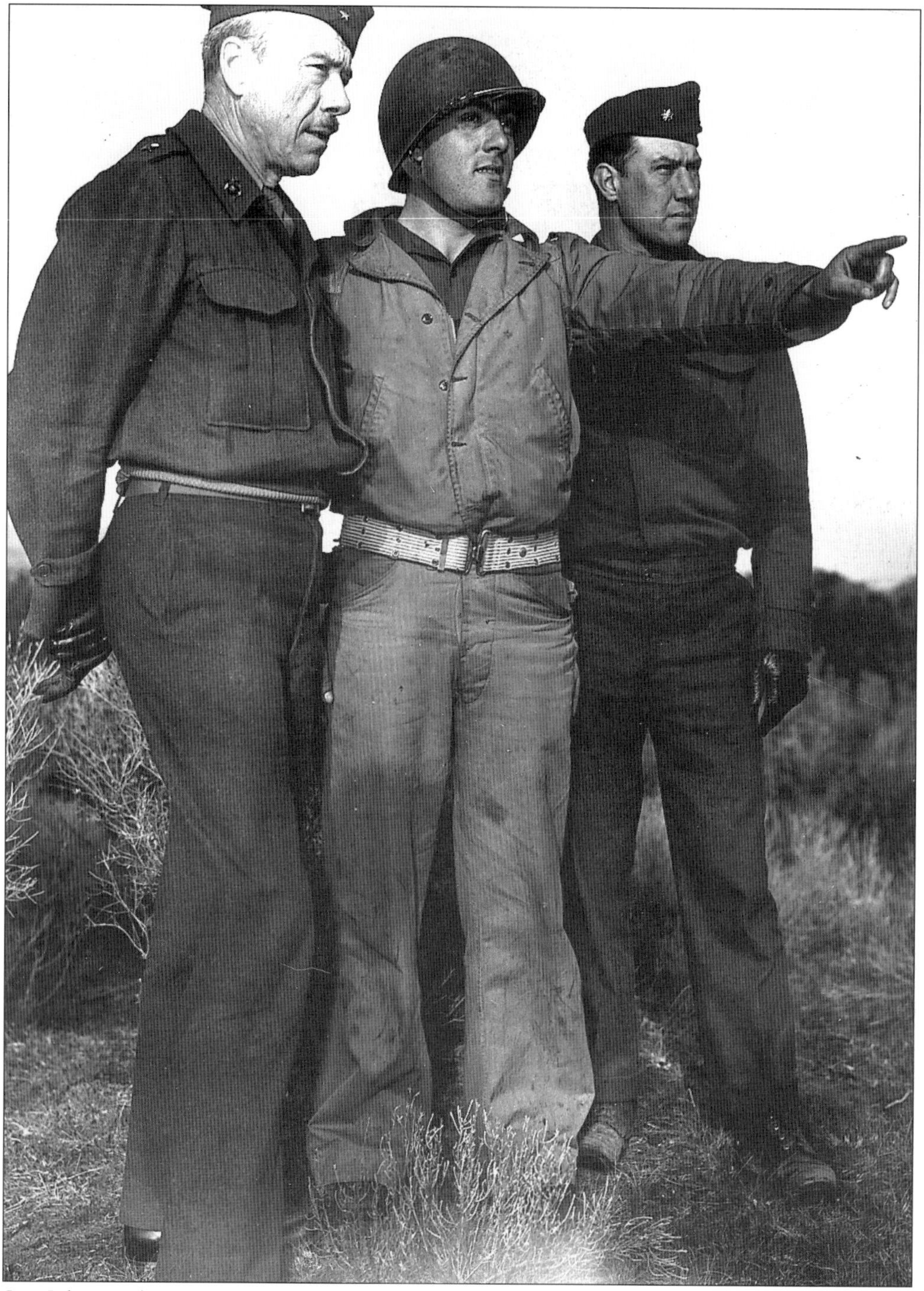

Sgt. John Basilone is pictured somewhere in the South Pacific with Maj. William H. Rupertus (left), commander of the 1st Marine Division, and Lt. Col. J.E. Weber. (Courtesy of the *Somerset Messenger Gazette*.)

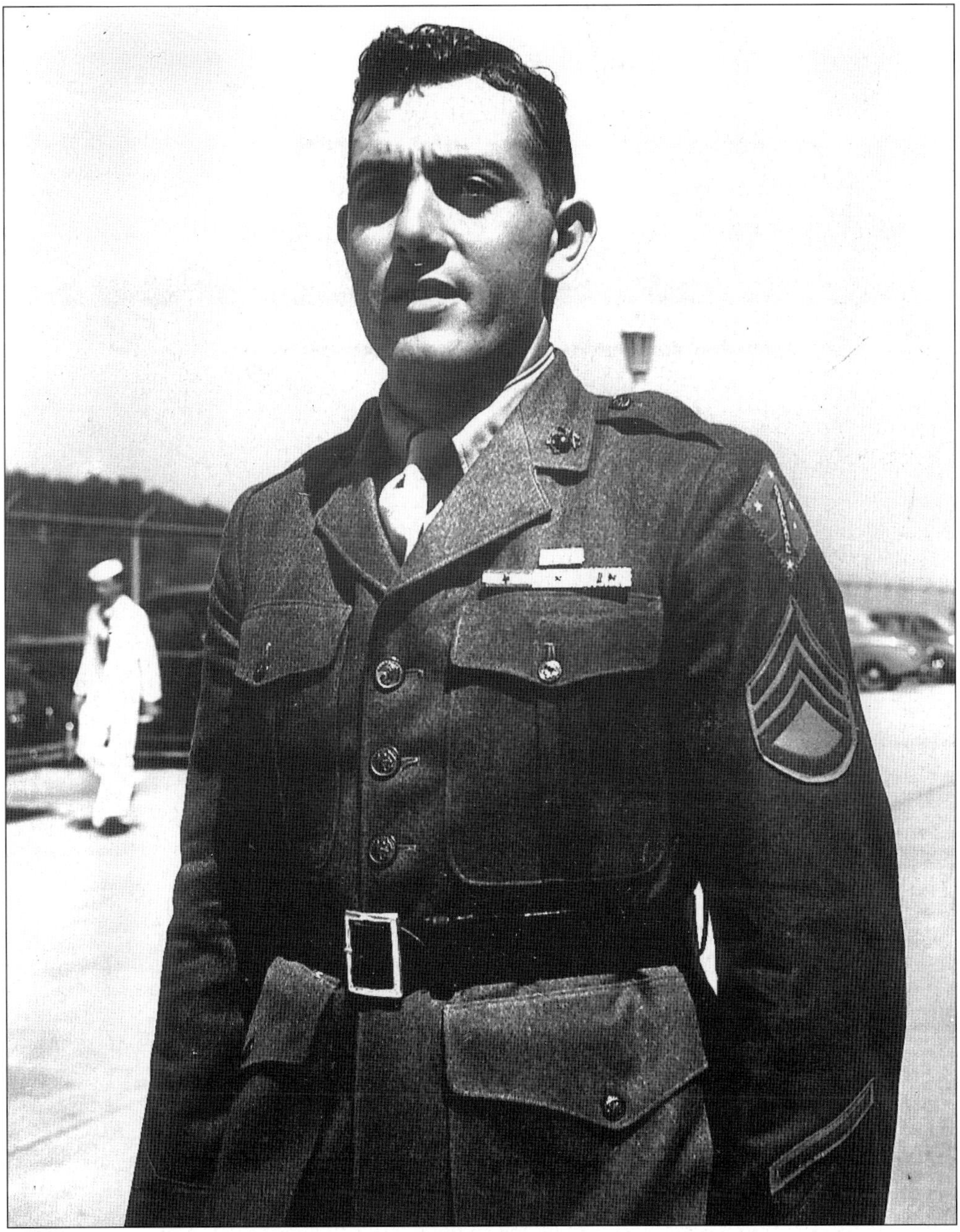

Sgt. John Basilone visits Marine headquarters in Washington, D.C. (Courtesy of the *Somerset Messenger Gazette*.)

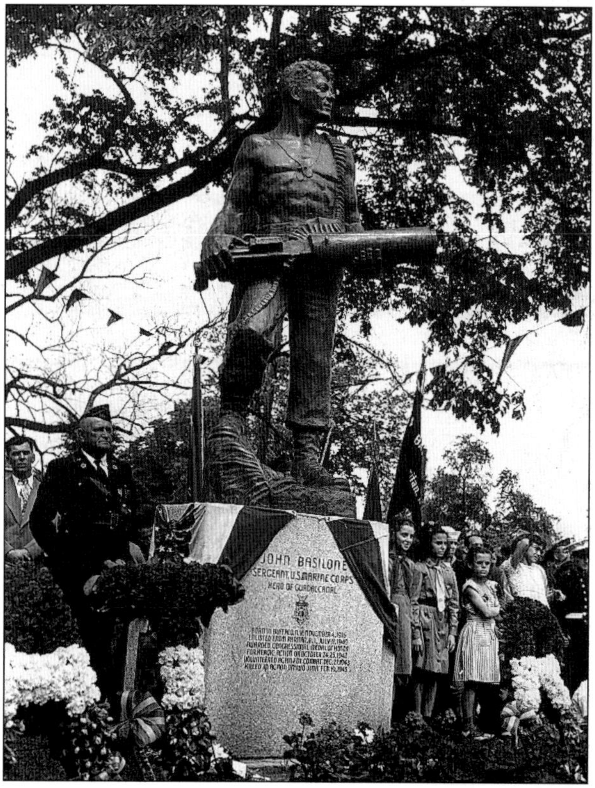

After World War II, the town commissioned Phillip Orlando to create a statue in honor of Sgt. John Basilone. In 1948, a special Basilone Day was held to commemorate the dedication of the statue. The tradition was revived in 1981 with a parade—the only parade in the United States dedicated to an enlisted man. This bronze statue stands as an everlasting tribute and memorial to Basilone's heroism. Notice how large Orlando sculpted the hands. This was done to emphasize Basilone's strength and gentleness. (Courtesy of the *Somerset Messenger Gazette*.)

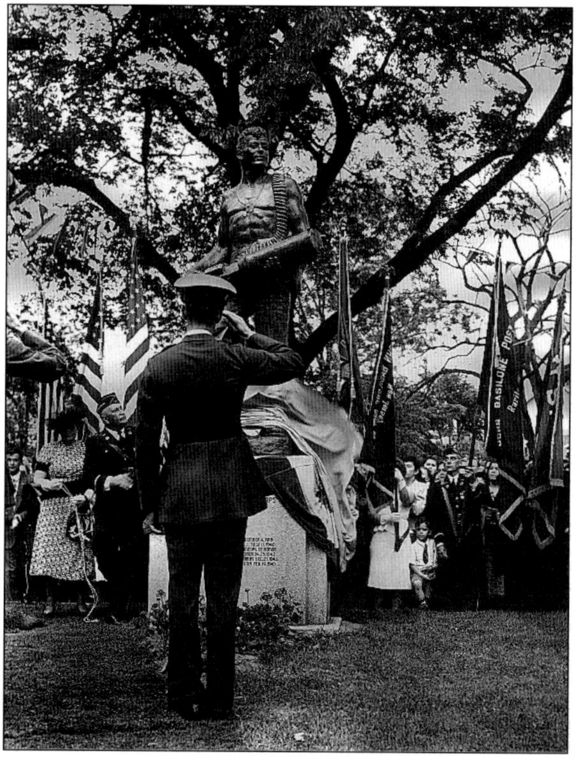

A young Marine salutes the newly unveiled statue of Congressional Medal of Honor winner Basilone. (Courtesy of the *Somerset Messenger Gazette*.)

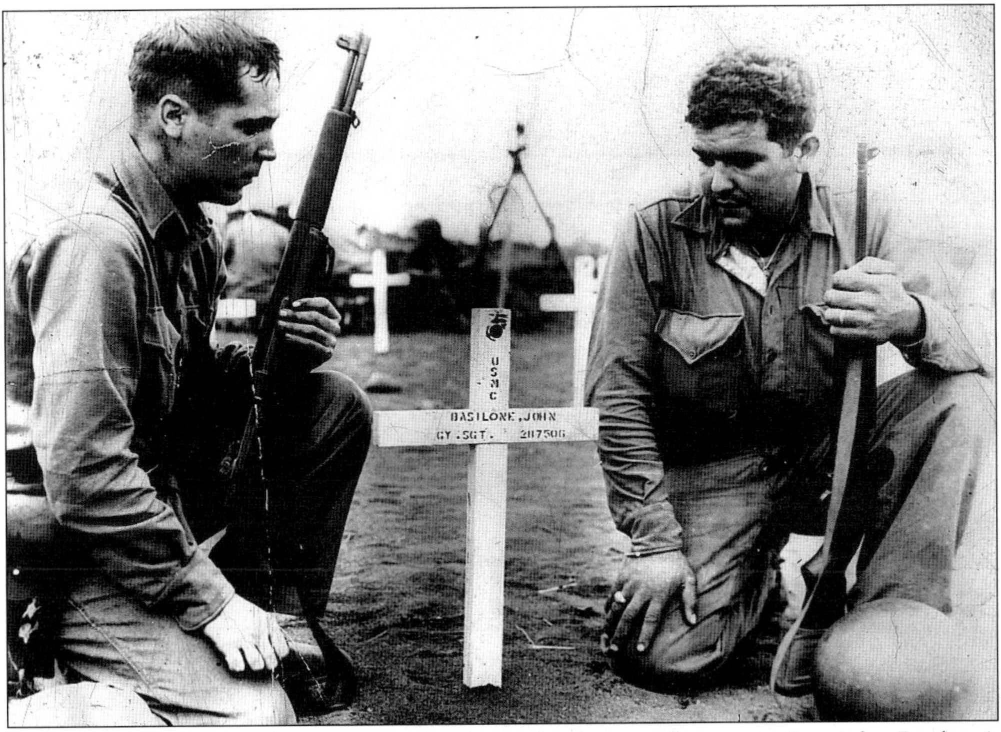

Marines Casey (left) and Cirello spend a few moments in reflection at Sgt. John Basilone's grave in Iwo Jima. His body was later moved to Arlington National Cemetery. (Courtesy of the *Somerset Messenger Gazette*.)

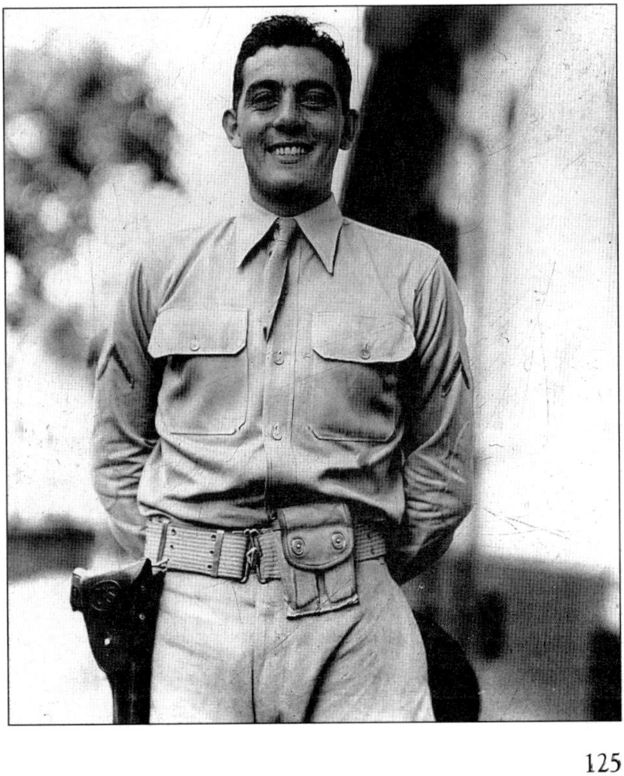

A restless and adventuresome John Basilone enlisted in the U.S. Army at the age of 18. This photograph was taken in the Philippines, where he acquired the nickname "Manila John." (Courtesy of the *Somerset Messenger Gazette*.)

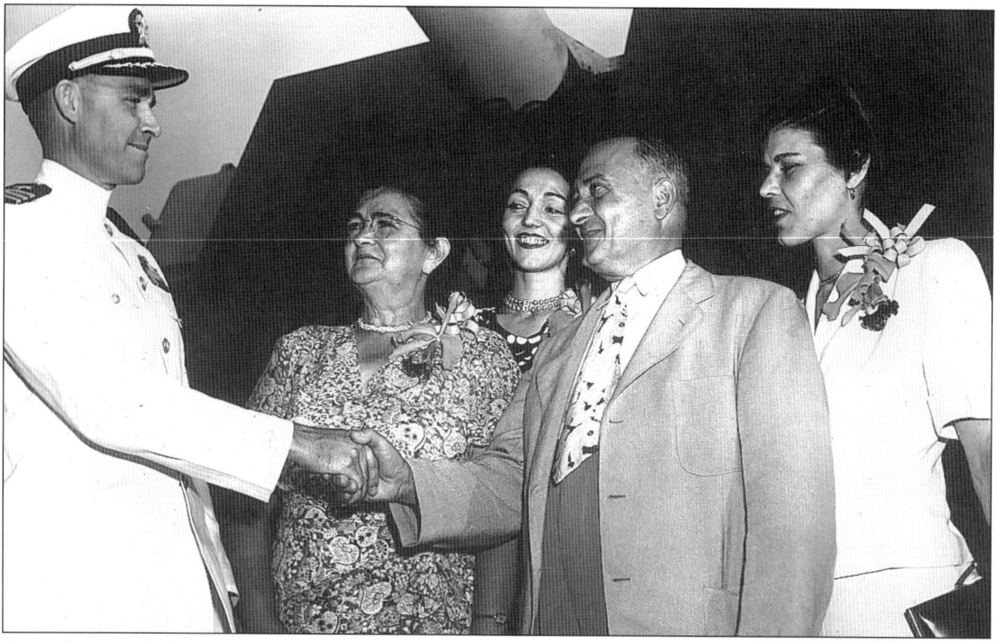

On July 26, 1949, members of the Basilone family are greeted by Commander Dennett (left), captain of the new USS *Basilone*, as they arrive to attend the commissioning of the destroyer named in Basilone's honor. From left to right are Theodora Basilone, Mary Basilone, Salvatore Basilone, and John's widow, Lena Rigi Basilone. (Courtesy of the *Somerset Messenger Gazette*.)

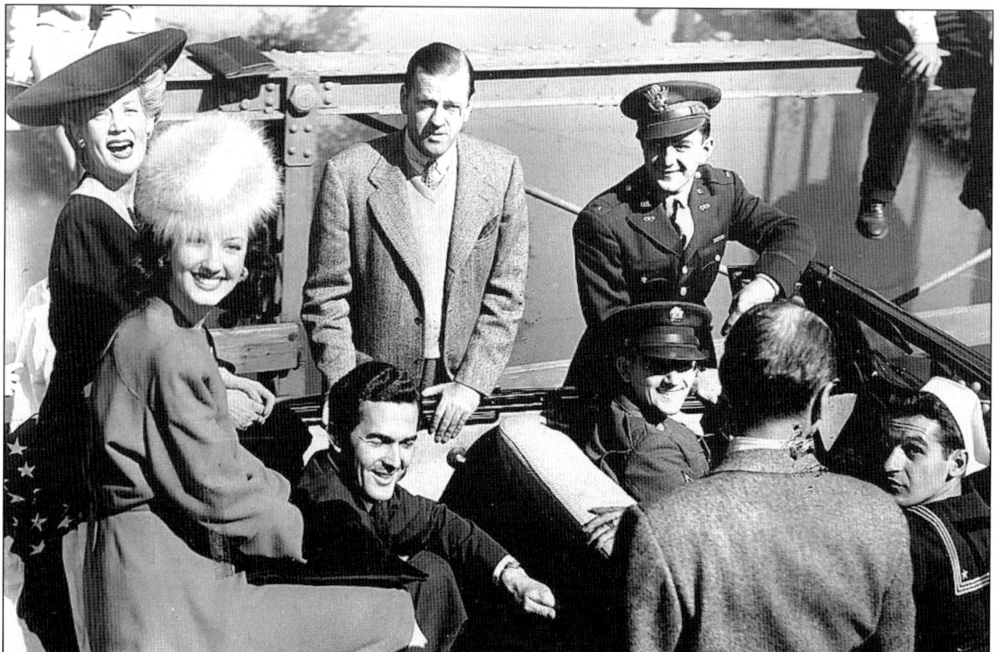

An estimated 20,000 supporters swarmed into Raritan on September 19, 1943, for the first Basilone Parade; it was a celebration fit for a hero. Hollywood celebrities including Louise Allbritton, Virginia O'Brien, and Danny Thomas took part in this parade to encourage the sale of war bonds. (Courtesy of the *Somerset Messenger Gazette*.)

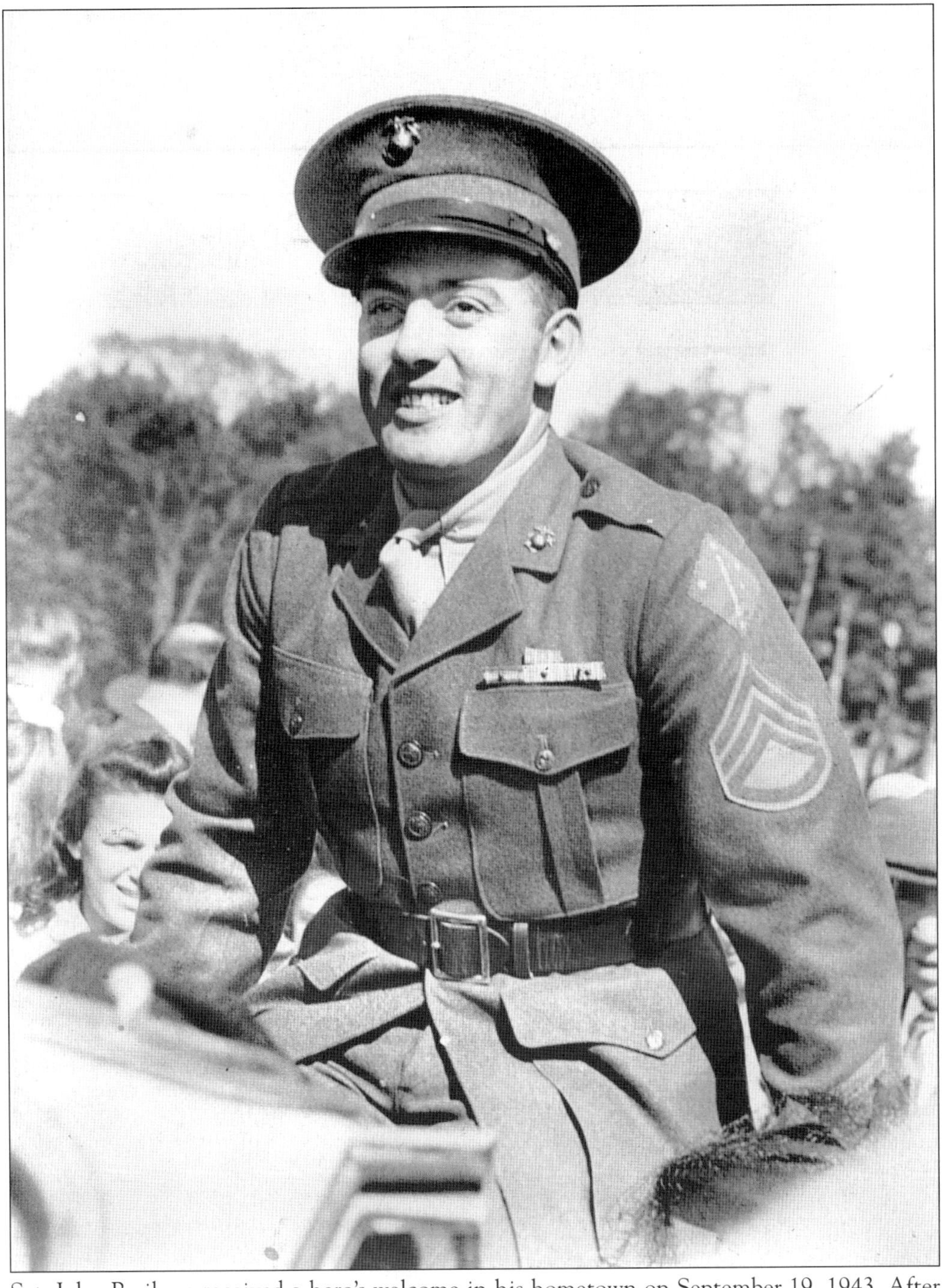

Sgt. John Basilone received a hero's welcome in his hometown on September 19, 1943. After attending Mass at his parish church and then a luncheon at a local restaurant, he rode in an open car during the huge parade in his honor. (Courtesy of the *Somerset Messenger Gazette*.)

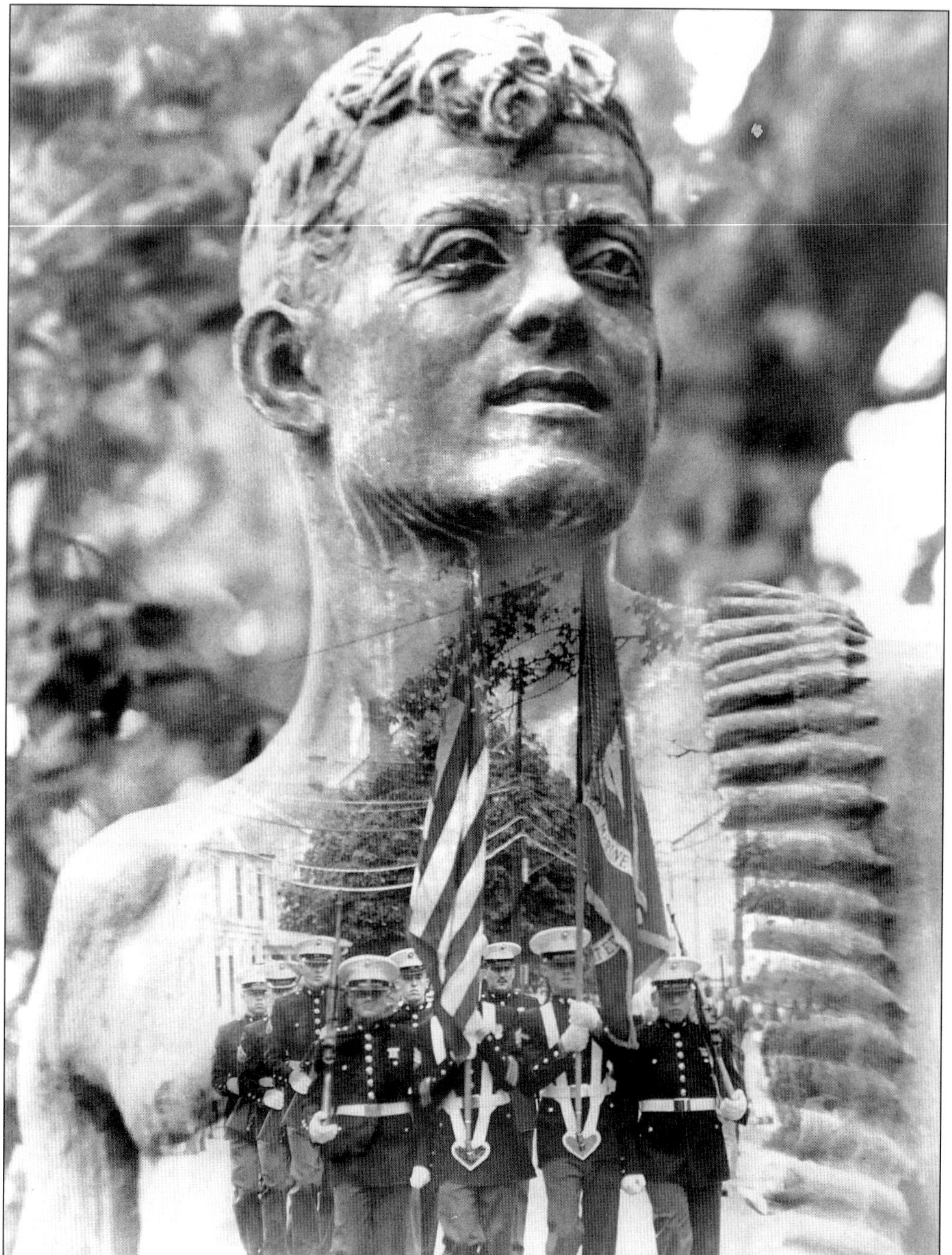

On February 19, 1945, a Japanese artillery shell stilled Gunnery Sgt. John Basilone's fighting heart. His bravery and valor live on, however, in the heart and soul of the Marine Corps. (Courtesy of the *Somerset Messenger Gazette*.)